Collective Insecurity

Law and Society Series
W. Wesley Pue, General Editor

Gender in the Legal Profession: Fitting or Breaking the Mould
Joan Brockman

Regulating Lives: Historical Essays on the State, Society, the Individual, and the Law
Edited by John McLaren, Robert Menzies, and Dorothy E. Chunn

Taxing Choices: The Intersection of Class, Gender, Parenthood, and the Law
Rebecca Johnson

Collective Insecurity: The Liberian Crisis, Unilateralism, and Global Order
Ikechi Mgbeoji

Unnatural Law: Rethinking Canadian Environmental Law and Policy
David R. Boyd

Murdering Holiness: The Trials of Franz Creffield and George Mitchell
Jim Phillips and Rosemary Gartner

People and Place: Historical Influences on Local Culture
Jonathan Swainger and Constance Backhouse

Ikechi Mgbeoji

Collective Insecurity: The Liberian Crisis, Unilateralism, and Global Order

UBCPress · Vancouver · Toronto

09 08 07 06 05 04 03   5 4 3 2 1

Printed in Canada on acid-free paper.

National Library of Canada Cataloguing in Publication Data

Mgbeoji, Ikechi, 1968-
Collective insecurity : the Liberian crisis, unilateralism, and global order / Ikechi Mgbeoji.

(Law and society series 1496-4953)
Includes bibliographical references and index.
ISBN 0-7748-1036-X (bound); ISBN 0-7748-1037-8 (pbk.)

1. Liberia–History–Civil War, 1989- 2. Peacekeeping forces–Liberia. 3. Africa–Politics and government–1960- 4. Africa–Ethnic relations. I. Title. II. Series: Law and society series (Vancouver, B.C.)

DT636.5.M42 2003   966.6203   C2003-910625-X

Canada

UBC Press gratefully acknowledges the financial support for our publishing program of the Government of Canada through the Book Publishing Industry Development Program (BPIDP), and of the Canada Council for the Arts, and the British Columbia Arts Council.

This book has been published with the help of a grant from the Canadian Federation for the Humanities and Social Sciences, using funds provided by the Social Sciences and Humanities Research Council of Canada, and with the help of the K.D. Srivastava Fund.

Printed and bound in Canada by Friesens
Set in Stone by Artegraphica Design Co. Ltd.
Copy editor: Francis Chow
Indexer: Christine Jacobs
Cartographer: Eric Leinberger

UBC Press
The University of British Columbia
2029 West Mall
Vancouver, BC V6T 1Z2
604-822-5959 / Fax: 604-822-6083
www.ubcpress.ca

Contents

Acronyms

AAFC	Allied Armed Forces of the Community
AFL	Armed Forces of Liberia
ALCP	All Liberian Coalition Party
ASEAN	Association of Southeast Asian Nations
CIS	Commonwealth of Independent States
CSCE	Conference on Security and Cooperation in Europe
ECOMOG	ECOWAS Cease-fire Monitoring Group
ECOWAS	Economic Community of West African States
INPFL	Independent National Patriotic Front of Liberia
JCMC	Joint Cease-fire Monitoring Committee
LAP	Liberian Action Party
LDF	Lofa Defence Force
LPC	Liberia Peace Council
LPP	Liberian People's Party
MOJA	Movement for Justice in Africa
NATO	North Atlantic Treaty Organization
NDPL	National Democratic Party of Liberia
NPFL	National Patriotic Front of Liberia
NPP	National Patriotic Party
OAS	Organization of American States
OAU	Organization of African Unity
OIC	Organization of Islamic Countries
PAL	Progressive Alliance for Liberia
PMAD	Protocol on Mutual Assistance on Defence
PPP	People's Progressive Party
PRC	Peoples Redemption Council
RUF	Revolutionary United Front
SADC	Southern African Development Community
TWP	True Whig Party
ULIMO	United Liberation Movement for Democracy in Liberia

UN	United Nations
UNGAOR	United Nations General Assembly Ordinary Resolution
UNMIH	United Nations Mission in Haiti
UNOMIL	United Nations Observer Mission in Liberia
UNTAC	United Nations Temporary Authority in Cambodia
UNTAG	United Nations Transition Assistance Group
UNTAMIC	United Nations Advance Mission in Cambodia
UP	Unity Party
UPP	United People's Party

Foreword

Conflict over territory and resources is as old as human history. The Westphalian state system as developed by the United Nations Charter was supposed to put an end to all such hostilities. The outlawry of war as a weapon of international diplomacy should have provided states and their citizens with security from the threat and the reality of foreign armed interventions. In practice, during the existence of the United Nations in the second half of the twentieth century, the world experienced more widespread conflict, violence, and terror than ever before. The African continent in particular has been mired in a multitude of recurrent wars that have shattered the security of life of millions of people.

Why has the UN system not worked to protect people and to enhance their welfare, as was intended, in Africa and elsewhere? Eschewing the popular but inadequate answer of blaming all of Africa's woes on past colonial division and rule, the author of this book searches out other roots of the failure of African states in the structure of international law itself. Turning over the very foundation stones of the international legal system, he exposes their weak facets and their core imperfections. Using the unhappy history of Liberia as a case study, Dr. Mgbeoji demonstrates the malleability of the principles of population, territory, government, and recognition from which the state is constructed, and the deficiency of the concept of non-intervention in its internal affairs in the face of massive human suffering and abuse of rights. He shows how multi-ethnic West African populations have become beset by inter-community strife that does not recognize state territory or boundaries. From a diagnosis of the varied failures of African governments and the recurrence of armed interventions, both aggressive and humanitarian, he calls forth a new vision of regional collective human security and introduces new parameters of legitimate governance under international law. It is a fresh construct of state and government in international law that is built on human realities and filled with human hope.

The origin of this book was a thesis presented for the degree of Master of Laws at Dalhousie University, Halifax, Canada. It earned Ikechi Mgbeoji the gold medal for the best student in all disciplines to graduate with a master's degree from the university in 1999. It was written in the course of the winter of that year, at the time the world's attention was directed to solving the problems of Kosovo. The intervention by NATO in the Federal Republic of Yugoslavia was not illuminated by the comparable intervention of ECOWAS in Liberia or by the lessons of that experience which Dr. Mgbeoji writes about with such brilliance, lucidity, and verve. Those lessons still need to be learned and this book is a splendid place to start.

Hugh M. Kindred
Professor of Law, Dalhousie University

Acknowledgments

In ruminating over some of the issues that form the subject of this book, I have consulted a lot of people and many events have combined to shape the views expressed here. I thank Hugh Kindred, Moira McConnell, and Dean Dawn Russell of Dalhousie University for their incredible support, guidance, and unstinting praise. Their incisive nudgings, questions, and suggestions have made this book readable. I am grateful to Wesley Pue of the University of British Columbia Faculty of Law and to Randy Schmidt of UBC Press, whose unflagging faith in this project brightened many a grey day in the library.

I also thank the emerging school of critical African scholars – Kofi Quashigah, Obiora Okafor, Makau Wa Mutua, Thuo Gathii, and Anthony Anghie – for their courage and inspiration. I have no doubt that because of their efforts, other scholars will begin to rethink the role and place of a reconstituted international law in relocating African states in the comity of nations. Their bold and pragmatic ideas have largely helped to shape the perspective that I have tried to bring to bear in this book.

My thanks and appreciation must be extended to members of my supportive and loving family: Elder Levi Mgbeoji, Ihuoma Mgbeoji and family, Eze Mgbeoji and family, Ebere Ohiara and family, and Uchenna Mgbeoji. I cannot forget to mention my mentors and colleagues at F.O. Akinrele and Company. I remember with gratitude Daa Chioma, Uncle Tony, and family. To my wife, Nkeiruka Mgbeoji, whose long-suffering love shortened my long hours, I owe a kingdom of gratitude. Finally, I dedicate this book to the memory of my sister, Eziaha Mgbeoji, and my mother, Victoria A. Mgbeoji. Their shocking and untimely demise shattered my world, but their memories are my daily inspiration. Adieu!

Introduction

The spate of civil wars in Africa has not only consumed people and resources but also raised issues regarding their latent causes and their impact on global security and on the regime governing the use of force in international relations. This book is a contribution to the discourse on these anxieties from a nuanced perspective, using the Liberian civil war as a case study. The approach has its obvious limitations, least of which is the danger of unfounded generalizations inherent in using one instance as representative of all. Liberia's emergence as a state and the corruption of its inherently defective polity has parallels in other African states, however.

These states emerged from the European colonization, exploitation, and dehumanization of Africa, a phenomenon that was packaged as a proselytizing mission to "save the heathen savages" of that continent. The territories in Africa, which subsequently emerged as states in the Eurocentric model, had little or no semblance to the pre-existing polities. African states therefore owe their modern blueprint and structures to the external urgings, understandings, and narratives of European (a)morality and reconfigurations of international law. It thus follows that Eurocentric conceptions such as race and racism, national security, transnational economics, and geopolitics would reverberate in Africa, sometimes with deadly consequences. At the same time, while the European partitioning of Africa created sociopolitical contradictions potentially inimical to a stable polity, it has to be conceded that a portion of the blame for the ubiquitous and chronic civil conflicts in Africa must be placed at the doorstep of the African ruling elite.

Through decades of corrupt and inept rule, systemic abuse of human rights, especially economic, social, and cultural rights, these states denied themselves internal legitimacy capable of withstanding the vicissitudes of external pressures and dynamics. Such is the case with Liberia. The internal contradictions in the new African states were papered over and ignored largely because of global preoccupation with the politics and intrigues of the Cold War. In that season of attrition, the massive flow of military aid and arms to Liberia and virtually all African states continued unabated. With the end of the Cold War, the seething discontent arising from the dysfunctional states rose to the surface. The surfeit of arms came in handy. The discontent in Liberia, which found expression in a violent rebellion, fanned across the subregion, aided by the inconsistencies of the African state boundaries dictated at the Berlin Conference of 1884-85 and an incompetent domestic leadership fostered by a cynical world. Faced with a defective global machinery for the resolution of armed conflicts, West African states intervened forcefully in the conflict, invoking their collective security interest in Liberia.

West African states also urged as justifications the invitation by Liberia's president at the time, and *ex post facto* ratification of their actions by the Security Council of the United Nations. The latter justification presents problems of abuse by powerful states, particularly in the context of new forms of threats to international peace and security. In these modern circumstances, the temptation to use force outside the machinery of the United Nations is great, hence the need for a critical assessment of the Liberian precedent. In examining these and other issues, this book posits that three measures – a reconstructed regime of African statehood, legitimate governance, and reform of the Security Council – are imperatives for a stable African polity in the post–Cold War era.

Collective Insecurity

Map of Liberia and neighbouring countries showing ethnolingual distribution of ethnic groups.

1
The Myth of African Statehood

African states have gained an unenviable reputation for chronic instability and strife, endemic corruption, and egregious waste of human and natural resources. In the popular media, it is becoming impossible to exaggerate the extent of African misery and socio-political incompetence. But certain hard questions must be asked. How did Africa come to this sorry pass? In what ways may the cradle of human origin and civilization regain its glory?

In this book, I undertake an inquiry into the dubious character of African states and their intrinsic capacity for collapse and insecurity. The analysis is in the form of a case study of Liberia and the crisis that has since convulsed the West African region. I argue that the corrosion of the African psyche and the mutilation of precolonial African political structures laid the basis for the modern crises afflicting the continent. Beyond the pernicious legacy of European imperialism coupled with the myopic, selfish, and impoverished leadership of the African elite, it seems clear that the solution to African political instability lies in a structural rearrangement of the African polity for the purpose of legitimate governance of African peoples. To the extent that the governments of various African states are structurally, philosophically, and ideologically incapable of responding to the aspirations of African peoples, such governments and states are illegitimate and thus prone to failure. The quest for legitimacy must transcend quick transplants of Eurocentric prescriptions on governance and economic well-being. Legitimacy in the African polity must bear the varied fingerprints of African peoples in the structure, substance, and process of domestic governance.

Liberia: Contrived Statehood and Political Instability

> *The civilized Liberian, to maintain his standing as a light and a ruler of the country, must live in some way aloof from the people he governs. This is the custom in America and it is far more necessary in Africa.*[1]
>
> – *Charles C. Boone*

Liberia is reputedly Africa's oldest state. Founded by freed Africans previously enslaved in the United States, this oligarchy of Americanized Africans held absolute sway over the country and dominated its pre-existing indigenous peoples. The settlers, barely constituting 5 percent of the entire Liberian population, ruled for over 125 years. As the wave of coups d'état swept over the continent in the immediate postcolonial era, Liberia appeared immune to that problematic phenomenon of state identity crisis in Africa.

It must be noted at the outset that the emergence of Liberia as a state was not necessarily a result of the decision of its indigenous nations to constitute themselves into a state, or of its capacity to be a viable state under the Eurocentric paradigm. Rather, like many African "states," Liberia was a creature of foreign political, economic, and cultural dictates. Further, like most African states fashioned in this crucible, the inability of its elite to create an indigenous idea of or consensus about its statehood exacerbated its internal contradictions, thus paving the way for socio-political attrition and the consequent failure of the state as a collective enterprise.

Liberia was conceived through political expediency in response to the paroxysm of racism in the post-emancipation era in the United States. It was conceived in fear by those who could not contemplate coexistence with black people in the post–Civil War era.[2] The institutionalized enslavement, exploitation, and denigration of the black race in the United States is an embarrassing proof of humanity's amazing capacity for orchestrated and systemic injustice.[3] In the course of the journey of the estimated 10-100 million blacks to the Americas, the West Indies, and different parts of the world for subsequent sale and degradation, millions of blacks perished at the hands of the enslavers.[4] The propagation of the practice of slavery by the early European Americans, who had themselves fled from medieval tyranny in Europe, is a riddle. As one writer observed, "it is stranger than fiction, yet it is true that the very same people who fled from British oppression to America to be free, as soon as they inhaled the first breath of freedom, they turned boldly and enslaved others."[5]

The economic impact of this diabolical trade in human beings on the basis of institutionalized racism is no less profound. The productive value of slave labour in the United States prior to independence is said to have been $2 billion in 1800s currency.[6] For Africa, it was an unmitigated social, economic, and political disaster, so much so that the world's second largest continent was set back for almost a thousand years and is still economically and politically dysfunctional. There were people in America who questioned the humanity and justice of slavery, as they believed that it constituted a violation of basic notions of civil liberty. Perhaps, however, this different attitude was not so much a result of moralistic outrage as it was a calculated reaction to the economic and political dynamics of the institution of slavery.

Arguably, the economic justifications for slavery were becoming increasingly weak in the face of modern industrialization.

As with most African states, the creation of Liberia was a consequence of several factors occurring beyond the shores of Africa. First, the rapid increase in the Negro population was already a matter of grave concern in the United States, as the industrial age was gradually undermining the economic raison d'être of slavery – cheap labour for agriculture.[7] Further, the clamour for the emancipation of blacks in the United States and the inclination of certain leading political figures there to make good the promises of freedom had helped congeal anti-slavery rhetoric into policy. It should be noted that by 1820 there were at least a quarter of a million freed slaves in the United States. As with the Biblical Jews in bondage in Egypt, there was the question of what to do with the increasing number of freed blacks in the US.

This question merged with the fear by the slavers of the looming prospect of equality at law with freed slaves. Indeed, the legislature of Virginia had requested its members in the US Congress to correspond with the President on the subject of purchasing land outside the US to resettle freed slaves without the limits of this state whither persons obnoxious to the law or dangerous to the peace of society may be removed.[8] It was at this historical juncture that the American Colonization Society was born. Its objective was to "rescue" free people of colour and to colonize them outside the United States, "where they might enjoy the blessings of liberty."[9]

In addition to this gratuitous racism, the season of unease and fear was further fuelled by the resistance of the American South to adjusting to a society founded on the principles of absolute human equality devoid of racial hierarchies. To complicate matters more, some African-Americans were beginning to engage in violent resistance to slavery. For example, there was the Negro revolt led by Nat Turner in August 1831. He organized an insurrection against slaveowners, in which over sixty slaveowners were killed. As a fearful precedent, this act of violent defiance struck terror in the hearts of several members of the establishment and strengthened the case for colonization of blacks outside the United States. The American Colonization Society persuaded the freed Negroes to emigrate to Africa, and those who bought the argument reasoned thus: "I am an African and in this country, however meritorious my conduct and respectable my character, I cannot receive the credit due to either. I wish to go to a country where I shall be estimated by my merits and not by my complexion."[10] It was to West Africa that they would eventually go.

For example, in 1816 Paul Cuffee, an African-American of mixed parentage from Massachusetts, performed the first experiment on emigration to West Africa when with pomp and merriment he set sail with thirty-eight freed slaves. Soon Alexander Hamilton, James Monroe, President James

Madison, Bushrod Washington (brother of George Washington), Daniel Webster, and Henry Clay were persuaded of what they termed the "peculiar moral fitness in restoring the Negroes to the land of their fathers." However, a large majority of the Negroes understood the salient racism behind the apparent benevolent objectives and activities of the American Colonization Society, dismissing them as unmerited stigma that was being cast upon the reputation of free people of colour. Undeterred, the society succeeded in gathering information about the African coast from the British Home Office and slavery abolitionist groups. The US Slave Trade Act of 1819 empowered the President to "make such regulations and arrangements as he may deem expedient to safeguard, support and remove Africans stranded in the United States."[11] This legislation provided the legal basis for the government's dispatching to Africa in 1820 of the vessel *The Elizabeth,* with 300 Africans rescued from slave-carrying ships.

On 25 April 1822, the immigrants landed on the west coast of Africa at a place called Montserrado and took possession of the Cape on the alleged barter with the natives for guns, gunpowder, beads, clothes, and so on. The seeds of Liberia had been sown. By 1837 the idea of a colony on the west coast of Africa for freed slaves from the United States had become an unfolding reality. The little band of colonists at Montserrado (later renamed Monrovia in honour of President James Monroe) organized and expanded their original territory by purchasing land from the natives. To convince the majority of the Negro population who remained in the United States to emigrate to Monrovia, the reports by the American Colonization Society spoke glowingly of a people who now "enjoyed the liberty once denied them and know nothing of that debasing inferiority stamped on us [them] in America."[12]

The new colony was threatened from diverse quarters and was denied status as a state. The British and the French encroached upon and significantly reduced the original extent of the colony, but the United States declined to intervene. In desperation, the young colony, on 26 July 1847, declared itself a republic. It is significant that the new state was actually an alien transplant on African soil, as it chose the name "Liberia" from the Latin for freedom – *liber* + *ria* for euphony. In other words, like most African states, the spiritual and genetic core of the Liberian state was rooted in foreign ideals, with only artificial linkage to its geographical location. In the climate of official racism that determined interracial relationships in the colonial era, it took the United States fifteen years to recognize Liberia, because the South resisted the idea of receiving a black envoy in Washington.[13] However, in the cynical geopolitical tradition that has largely influenced European relations with Africa vis-à-vis the United States, recognition of the new republic was quick to come from Great Britain, Denmark, Belgium, and France. In a sense, the young colonial state, like other African states, was at its inception a pawn on the international chessboard.

Again, the young state of Liberia, divorcing itself from its African roots and heritage, blindly copied foreign norms, structures, and prescriptions on governance. For example, the mode of governance in the young republic was uncritically tailored after that of the US. Its Declaration of Independence read like the American Declaration of Independence. And, as in the American original, no native or indigenous "Liberian" was signatory to the all-important document. The republic's constitution defined "Liberians" as "originally the inhabitants of the United States of America."[14] To complete the ludicrous acceptance of everything American, its motto reads: "The love of liberty brought us here." In effect, the African natives originally inhabiting the "Liberian" geographical and cultural space who were not "former inhabitants of the United States" were not deemed to be "Liberians." The politics of Americanized elitism and exclusion had begun. Liberia was thus a colony and a material projection of a distorted polity and bizarre sense of intraracial superiority.

It is no surprise that, having been fed on a diet of racism and notions of racial superiority on the basis of skin pigmentation, the state of Liberia was founded upon and sustained on the supposed superiority of the light-skinned Americo-Liberians (the elite) over the darker-skinned natives. As Liebenow lamented: "The experiment in colonization was not the 'in-gathering of' Africa's lost children. These were Americans, and their views of Africa and the Africans were essentially those of nineteenth-century whites in the United States. The bonds of culture were stronger than the bonds of race, and the settlers clung tenaciously to the subtle differences that set them apart from the tribal 'savages' in their midst. It was not then (nor is it today) unusual to hear tribal people refer to the Americo-Liberians as 'White' people."[15] In living out their American fantasies, early "Liberians" became more American than their former masters in the United States,[16] making a fetish of their exposure to the West. As they regarded the natives as the country's greatest problem,[17] a state policy of political and economic exclusion of the natives was created, thus subverting the very logic behind their colonization in Africa.

A state founded for Africans long torn from their roots and with the fond hope that they would feel at home in Africa amid their kin was determined to distance itself culturally and spiritually from its African roots. It looked up to America as the proverbial beacon on the hill and desired everything American. A people rejected by America was bending over backward to love America. Yet the love was hardly reciprocated. According to Merran Fraenkel, whose incisive work on Liberia remains a classic: "They identified themselves closely with the way of life of the 'New World,' despite their repudiation of the role in which they had been cast in it ... They were expatriates rather than repatriated: they were not buoyed up ... by the idea that they were returning to their ancestral continent. Indeed, the entire Declaration contains no mention whatsoever of Africa as the land of their forefathers, despite the fact that, for some of them, Africa may have been only one or two generations back ... Africa was a strange and barbarous continent; their 'native land' was America."[18]

This rejection of their African heritage was also reflected in the country's foreign policies and in its attitude towards the struggle for independence by colonial Africa. The prevailing emotion exhibited by the ruling class in Liberia to the emergent wind of freedom and to the end of colonialism in Africa was sheer apprehension. According to the Liberian Secretary of Defence in his annual report for 1960: "With the attainment of independence of ... Africans ... contiguous to our borderline, problems which we never thought of are arising and have to be grappled with every degree of efficiency and alertness. Not only are the problems of the crossing into our territories of citizens of other states involved but also the question of national ideologies, some of which are divergent to ours and destined to threaten and uproot the very foundation upon which our democratic institution was founded."[19] The young Liberian state thus denounced the pan-African[20] stance of Marcus Garvey on "Africa for Africans," and at the San Francisco debates on the proposed United Nations, the Liberian legation reminded pan-Africanists that Liberia was there to represent a nation not a race.[21] In the prescient insights offered by Fraenkel, the self-identification of the Americo-Liberians as "inhabitants of North America" and their apparent lack of any feelings of cultural attachment to Africa were of vital importance in determining the manner in which the new settlement developed. It deserves to be noted that the elitist aloofness and disconnection from the average African was not a Liberian peculiarity. It was largely a continental phenomenon, often reflected in an abiding fascination of African elites with values, institutions, and legacies of the retreating colonial masters.

In Liberia, this attitude set the stage for the tyranny of Samuel Doe and consequent state failure. In effect, the phenomenon of state failure in Africa is a multifaceted one, implicating the racial theories and praxis of the colonial age, the erasure and denial of African contributions to global civilization, distortion of the African psyche, and mutilation of the autochthonous and time-tested political structures and jurisdictions of precolonial African states. Having been robbed of its dignity and pride of place by the racist historiography of the annals of human civilization, the colonial and postcolonial African elite, particularly the Liberian variant, was a cultural oddity with schizophrenic personalities on matters of politics, culture, and worldview. It was a hybrid of sorts, neither African in the authentic sense nor fully Europeanized and accepted by Europe as an unblemished bearer and transmitter of European values.

Consequently, the first Americo-Liberian settlers had pretensions to superiority over some of their class. In line with the racist assumptions and beliefs carried over from their experiences in the United States, the possession of a lighter skin pigmentation was associated with greater intelligence, ability, and civilization. Thus, mulattos affected superiority over their contemporaries of darker pigmentation, and for some time monopolized politics and commerce on the basis of skin colour. The Negroid West Indian statesman Edward Wilmot Blyden, who emigrated to Liberia in 1855, was politically frustrated by the mulattos on the basis of colour and broke ranks with the ruling Republican Party in 1867 in opposition to what he termed the "mulatto oppression."[22]

In the fullness of time, the mulatto oligarchy naturally withered away and metamorphosed into an oligarchy of the very dark pigmented Americo-Liberians. The abiding tie or bond was their American roots and experience. In all this ebb and tide of class and race power in Liberia, the lot of the natives stagnated. Worse still, the Americo-Liberians were in political control even in the remote hinterlands. In effect, the clear stratification of Liberian society at the nation's inception was both a tool and an elitist consequence of intraracial economic exploitation and political exclusion of the natives. This illegitimacy of governance and the aloof elitism of the ruling class were not peculiar to Liberia. Indeed, virtually all states created by Europeans from precolonial African nations exhibited identical inclinations and anomie.

In addition to this testy relationship with the natives, who themselves had diffuse geographic boundaries, the encroachment on the young republic's territory by European powers continued. Between 1847 and 1910, Liberia lost 44 percent of its original territory. The scramble for Africa by European powers was beginning to intensify. By virtue of the Berlin Conference, General Act of 26 February 1885, Great Britain forced Liberia to cede a sizable portion of its coastline to British Sierra Leone. This phenomenon attracted the anger, if not the action, of the United States, which in the Taft Commission Report of 1909 lamented that Liberia as an independent power might speedily disappear from the map.

For 125 years, the Americo-Liberians, who constituted less than 5 percent of the Liberian population, excluded the natives from the government of Liberia and monopolized all political, economic, and social positions of eminence. It was only in 1963 that an attempt was made to integrate the disparate native groups.[23] If democracy is to be understood as the diffusion of potential political power to wider groups in society, it stands to reason that there was no democracy in Liberia. The oligarchy of the True Whig Party (TWP) was a government of the many by the few and for the few: the epitome of aristocratic dictatorship. In spite of the occasional political differences among the elite, there was one body against whom they were united – the natives. Thus, when the ruling class disintegrated or became disaffected, the entire country followed suit.

It should be mentioned again that prior to the arrival of the settlers from the United States, the political structure of the disparate native groups in the geographic space later known as Liberia was fully established. Until the renaissance of African historiography, it was the dogma in many circles that Africa had no sophisticated states in the precolonial era. In modern times, the works of Cheikh Anta Diop, Basil Davidson, Kenneth Dike, and others have dispelled this false notion. With particular reference to Liberia, it is hardly in doubt that there were various types of pre-existing political structures among the ethnic groups in that region. Modern scholars agree that the complexities and varieties of domestic political structures in precolonial Liberia defy easy categorization.[24] Although the area now known as Liberia had formed parts of ancient and formidable empires in past millennia, most Liberian native groups had morphed into political structures with indicia of statehood that were different from Eurocentric models. In effect, the prevalent notion of the Americanized African or the European as the "bearer of light and civilization" was as erroneous as it was conceited.

In precolonial Liberia, the political structure of the native groups was primarily based on kinship cemented by complex social ties. The diffuse nature of political authority, built as it were on linguistic, cultural, religious, and historical peculiarities, was alien to the settler-elite and Eurocentric conceptions of statehood. Commenting on the fluid nature of precolonial boundaries and societies among Liberian ethnic groups, Liebenow further observes that "there has always been a certain amount of fluctuations of ethnic boundaries. The constant search for new agricultural lands or the flight from arbitrary rulers have constantly driven people into previously uninhabited and uncharted sections of Liberia."[25] For some of the ethnic groups, membership in a group came about by self-identification or through a sense or consciousness of belonging. Thus, the political boundaries and substance of the indigenous nations of Liberia was defined by autochthonous criteria rather than Eurocentric parameters.

Again, as with other African natives, the eventual control and domination of the natives in Liberia by the settlers or colonialists were accomplished by an adroit combination of various methods, including conquest aided by superior firepower, divide-and-rule strategies, and fraudulent "deeds of cession" of landed territory. Consequently, the state of Liberia, like most other African states, was a contrivance devoid of a common national psyche and sense of destiny. In the absence of a nation properly so called, it would seem unconvincing to speak of nation building and nationalism in such emergent states conjured up by the idiosyncrasies of external dictates. The imposition of Western education as a criterion for participation in governance and the relative poverty of the natives were tools with which the settlers perpetuated their hegemony. For instance, electoral franchise was dependent upon proof of literacy in the English language, and possession of property was dependent on jurisprudence of property fashioned in Europe.

Hence, even though some of the native groups such as the Vai had developed indigenous letters and characters of literacy, proficiency in such autochthonous writing cultures was discountenanced. With respect to Eurocentric literacy tests, it is remarkable that while the natives lived in the hinterlands, the schools where literacy in English language could be acquired and foreign values imbibed were located in the distant coastal areas inhabited by the settlers. Consequently, the earliest natives who acquired the franchise were those who served and waited on their elitist overlords in the cosmopolitan coastal cities. It is equally noteworthy that this pattern of rural/urban dichotomy has significantly affected the character and stability of postcolonial African states.

In order to increase the number of foreign-trained elites or "civilized" elites, the government opened its doors to freed slaves from the West Indies. This ingenious plan failed largely as a result of the growing emancipation of slaves in the United States and tales from Liberia in the United States about the numerous conflicts between the settlers and the natives. In futile rejection of this internal colonialism, the Krus, a seafaring native group, revolted in 1915, and the Golas also engaged the settler government in a bloody war in 1918. These were military efforts by the natives to throw off the yoke of the settlers. In a response that was to be replicated in various postcolonial African states by other Western states such as France and Belgium, these internal violent attempts to reject a distorted polity and oppressive regime were viciously put down with the arms and soldiers of the US Army. The outcome of these conflicts, to borrow the words of Maugham, was that the natives were broken and "no more troubles were experienced"[26] from them.

The political and cultural hegemony of the settlers was further sustained by a monolithic political machinery built around the True Whig Party.[27] Membership and ascendancy in the TWP were a direct function of membership in the Masonic Lodge, which refused admission to the natives.[28] This ubiquitous and powerful organization, founded in Liberia in 1867, literally controlled Liberian politics and economy.[29] What was good for the members of the Masonic Lodge was good enough for the party and, in turn, the state. In effect, it is fair to argue that, contrary to the impression created by periodic elections, campaigns, and the usual accoutrements of democracy, the ominous reality was that the average Liberian was under a dictatorship of a few self-proclaimed patricians who merely mimicked the outward forms of American democracy.

The emergence of William Tubman in 1944, with his promise of enhanced native participation in the governance of Liberia, wilted as the ruling elite once again preferred to inject "new blood" of their own "race." This was a revival of the policy of encouraging the immigration of emancipated Negroes from the West Indies. When this project failed to stem the tide of native agitation for equal access to power, the elite resorted to terror and intimidation. Thus, when Didhwo Twe, a native and leader of the opposition Reformation Party, opposed Tubman's re-election bid for the presidency in the 1951 elections, he was speedily charged with treason on spurious evidence. He fled the country and Tubman won the election.

Later, Tubman sought to integrate the natives but a large number of the elite were opposed to the idea. The position of Tubman was a response to the prevailing climate in Africa at the time. The other natives in colonial Africa were agitating for self-rule. Politically inspired riots were already widespread in Sierra Leone, Guinea, Ghana, Nigeria, and other West African countries. Liberia thus operated a form of internal colonialism, a subtler form of apartheid that the natives could not understand. Given that all the other countries in Africa were labouring under white colonial rule, it was natural to reduce colonialism to a white-against-black paradigm. To be colonized and suppressed by their own race was beyond the comprehension of the Liberian natives, and unlike their kith and kin in colonial Africa who were eagerly looking forward to seeing the backs of the European colonizers, the Liberian natives were stuck with the Americo-Liberians.

Hence, Tubman's resolve to quickly integrate natives in the politics and governance of Liberia may be seen as a masterstroke to save the status quo.[30] Tubman quickly liberalized Liberian citizenship rights to grant citizenship to all native Liberians. The franchise was also apparently liberalized. As a skilled politician, he formulated a system of cosmetic integration of natives that essentially sustained the settler domination of Liberia. Thus, in 1946, although natives constituted ninety-five percent of the population, they had only twenty percent of the seats in the Lower House. Worse still, the native seats were perceived to be held by Tubman's lackeys.

It thus followed that in Liberian elections, the presidential ballots were often rigged in favour of the monolithic, all-powerful True Whig Party. For instance, in the 1959 election, Tubman scored 530,474 votes versus 55 votes recorded for his opponent. In fairness to Tubman, similar feats had been recorded by past Liberian presidents and, indeed, in many African postcolonial democracies. For instance, in the 1923 elections in which 6,000 voters had been registered, President King had miraculously returned 45,000 votes to clinch the presidency! The inescapable inference here is that the uncritical adoption of Western models of governance without adequate calibration to accommodate indigenous and time-proven methods of legitimate governance was a major factor in the ubiquitous tales of conflicted statehood in postcolonial Africa.

More surprising is the ease and unaccountability with which well-meaning but misguided Western powers and policy makers espouse elections as the ready-made band-aid for serious and complicated African political crises. As Nicholas Kristoff recently observed, "without much of a sense of gritty realities in the developing world, we in the West tend to regard 'democracy' as simply elections. When trouble erupts – in Cambodia, Somalia, East Timor, Afghanistan, Angola – we prescribe elections, bless the results as democracy, and hurry off."[31] This simplistic and inordinate emphasis on elections alone partly explains why such unrealistic and uninformed conceptions of democracy are at the root of the inability of such democracies to yield the much-desired results that ought to be derived from legitimate governance. Needless to add, allegations of fraudulent or stolen elections in Africa often constitute the first early-warning signals of imminent political strife, civil mayhem, and possible state failure.

In Liberia, the Western-educated native elite were not spared by the elitist Americo-Liberians. In 1968 Edward Fahnbullah, a Liberian diplomat of native extraction, was charged with treason; in spite of the scanty and dubious evidence presented, he was convicted and his property was confiscated. The trial further polarized the settler elite and the budding indigenous elites. Three years after the spectacle of the Fahnbullah trial, President Tubman died and was succeeded by his deputy, William Tolbert. The latter tried to heal the wounds of the trial by rehabilitating Fahnbullah. In spite of Tolbert's liberal posture, the upper levels of government and the economy were still controlled by about a dozen interrelated Americo-Liberian families.

The declining economic fortunes of the country further worsened the situation. Opposition against the regime gained strength. The heart of this newly strengthened attitude lay in the student body, especially inside the University of Liberia. The Togba Tipoteh–led Movement for Justice in Africa (MOJA) was the most prominent of these groups and was also supported by external bodies of opposition such as the US-based Progressive Alliance of Liberians (PAL) led by Bacchus Gabriel. The PAL soon metamorphosed into a political party – the People's Progressive Party (PPP) – and declared its readiness to oppose Tolbert in the elections,[32] but the Tolbert regime refused to register the PPP.

Following a controversial subsidy placed on the price of imported rice (Liberia's staple food), the MOJA issued a "General Declaration of Rice and Rights," enjoining the populace to march in protest against the rice subsidies. According to Amadu Sesay, "the rice riots of April 1979 marked a turning point in the history of Liberia."[33] The government subsidy on imported rice was perceived as another largesse for the merchant ruling class of Liberia.

Consequently, the PAL called for a public demonstration against the rice subsidy. The rice protests were brutally crushed, and it became obvious that the Tolbert government, like other "sit-tight" rulers in postcolonial Africa, was running short of ideas for the rational governance of Liberia.

Illegitimacy of Governance and State of Rebellion

> *Had we been candid about the standards of government in Liberia it would have been very damaging to US interests ... Great powers don't reject their partners just because they smell ... We had the Liberian Executive Mansion pretty well wired. So we knew what was going on in the Mansion ... Womanizing until 3 am.*[34]
>
> *– Chester Crocker, US Assistant Secretary of State for African Affairs (1981-88)*

> *Perhaps I made a wrong career choice if it was people like that I was going to meet. Doe was unintelligible.*[35]
>
> *– George Schultz, US Secretary of State (1980-88)*

On the night of 11 April 1980, a group of seventeen semi-literate junior soldiers of native background led by scruffy twenty-eight-year-old Master Sergeant Samuel Kanyon Doe struck a fatal blow to the 133-year-old oligarchic rule in Liberia. In that night of the long knives, President Tolbert and twenty-seven of his guards were butchered. Like all coups d'état, it was a secretive plot that upstaged the prevailing political order.[36] In its maiden broadcast to the nation, the military junta read out a litany of evils allegedly committed by the defunct oligarchy. It imposed a dusk-to-dawn curfew, closed all Liberian borders, and set up a military tribunal to try the members of the defunct regime for alleged corruption, treason, and violation of human rights.

This body of seventeen was composed of seven sergeants, eight corporals, and two privates. None was educated beyond high school. Their modest ranks were soon to be dropped for more glorious epaulettes. The junta called itself the Peoples Redemption Council (PRC). The first few days of the coup were marked by excesses in vendetta and widespread looting of the assets of the vanquished elite, who were punished with extra-judicial killings.

This penchant for bloodshed was to characterize the regime. Besides declaring martial law, it dismissed the top echelon of the Liberian civil service, assumed both legislative and executive powers, suspended the constitution of Liberia, and disbanded the Supreme Court. Assets and property of the top members of the True Whig Party were summarily confiscated, and bold promises to right the wrongs of the past were announced. While the coup d'état was welcomed by a large majority of Liberians as it disposed of the hated oligarchy of the True Whig Party, its excesses were condemned, albeit tamely, by some African countries for at least three reasons.

First, the assassinated President Tolbert was at the time the chairman of the Organization of African Unity (OAU) and was widely respected by his colleagues, with whom he had developed some deep personal relationships. One of Tolbert's sons was married to a daughter of the late Ivorian head of state, Felix Houghouet-Boigny. His murder by Doe's forces at the premises of the French embassy, where he had sought refuge, was to play a significant part in Boigny's subsequent support for the rebellion against Doe.

Second, although a considerable number of African rulers had come to power through coups d'état, Doe's coup was by all comparative standards excessively bloody. No fewer than 200 persons were killed in the first three days. This bloodletting continued with the brutal execution of the thirteen top members of the Tolbert regime. The procedure adopted in their hasty trial and execution did not have any redeeming qualities. They were summarily tried without any legal representation, and in spite of weak and sputtering international protests, were executed in a gross and sadistic manner: tied to stakes and without blindfolds, they were machine-gunned to death before a gleeful crowd. The International Commission of Jurists issued a statement on 23 April 1980 describing both the trial and execution as violations of accepted international norms, yet no sanctions or other serious normative measures were adopted or pursued by the international community against the Doe regime. Finally, Doe's coup came at a time when Africa was coming to terms with the tragedy of Idi Amin's tyranny in Uganda[37] and Bokassa's excesses in the Central African Republic.[38]

For these and other reasons, Liberia's delegation to the contemporaneous special session of the OAU Council of Ministers was refused admission to the conference venue in Lagos, Nigeria. Similarly, the Liberian delegation led by Doe himself was refused participation at the Economic Community of West African States (ECOWAS) Summit convened in Lome, Togo. Commendable as these measures were, they embodied a far more complex and unresolved dilemma in the search in Africa for governmental legitimacy and stability in the continent. Reference must therefore be made to the complexity of the concept of governmental legitimacy and to the limitations of the international legitimation process. The unreliability of international legitimation mechanisms, especially the self-interest of states, as the barometer for measuring the domestic legitimacy of government in Africa needs to be critically examined. It is to these issues that scholars of African political instability ought to devote the full rigour of their analytical powers. It is perhaps prudent to deal with the question of governmental legitimacy briefly before delving into the issue of inconsistencies in the global process of legitimation.

From the beginning of the Liberian state, indeed virtually all African states, the structure and process of governance were determined beyond the shores of Africa by institutions and persons with little or no knowledge of African realities and history. Beyond racial contempt for Africans, the dominant sentiment of the colonial overlords was a feeling of paternal stewardship towards Africans. The continent was thus in the position of receiving rather than partaking in the normative processes that led to the emergence of Eurocentric statism in Africa. Neither the consent of Africans nor the aspirations of the African citizenry mattered in the events and incidents that gave rise to colonial African statehood. Accordingly, African states were in their conception, gestation, and birth alien and strange contraptions foisted on the continent by imperialist forces who hardly thought of Africans as human beings imbued with reason. Modern Africa was thus conceived in fraud, chicanery, rapacity, and racist condescension. Imbued with this intrinsic illegitimacy, it is fair to say that *ab initio,* African states were devoid of internal legitimacy.

Legitimacy of governance is essentially characterized by the structural and procedural ability of the citizenry to influence decisions that affect their day-to-day happiness.[39] In the circumstances, the imposition of ludicrous boundaries on the African landscape, the introduction of strange precepts of governance, and the mutilation of the African identity by imperialistic forces succeeded in denying postcolonial Africa the needed domestic legitimacy, nationalistic coherence, and organization with which to hold its place in the comity of nations across the globe. Beyond the aberrations of colonially imposed boundaries, the structural inability of the emergent African states to create the enabling environment for the economic well-being or prosperity of the citizenry obliterated any extant vestiges of internal legitimacy. Encumbered by their colonial legacies, the emergent African states were easily held hostage by the swinish scramble of the domestic elite for the offices and remnants of the colonial loot left behind by the retreating colonialists. In Liberia, as in most postcolonial African states, the elite lived large while the citizenry struggled for the crumbs.

With respect to the problems associated with international legitimation and the discordant tunes played by African states in response to Doe's savagery, it is common knowledge that national self-interest, as opposed to any transparent *a priori* rules, determines or at least heavily influences international attitudes or responses to crises of governance in Africa. For example, Jean-Bedel Bokassa of the Central African Republic violently overthrew David Dacko and crowned himself emperor, but because he gave the French free rein over the mineral wealth of the country, his debauchery, violence, and egregious abuses of human rights were tolerated. It was only when he became rather too infamous that French troops were used to depose him.[40]

Similarly, the dysfunctional government of Côte d'Ivoire elicited no global concern until the political strife there erupted and threatened global cocoa prices. Côte d'Ivoire is the world's leading supplier of cocoa beans, the key ingredient in the production of chocolate. Again, thirty years after the event that has since plagued Zaire, Belgium recently apologized for its assassination in 1961 of Prime Minister Patrice Lumumba.[41] According to the apology tendered by the Belgian foreign minister, Lumumba was killed with logistics supplied by the Central Intelligence Agency (CIA) because he was reputed to have communist sympathies. Similarly, as a result of growing and chronic instability in the Middle East, the United States is papering over the illegitimacy of some governments in West Africa as it seeks new oil supplies in that region.[42] The list of examples of international hypocrisy in matters relating to legitimate governance in Africa and the primacy of perceived domestic self-interest in the process of international legitimation is virtually endless.[43]

This cynical approach to questions of governmental legitimacy at the international level is, regrettably, a common a feature of international relations, especially First World versus Third World engagement. As Nicholas Kristoff recently observed with respect to the United States' relations with General Pervez Musharraf of Pakistan: "If there was a form of government that produced autocrats who sponsored terrorism, stole millions of dollars while impoverishing their citizens, shredded public education and health, permitted child bondage, tortured dissidents and tolerated pogroms, then we should condemn it. Except that in South Asia such a system is called democracy ... President Bush has winked as Gen. Musharraf steamrolled over a democratic system so as to maintain the army's hold on power. Mr. Bush's stand is hypocritical and threatens to undermine everything we stand for."[44] Notwithstanding the question of inconsistencies in and the hypocrisy of the international political order on issues of legitimation of governments,[45] it is arguable that for whatever it was worth, the international community should have completely refused to accord the Doe regime any international legitimacy at all.

Another significant factor that compels this viewpoint is the immaturity and rashness that was apparent in the earliest days of the Doe regime in Liberia. Doe's response to the punitive measures imposed by some African states betrayed his unsuitability for the high office he occupied. He recalled the Liberian ambassadors in Nigeria, Côte d'Ivoire, and Sierra Leone, and on 14 June 1980, Liberian troops invaded the French embassy and arrested Adolphus Tolbert, the brother of the slain President Tolbert. Similarly, in February 1983, when a Sierra Leone newspaper allegedly libelled him, President Doe unilaterally closed the borders between Liberia and Sierra Leone and threatened to keep them closed until the Sierra Leone government shut down the offending newspaper. This contempt for the due process of law portended the greater bloodshed and severe regional dislocations that Doe's heavy-handedness would precipitate.

The new helmsmen obviously lacked the sobriety required by their new station in life. Barely a fortnight after taking power, they announced rapid promotions for themselves. Noncommissioned officers suddenly assumed dazzling ranks. Doe leapt from the lowly rank of Master Sergeant to the dizzying height of a five-star General of the Liberian Army[46] and increased the salaries of the military by 150 percent. It is equally significant that of the twenty-seven cabinet members constituted by the PRC, ten were from the Krahn-speaking part of Liberia, the same ethnic background as Doe; five members were from the Kru-speaking part, seven from the Dan/Gio-speaking region, and four from the mixed Lofa-speaking parts of Liberia. In effect, the soldiers had learned the politics of divide-and-conquer from the defunct order.

Within the caucus of the PRC, cracks soon appeared. It was becoming clearer that Doe's rhetoric on "African socialism" and diatribes against the "corruption of capitalism" were a subterfuge for his quest for ultimate personal control of Liberia. For instance, when some members of the PRC preferred leaning towards the communist Soviet Union, this attitude appeared not to go down well with Doe and his then deputy, Brigadier General Quiwonkpa, who preferred to sustain the Liberian connection with the United States.[47] Doe's camp prevailed and the pro-socialist camp led by Major General Weh Syen was marked for destruction. The pro-American camp ordered the Soviet embassy to reduce its embassy staff by half for acts described as an unbecoming attitude. The Libyan legation, called the "Peoples Bureau," was asked to shut down and leave Liberia within two months. This antagonism with Libya was to become a critical factor in the subsequent crisis, as the rebels were alleged to have Libyan support.

Three months after this split, thirteen lower-ranking officers sympathetic to the Weh Syen camp were implicated in an alleged coup plot against Doe and executed for treason. Three months after the executions, Weh Syen himself and four members of his camp were allegedly implicated in another coup plot and also executed for treason. Doe constantly changed his cabinet and fostered a personality cult. By December 1991, only two of the original seventeen members of the PRC were alive and in Liberia. The rest had been either exiled or killed. The only potential threat to Doe's personal rule of Liberia was his charismatic deputy, General Quiwonkpa, a Dan/Gio of the Nimba County of northern Liberia. The Dan/Gio nation straddles Liberia and Côte d'Ivoire. Doe's prompt demotion of Quiwonkpa was rejected by the latter. Quiwonkpa was then dismissed from the Liberian Army and expelled from the PRC.[48] One month later, he was implicated in a "plot" to overthrow Doe allegedly sponsored by the defunct Soviet Union and Ghana. In spite of their protestations of innocence, the ambassadors of both countries were asked to leave Liberia within forty-eight hours.[49] General Quiwonkpa fled to Côte d'Ivoire through Nimba, but Doe quickly rounded up those suspected to be sympathetic towards him and had them tried for treason.

Doe's crackdown on the perceived opposition and rivals was not restricted to his primary constituency – the military – or to the political class. It extended to civil society, especially the student body in Liberia. Liberian students had expressed shock and disapproval of his brutal execution of the thirteen members of the Tolbert cabinet and were agitating for reforms. Doe banned by decree the holding of parties in higher institutions of learning in Liberia on the grounds that they were a subterfuge for inciting the youths against his "revolution." In 1984 a civil demonstration was brutally quelled by Doe's security forces and at least forty people were killed in the process. In addition, the regime was mired in fraud and corruption.

The clamour for a speedy return to civil rule did not affect Doe's intention to succeed himself as the elected president of Liberia. A committee headed by Amos Sawyer was set up to draft a new constitution for Liberia.[50] Doe formed the National Democratic Party of Liberia (NDPL) and named himself the party's presidential candidate. Other political parties, such as the United People's Party (UPP) led by Gabriel Bacchus Mathews, the Liberian People's Party (LPP) led by Amos Sawyer, the Liberian Action Party (LAP) led by Tuan Wreh, and the Unity Party (UP) led by Edward Kessely, were floated. As the new Liberian constitution pegged the qualifying age for the presidency at thirty-five years, Doe's true birth date of 6 May 1952 disqualified him from running, but by diverse means, his age was "corrected" to show that he was born in 1950.

To make doubly sure, he rescheduled the election timetable and fixed the presidential elections for 8 October 1985. On 19 August 1985, he "uncovered" a "plot" by Amos Sawyer to overthrow him. Sawyer was arrested with three others and immediately charged with treason. According to an official statement, Sawyer's alleged plot consisted of a campaign "to create confusion, fear, distrust and division among the people" and thus secure the resignation of President Doe. Once again, the students demonstrated against Doe's increasing tyranny; in response, his presidential guards opened fire on them.

Bolstered by the huge amounts of aid and other money pumped into Liberia by the United States, Doe had ample resources for his unprecedented repression of the Liberian people. Between 1980 and 1985, he received over US$500 million in aid and military wares from the US. While this aid was supposedly meant to bolster Liberia's defence against the forays of Libya's Ghaddafi, it is unlikely that President Doe would have been able to entrench himself in power without this unconditional support. The salient point here is that a considerable number of despotic governments in Africa have been sustained by external support anchored on the cynical self-interests of powerful states in Europe and of the United States. Consequently, the normative significance of external support for African governments should not be exaggerated. Basking in such support, Doe dissolved the PRC and constituted an Interim National Assembly with himself as the head.[51] Under Doe's regime, his ethnic group, the Krahn-speaking part of Liberia and the Mandingoes, gained relative political ascendancy over other groups by dominating political appointments in Liberia.

As the election date drew near, Doe banned the embattled Amos Sawyer's popular Liberian People's Party on the ground that it advocated "foreign ideologies"[52] and had thus infringed the electoral laws. In addition, some opposition figures were arrested for allegedly spreading lies, rumours, and misinformation, and were charged with treason. It was under these circumstances that the presidential election was held on 15 October 1985. The electoral commission had as its vice chairman David Gbala, an NDPL (Doe's political party) activist. Despite credible allegations of electoral irregularities, on 29 October 1985 Doe was proclaimed the winner with 50.9 percent of valid votes cast. The opposition parties protested and contended that Jackson Doe (no relation to President Doe) of the Liberian Action Party (LAP) had won the election with 63 percent of the total votes cast. The other results showed that Doe's NDPL had won 22 of the 26 Senate seats and 51 of the 64 Lower House seats.

The opposition parties refused to take their seats in the Congress, describing the elections as a mockery of the law and of the people of Liberia. Amid the confusion, General Quiwonkpa, who had fled Liberia to Côte d'Ivoire on allegations of treason, launched a dramatic but tragic coup attempt on 12 November 1985. During his exile in Côte d'Ivoire and in the United States, Quiwonkpa had made public his resolve to return to Liberia and depose Doe. The coup attempt lasted three days and unofficial accounts put the death toll at more than 1,000.

Doe recalled the Liberian ambassador in Sierra Leone for alleged complicity in the coup attempt. Nationals of other West African countries, such as Ghana, Guinea, and Côte d'Ivoire, were allegedly involved in the coup attempt.[53] The Dan/Gio people of Nimba County, Quiwonkpa's ethnic group, were routinely victimized for their alleged support for the coup attempt. As the economic situation worsened,[54] Liberia's political isolation increased. In spite of his transformation into a civilian president, Doe's heavy hand pressed the opposition relentlessly.[55] The opposition from Nimba County[56] reared its head again on 4 September 1987, giving rise to a Treaty of Non-Aggression and Security Co-operation between Liberia, Sierra Leone, and Guinea. Official allegations of coup plots[57] became the routine pretext for decimating opposing ethnic groups[58] and potential rivals.[59] The fatal threat to the Doe regime was to start on 24 December 1989, however.[60]

A Brutal and Fractious Rebellion

On the fateful night of Christmas Eve 1989, twenty-four armed men of different West African nationalities[61] crossed over into Nimba County[62] from neighbouring Côte d'Ivoire and attacked a border customs post, killing an army officer. The exiled Charles Taylor[63] claimed that a group led by him, the National Patriotic Front of Liberia (NPFL), was responsible for the rebellion. As the rebels increased in number and acquired more weapons, its ethnic tendencies[64] began to emerge. Taylor, half Americo-Liberian, aligned himself with the Dan/Gio of Nimba County who had borne the brunt of Doe's excesses. They now seemed to be exacting retribution for the oppression[65] meted out to them by Doe's Mandingo/Krahn-dominated Liberian Army and government. The Mandingoes and Doe's Krahn ethnic group, who were alleged to be the backbone of Doe's regime, bore the brunt of the excesses of the rebellion. Within a few weeks, a massive refugee crisis had developed and the conflict had uprooted "60 per cent of Liberia's estimated population of 2,500,000."[66]

The NPFL's[67] rapid conquest of Liberian territory suggested the probability that it had substantial support both inside and outside Liberia. The NPFL increased its numbers by sheer terror, summarily executing unwilling recruits and using child-soldiers, some as young as six. Within the first two months of the rebellion, however, the NPFL suffered a split. The splinter group called itself the Independent National Patriotic Front of Liberia (INPFL) and had Yormie Johnson as its leader. Johnson had allegedly left the NPFL after Taylor accused him of summarily executing his own troops, and he was determined to stop Taylor from seizing power. Allegations of atrocities dogged all the rebel groups. As the rebellion mounted, Doe's lackeys deserted him and fled abroad. Within six months, the rebels controlled 90 percent of Liberia and were marching speedily to the capital, Monrovia. In addition, the rebels controlled very strategic points, including the airports and seaports. By mid-June 1990, the NPFL rebels were within fifty kilometres of Monrovia, and by 28 June they had seized the principal road links to the capital. In short, Doe and his remaining cronies were besieged.

Ethnically motivated atrocities against civilians were rampant, and probably reached their peak with the massacre by the Krahn-dominated regular army of 600 Dan/Gio civilians seeking refuge in a church compound in Monrovia. Interestingly, Liberia's benefactor and friend, the United States, which had lent considerable support to Doe's government, merely stationed 2,000 marines to safeguard American citizens and installations, especially an Omega communications system tracking shipping and submarine movements in the Atlantic. Other strategic assets included a powerful Voice of America radio transmitter situated near Monrovia, a communications and information-gathering centre at the embassy for contact with US embassies throughout Africa, and refuelling facilities at the Robertsfield International

Airport for the US Air Force. The US marines were ordered only to evacuate the remaining American citizens and protect the American embassy. It is remarkable that the protection of foreign self-interests in Africa during moments of political crisis represents an unbroken pattern, as evidenced in several African hot spots such as the Rwandan genocide, the Madagascar standoff in 2002, the Somalian meltdown, the Zairean conflict, and, lately, the conflict in Côte d'Ivoire.

There was an impasse as the various factions would not let Taylor seize the whole of Monrovia. The deadlock over the capture of Monrovia by the NPFL is attributable to the breaking away from the NPFL of its advance group, commanded by Yormie Johnson, who formed the INPFL. Thus, at the moment when ultimate victory was within the NPFL's grasp, Yormie Johnson not only frustrated Taylor's bid for control of the capital but set the stage for further factionalization of the rebellion against the Doe regime.

The Economic Community of West African States (ECOWAS) emerged as the solitary initiator of a settlement of the conflict, as the United Nations and the Organization of African Unity, save for scattered homilies on the wisdom of peaceful settlement of crises, did nothing to resolve the crisis. The ECOWAS approach was primarily aimed at a peaceful and negotiated end to the crisis. However, Taylor's NPFL faction, in the hope of wresting control of the capital city and the presidential mansion from the other contending factions, initially avoided all peace talks. Taylor's conduct and attitude can probably be explained on two geopolitical and juridical grounds.

First, the NPFL had effective control over a substantial part of Liberia, and although the breakaway INPFL controlled the Monrovia seaport and major land access to the capital city, it did not have Taylor's superior firepower. Taylor reckoned that sooner rather than later, the INPFL would yield to his superior numbers and firepower. In addition, the rump of the Liberian Army, which had control over the presidential mansion and its immediate environs, showed itself to be undisciplined and rapacious. Taylor thus reckoned that it was only a matter of time before his forces gained control over the capital city and the presidential palace.

Second, Taylor's determination to capture the capital city and the presidential palace was a reflection of a long-standing attachment to the political significance of both symbolic locations. The military and political significance of this situation is that in the immediate postcolonial African political experience, contenders for state power generally regard control over the capital city and the presidential mansion as the ultimate symbol of effective political control in a state.[68] It matters little that the force in control cannot extend similar control over the hinterlands of the country in question. Politically, effective control of other territories in an African country, no matter how extensive, is not the same as effective control over the capital city. On the basis of this juridical notion, the power that controls the capital city and the presidential mansion is the president, and the forces in control of other parts of the country remain rebels until they have overrun the capital city and installed one of their own in the presidential mansion. In other words, Taylor would remain a rebel unless and until he exercised control over the presidential palace and the capital city of the state of Liberia.

Thus, control over the capital city differentiates the "rebel" from the official "government." Proof for this proposition may be found in the cases of the chronic rebellions in Angola, Zaire, Uganda, Mozambique, and other countries. Taylor therefore believed that given more time and in view of his considerable control over large areas of Liberian territory, the other factions would weaken or self-destruct, thus enabling him to achieve his objective of ultimate control over Liberia. Taylor simply could not afford to let go of Monrovia and the presidential mansion. These were the lamentable yet irreplaceable indicia of legitimacy of power in Liberia, and indeed throughout Africa.

On the other hand, this famished conception of legitimacy of power in African politics partly explains Doe's tenacious grip on the presidential mansion and Yormie Johnson's stranglehold on the main access to the capital city. Their roles in the complex equation of relevance and power in the troubled state lay in how tenaciously they could cling on to those symbols of power. In Taylor's calculation, the ECOWAS peace proposal would rob him of the momentum he had gained and would give his opponents a much-needed respite and time to search for more arms and troops. It is therefore understandable why Doe and Johnson's INPFL welcomed the ECOWAS interference and Taylor opposed it. Taylor's misgivings were further fuelled by the closeness between Nigeria's President Babangida and Doe.

What has baffled scholars is why Babangida played such an active role in the Liberian crisis, spending well over US$8 billion of scarce Nigerian resources in a conflict that posed only a remote threat to Nigerian security and for which there was "little solid gain for Nigeria."[69] In a continent with non-existent or weak institutional structures for legitimate governance and for transparent formulation of foreign policies,[70] it is imperative for scholars to go beyond the national interest paradigm in understanding the reasons for Nigerian leadership in the ECOWAS intervention in Liberia.

It has been speculated that both dictators shared sympathies and mutual business interests that possibly translated into military support for the beleaguered Doe. There is anecdotal evidence that a significant number of foreign policies made by African states are in fact decisions made by heads of states on the basis of their personal or business relationships with their counterparts. It is therefore not unusual for one African head of state to commit state resources or troops towards helping or salvaging a beleaguered colleague even if there is no national benefit accruing to the state from such enormous commitments of resources and personnel. Because of the personal and perhaps business relationship between Doe and Babangida, Taylor deeply distrusted the Nigerian-inspired ECOWAS peace plan for Liberia. By 20 July 1990, Doe had grudgingly (after realizing that ECOWAS was determined to do away with his presidency) accepted an ECOWAS peace proposal. This provided for a ceasefire, deployment of a peacekeeping force in Liberia, and the formation of a government of national unity.

Doe's final isolation occurred on 21 July 1990, when all his ministers signed a public statement urging him to resign in order to save Liberia from further destruction of life and property, and also to ensure his personal safety. The solitary efforts of ECOWAS[71] continued at its Thirteenth Summit of Heads of States in Banjul, Gambia, on 28-30 May, where it resolved to send a peacekeeping force to Liberia. The objective of the peacekeepers was to oversee the ceasefire agreement and bring the civil war to an end. Johnson's INPFL (with its secure access to the capital city) welcomed the ECOWAS initiative. However, Doe's personal end was drawing near. In a meeting arranged by the ECOWAS Cease-fire Monitoring Group (ECOMOG) with the INPFL on 11 September 1990, he was apprehended, tortured, and killed by the INPFL rebels. To this date, the circumstances under which Doe died remain controversial, and they radically altered the role, perception, and stance of ECOMOG in the conflict. Although Johnson and his INPFL forces ultimately killed Doe, the incident took place in ECOWAS-controlled premises.

It has remained a mystery how Johnson and his armed escorts, in spite of the presence of ECOMOG security operatives, were allowed to bear arms and attend a meeting uninvited, especially when Doe's military guards had already been disarmed. Speculation surrounds how Johnson got intelligence reports indicating the time and venue of that fatal meeting. The sequence of sloppiness, fuzziness, improbable coincidences, and unanswered questions about the exact roles of the parties in the apprehension, torture, and killing of Doe largely fuelled the impression of ECOMOG's complicity in Doe's death. This in turn affected the credibility of ECOMOG as an impartial arbiter in the Liberian crisis.

Contrary to general assumptions that the departure of Doe – dead or alive – would bring peace to beleaguered Liberia, however, the factions persisted in their fighting, massacring Liberians and foreigners caught in the conflict. While ECOWAS insisted on a democratic transition, some of the factions, believing that they could win power by force or use their respective degrees of control over Liberian territory as bargaining chips, insisted on prolonging the conflict. For example, the remnants of the Armed Forces of Liberia (AFL), having secured access to the presidential mansion, believed themselves to be in possession of the symbol of power in Liberia.

For his part, Charles Taylor, in effective control of more than 80 percent of Liberian territory, laid claim to the presidency. Meanwhile, ECOWAS organized a conference of all leading Liberian politicians, during which Amos Sawyer was appointed the Interim President.[72] Simultaneously, the NPFL forces resumed its bombardment and shooting of ECOMOG troops in Monrovia. It was under these circumstances that the ECOWAS peacekeepers, acting on an enhanced mandate to use "all necessary means"[73] to bring the conflict to an end, practically joined the fray as combatants by deploying and using military force against the warring factions.

By October 1990, ECOMOG had taken Monrovia from the rebels and established a buffer zone of 20 kilometres around its perimeter, creating havens for the mounting number of refugees fleeing the hottest areas of the conflict. Frustrated in his goal of seizing the capital, Taylor declared himself president of Liberia, moved into the Liberian hinterland, and established his operational headquarters at Gbarnga, 150 kilometres northeast of Monrovia. One of the foreign factors in the conflict betrayed itself when the NPFL insisted to no avail that Libyan troops be added to the ECOMOG contingent. This request was rejected by the Nigerian-led ECOMOG, as the Libyans had been fingered as one of the major financiers of the NPFL. Taylor's intransigence mellowed, however, after a delegation from Nigeria persuaded Ghaddafi, on 21 November 1990, to reconsider his support for Taylor.

Similarly, the government of Burkina Faso, which had dispatched 400 soldiers to help Taylor's rebellion, was advised by the United States to desist from aiding the NPFL rebels. According to Herman Cohen, "we informed the President of Burkina Faso that we disapproved of his sending arms to the NPFL in transit from Libya." This cleared the way for further negotiations, leading to the Bamako Accord of 28 November 1990, which provided for a ceasefire agreement.[74] The NPFL, however, disagreed with ECOWAS on the proper status of the Sawyer-led interim government. This necessitated further talks at Yamoussoukro, Côte d'Ivoire, between all the relevant parties, leading to the signing of another peace accord in October 1991. While the ceasefire agreement held, the disarming aspect failed as the NPFL accused ECOMOG of supporting the interim government at Monrovia headed by Amos Sawyer.[75]

New factional groups with clearly ethnic agendas soon emerged. One of them, the United Liberation Movement for Democracy in Liberia (ULIMO),[76] which had its base in Sierra Leone, launched armed attacks against the NPFL from the northwestern part of Liberia bordering Sierra Leone. The Yamoussoukro Accord finally collapsed when the NPFL executed six Senegalese soldiers of the ECOMOG contingent and committed other atrocities, one of the most shocking of which was the murder of five American nuns in late October 1993.[77]

As the crisis degenerated, the Permanent Representative of Côte d'Ivoire at the United Nations addressed a letter dated 15 January 1991 to the president of the Security Council,[78] requesting that body to consider the Liberian crisis in its deliberations and to support the appeal for humanitarian aid to Liberia. The conflict was spreading to neighbouring countries, particularly Sierra Leone. On 10 April 1991, Sierra Leone wrote to the Security Council detailing the attack on its territory on 23 March 1991 by NPFL bandits. Sierra Leone warned that "because of the seriousness of and persistence of the attacks she reserved the right to use all necessary means, including assistance from friendly countries, to protect the lives of its people and defend its territorial integrity."[79] It is significant that the fears raised by Sierra Leone later materialized into one of the most brutal conflicts in human memory.

With this looming prospect of an exacerbated regional crisis, the United Nations accepted the ECOWAS invitation to participate in and oversee the proposed Yamoussoukro talks on peaceful settlement of the conflict. But the ink on the Yamoussoukro Accord had hardly dried when the rebels took up their arms again. Another peace accord was concluded in Geneva under the auspices of the UN and ECOWAS; it was signed in Cotonou, Benin, and replaced the Yamoussoukro Accord. It provided for another interim government, reduction of the Nigerian contingent in ECOMOG, and disarmament of the warring factions. Once again, Taylor refused to permit the disarmament of NPFL troops on the grounds that the Nigerian quota in ECOMOG had not been reduced.

To reduce the NPFL's suspicion of the alleged partiality of ECOMOG in the disarmament process, ECOWAS, in a letter dated 29 July 1992, invited the United Nations to set up an Observer Mission in Liberia (UNOMIL). UNOMIL was also to cooperate with ECOWAS and the OAU in supervising the transitional process and overseeing the elections proposed under the Cotonou Peace Accord. Renewed hostilities occurred as another armed faction, called the Liberia Peace Council (LPC), headed by Dr. George Boley, emerged, further complicating an already bloody and fractious battlefield. This group was like the ULIMO-J made up of Krahn-speaking Liberians, and soon engaged the NPFL in bloody battles in alleged protest against atrocities committed by the NPFL.[80] Another rebel group, the Lofa Defence Force (LDF), also emerged to pursue an ethnic agenda. The Cotonou Peace Accord of 25 July 1993 was partly implemented as an interim government headed by David Kpomakpor[81] was constituted and troops from Uganda and Tanzania joined the ECOMOG force in order to reduce the Nigerian contingent.

By this stage there were six different groups fighting one another in Liberia: the NPFL, ULIMO-J, ULIMO-K, LPC, LDF, and AFL (the remnants of the Liberian Army). Fighting continued, with all the factions committing atrocities against the civilian population.[82] Amid the chaos, some of the rebel groups, such as the NPFL, suffered internal crises of leadership.[83] Another peace agreement initiated by President Rawlings of Ghana was signed by the leaders of the NPFL, the AFL, and the ULIMO-K at Akosombo, Ghana, on 12 September 1994. The unwillingness of the warring factions to comply with the series of peace agreements frayed the patience of the UN, the OAU, and ECOWAS. Thus, the governments of Ghana and Nigeria declared their readiness to reconsider their participation in the peace process if the rebels persisted in the war. These threats were made good when Ghana and Nigeria began withdrawing their soldiers from the ECOMOG force and UNOMIL followed suit by reducing its numerical presence.

The brutalized Liberian civil population rose up to "call on the ECOMOG Peace Keepers to be decisive in enforcing compliance of the factions in heeding ceasefire regulations so as to save the Liberian Peace Process to which they have committed so much in human and material terms from collapse."[84] The rebels then showed a discernible attempt to keep within the terms of the Akosombo Accord. However, reports of further fighting and atrocities continued as NPFL troops were reported on 8 September 1994 to have seized forty-three members of the UN observer mission. The last attempt to find a peaceful settlement to the crisis took place in Abuja, Nigeria,[85] when all the warring factions agreed to a comprehensive peace plan. By this time, over 200,000 Liberians had perished in the fratricidal conflict that had lasted for five years.[86]

Pursuant to the Abuja Accord, a transitional Council of State was inaugurated on 1 September 1995 and the ECOMOG troops were widely distributed in Liberia to oversee the return of Liberians to their war-torn country. The number of Liberian refugees returning from Guinea was put at 410,000, from Côte d'Ivoire 305,000, and from Ghana 15,000. ECOMOG began disarming the estimated 60,000 troops loyal to the various warring groups,[87] as the armed factions began transforming themselves into political parties to contest the elections slated as part of the peace process. The NPFL became the National Patriotic Party (NPP) and ULIMO-K became the All Liberian Coalition Party (ALCP).

The peace process gained impetus as francophone countries in the subregion sent 2,300 soldiers to build up the ECOMOG contingent to 13,000. Similarly, the United States and Great Britain sent military aircraft for the airlift of those troops. As the return to political activities heated up, thirteen candidates emerged to contest the Liberian presidency. With his stronger organization and finances, Charles Taylor, in spite of allegations of rigging and electoral malpractice, realized his ambition of becoming Liberia's president. He was sworn into office in August 1997 and the Liberian Constitution of 1985 was reinstated.[88]

From this short account of the transformation of violent rebel groups into political parties, certain troubling conclusions must be drawn. First, the ease with which the global community seems to accept the indispensability of mere elections as the cornerstone of political stability in the industrializing world is a matter of grave concern to astute observers of state failure in postcolonial Africa. The naivety in the notion that elections hurriedly organized and supervised by retired politicians from the West are sufficient in themselves to redress historical inequities and heal visible wounds of egregious abuses of state power is beyond belief and calls into question the resolve of the global community to avoid crises in Africa.

Second, it is simplistic to assume that violent rebel groups are potential political parties in the Western sense. The astonishing speed with which violent rebel groups metamorphose into political parties at the insistence of the international community raises serious questions about the genuineness of such transmutations. It is a culture that promotes impunity. Consequently, it would seem imprudent for any experienced or shrewd analyst of political strife in Africa to place any faith in the lasting effects of such barefaced metamorphoses.

Colonialism and the Failed-States Syndrome in the Post–Cold War Era

> *The first Liberians to be enlisted by Taylor were a 40-strong group assembled by Cooper Miller, a former soldier who had gradually brought his followers into the Ivory Coast ... They were taken to Danane ... from there they took the bus to Ougadougou (Burkina Faso) and were installed at a military base outside the city. From there they were transported by plane to Libya.*[89]
>
> – *Mark Huband*

Although the cause of the Liberian conflict has been characterized as a purely internal matter by some observers, prescient analysts have pointed to the mutilation of precolonial African nations into ahistorical units run by self-indulgent elites as a time bomb waiting to explode.[90] In effect, the collapsing artifices known as African states create an inherent demand for foreign intervention.[91] In order to appreciate the regional dimensions of the Liberian conflict, the historically interlocking nature of West African, nay, precolonial African, indigenous peoples and the innate instability of the entities created by colonial overlords at the 1884-85 Berlin Conference need to be considered.[92]

It is also in the context of this historical and egregious display of racist and colonial fiat that certain actions taken by some West African states in response to the collapsing state of Liberia can best be understood. Of course, it can hardly be denied that some countries in the subregion played questionable roles in organizing, encouraging, and fuelling the conflict. Furthermore, the global factors that catalyzed the unravelling of some African states, especially Liberia, Zaire, and Somalia, and the impact on regional stability and security, deserve critical appraisal. A consideration of the Liberian conflict from these perspectives belies the notion that the Liberian crisis was a domestic problem.

A holistic appreciation of Liberian and African political history and the manipulation of that continent by external forces and their domestic clients enables an insightful examination of the rationale for the ECOWAS intervention. In addition, this approach implicitly questions our contemporary appreciation of the narrative of international law on non-intervention in the domestic affairs of states. It is prudent to deal first with the Sisyphean problems of African state boundaries and the consequent dysfunction of the postcolonial African state in the post–Cold War era.

As already adumbrated, most African states are colonial contrivances brought into existence by non-African political and economic powers with little or no knowledge about the peculiarities of Africa. Prior to the normative and practical rejection of colonialism, European and American hegemonic powers indulged in the mutilation of African precolonial nations for their own economic and political ends. The products of this colonial fiat had little or no resemblance to precolonial territories and political identities. The colonial project proceeded as if Africa was a tabula rasa for the inscription of colonial values, whims, and interests. Indeed, of the fifty-three African states in modern times, only ten (Botswana, Burundi, Egypt, Ethiopia, Lesotho, Madagascar, Morocco, Rwanda, Swaziland, and Tunisia) have some similarities to their precolonial political identity. The rest, as well as these, were either "partitioned or bounded by the expediency of colonization."[93]

It was by colonial fiat that decisions were made as to whether a part of one ethnic group was to fall into Nigeria or Benin. Indeed, as Ali Mazrui has pointed out, even the term "Africa" and its derivatives, such as "African," are not indigenous to the continent; they, like the colonial state, are European impositions.[94] In effect, the colonial delineation of Africa at the Berlin Conference of 1884-85 irresponsibly carved out and dispersed homogeneous ethnic groups into the disparate units now known as African states.[95] Unlike most modern European states, which have congealed into discernible expressions of primordial ethnic and cultural affinity, African states are profoundly artificial, devoid of authentic national, cultural, and cohesive psyche and identity. If one may ask, what does it mean to be a Nigerian? Who is a Ghanaian? Thus, unlike the Scots of Scotland or the French of France, African peoples boxed into artificial states have not yet cohered into nations or developed commonalities of culture, institutions, and frameworks within the artificial boundaries of the Eurocentric states inherited from the colonial era. In short, colonization and the violent disruption of the African political order savaged and stultified the evolution and vitality of precolonial African nations and cultures.

With particular reference to Liberia and its neighbours, it is generally agreed by scholars that almost all Liberian ethnic groups are also found in neighbouring postcolonial countries.[96] The same pattern is replicated in virtually all African states. This is one major potential and actual catalyst of disputes in Africa. Burkina Faso and Mali have fought three bitter wars in a period of ten years over disputed colonial boundaries, and there are over 103 examples of borders that divide nations across different African states. In the "scramble for Africa," the Berlin Conference was motivated by European concerns for the convenient economic exploitation of the continent.[97]

It would be simplistic, however, to attribute African postcolonial instability solely to the imperialistic mutilation of precolonial African states and peoples and the pillage of African resources. A more insidious and devastating consequence of the colonial ravage of Africa is the loss of African self-esteem through the process of racialization of knowledge and African historiography and the erasure of precolonial African contributions to human civilization. In effect, the physical occupation and appropriation of African resources and geography was only a part of a more complex enterprise in which African peoples were humiliated and debased, and their time-tested contributions to human development expunged and denied. Hence, although previous European scholarship had clearly attested to the African origins of world civilization,[98] the colonization of Africa was justified by the argument that Africans were primitive, racially inferior to Europeans, and thus a moral burden on Europeans.

This unfortunate ideology, which held sway in the colonial era, gave rise to the erroneous notion, even among Western-educated African natives, that the history of Africa began only after the continent was colonized by Europe. In other words, the denial of African precolonial history served to rob a large segment of the first generation of Western-trained African bureaucrats and elite of the sense of history, competence, and confidence necessary to confront the challenges of the age. This sense of inadequacy and inferiority to the "Whiteman" was particularly acute in the Americo-Liberian elite as well as the emergent elite who disdained anything African. Having been fed on a diet of shame and disdain for their African heritage, they believed in the omniscience of American ideologies, institutions, and way of life.

Further, in the self-imposed messianic and civilizing role of the colonizing Europeans, the mutilation of African precolonial societies was executed with little or no regard for the cultural and ethnic homogeneity of affected African peoples. Without overstating the importance of ethnic homogeneity in the creation and sustenance of states, the experiential reality is that the forced combination of disparate African nationalities into artificial political straitjackets has largely become a controversial instrument for the acquisition and maintenance of power in Africa by the ruling cliques that inherited the colonial contraptions from the retreating European powers. This trend has become more pronounced since the eclipse of the ideological divide between the East and the West and with the growing sense of ethnonationalism and geopolitical irredentism.

This phenomenon gives rise to accusations of ethnic irredentism and politics of ethnicity. The late Kwame Nkrumah of Ghana was given to reminding Togo of the large number of members of the Ewe nation in Togo. Indeed, the first Togolese leader, Sylvanus Olympio, was Ewe. For Liberia and West Africa, Table 1 illustrates the population spread and division of some of the native ethnic groups in and around Liberia.[99]

Characterized by ignorance about the political dynamics and structure of the continent, the colonial scramble for Africa yielded arbitrarily carved units cast into ahistorical straitjackets. These bizarre geopolitical entities known to contemporary international law and relations as African states have since haunted global tranquillity and disoriented the place of Africa in global affairs.

According to Makau Wa Mutua, the mapmakers proceeded as though Africa were a blank slate, devoid of history, uninhabited by rational human beings, and ripe for Europeans to inscribe their fancies on.[100] Indeed, the observations and attitudes of imperial statesmen towards African peoples during the colonial era is very revealing. The unmistakable feature of colonial attitudes towards precolonial African states and peoples is a ruthless and whimsical display of raw power and unquestioned discretion. Quoting

Table 1

Distribution of ethnic groups in and around Liberia

	Liberia	Mali	Guinea	Sierra Leone	Côte d'Ivoire
Bassa	347,000	–	–	5,000	–
Gola	99,300	–	–	8,000	–
Kru	184,000	–	–	8,000	–
Mandingo	33,800	200,000	1,816,500	90,000	–
Mende	19,700	–	–	1,240,000	–
Vai	89,500	–	–	15,500	–
Kissi	115,000	–	–	85,000	–
Krahn	47,000	–	–	–	12,200
Dan/Gio	200,000	70,000	70,600	–	800,000

Note: Data taken from <http://www.christusrex.org/www3/ethno/Libe.html>, accessed 25 February 2003.

a British colonial official, Africa scholar J.C. Anene notes that "in those days we just took a blue pencil and a rule, and we put it down at Old Calabar, and then drew that line to Yola ... I recollect thinking when I was sitting having an audience with the Emir [of Yola], surrounded by his tribe, that it was a very good thing that he did not know that I, with a blue pencil, had drawn a line through his territory."[101]

As Anene further observes, the manner in which the boundaries were made was often a subject of after-dinner jokes among European colonizers and officials. In many cases, distant territories not yet known to the colonial masters formed the subject of the partitioning of Africa. For example, quoting Anene again, Makau Wa Mutua notes that in 1890 Lord Salisbury, the British Prime Minister, found it amusing that "we [the colonial masters] have been engaged in drawing lines upon maps where no white man's foot ever trod; we have been giving away mountains and rivers and lakes to each other, only hindered by the small impediment that we never knew exactly where the mountains and rivers and lakes were."[102] It is significant that in recent times the disregard for African history that characterized the colonial mutilation of precolonial communal boundaries among peoples of modern-day Nigeria and Cameroon has forced both states into protracted legal disputes at the International Court of Justice, as evidenced in the Bakassi matter.[103]

For Liberia, this exercise of colonial whim was particularly damning. The majority of the sixteen Liberian ethnic groups straddle the borders between Liberia and the neighbouring states of Sierra Leone, Guinea, and Côte d'Ivoire. In some cases, such as the Mende, the major portion of the ethnic group resides across the border. Even today "the majority of Liberians identify much more with their ethnic group than they do with the modern state of Liberia."[104] A close study of Table 1 partly explains why the ULIMO-K (predominantly Mandingo) in the Liberian civil war had considerable support from Mandingoes in neighbouring Guinea.

Similarly, the Dan/Gio (mainly in Nimba County) were alleged to have considerable support from their kith and kin in neighbouring Côte d'Ivoire and Guinea. This tendency also helps to explain the relative ease of cross-border refugee movement in times of humanitarian crisis. Indeed, a humanitarian disaster is not needed to trigger massive human migration in that part of the world. The precarious structures of African states are independently capable of generating refugee flow. As Liebenow presciently noted, artificial and largely unregulated international boundaries have provided no "obstacle to Mende, Gola, Kissi, and Vai, who move back and forth to renew old ties with kinsmen in Sierra Leone; to Grebo, Kru, and Krahn who visit their relatives in the Ivory Coast; to Loma, Kpelle, Mandingo, Mano, and Gio who have maintained their economic and social links with kinsmen in Guinea."[105] The African state is simply a leaky vessel.

This phenomenon, aptly described by James Minahan as "nations without states," repeats itself across Africa and must be redressed if Africa is to have a modicum of stability. For instance, the Ibibio nation, with its political and spiritual capital in Calabar in present-day Nigeria (which had as early as 1472 established formal trading and diplomatic relations with the Portuguese), has 5,200,000 of its people on the Nigerian side and nearly 900,000 in neighbouring Cameroon.[106] Similarly, the Karembu of the famed Kanem-Bornu empire have 4 million of their people in present-day Nigeria and over 3.7 million in the adjacent states of Niger, Chad, and Cameroon.

Yet the colonial boundaries made by Britain, France, Portugal, and Germany have not diminished the fervour and passion among the Karembu for their strong cultural links, reinforced by traditional festivities such as the durbar. The resultant cartographical and cultural disorientation creates a delicate mix of tension and explosiveness, especially in the context of contrived nation-statism under Eurocentric conceptions of statehood. A serious strain on the bilateral and multilateral relations of the West African states is thus imposed by these factors. The tension is heightened by ethnic politics and clientelism of alienated African rulers and elites, who are the most vocal supporters of maintaining inherited colonial boundaries regardless of the inherent problems and contradictions that they entail.[107]

It is a profound irony, perhaps a vestige of the uncritical African faith in the "wisdom of the Whiteman," that absolute respect for the integrity of the colonial boundaries is a fundamental norm of the OAU Charter and state practice in Africa.[108] Indeed, of the fifty-three African countries, only Eritrea has successfully overturned the integrity of a colonial boundary and attained recognition as a sovereign state by breaking away from Ethiopia.[109] The doctrine of *uti possidetis juris,* adopted in Latin America, recognizing the juridical validity of colonial boundaries, has been so rigorously enforced in Africa by postcolonial Africans that it is virtually treasonable, even in recent times, to engage in a debate on the utility of the colonial boundaries in the modern age. As already indicated, this attitude, a holdover of what the famous Africanist musician Fela Anikulapo-Kuti described as "colonial mentality," has combined with a fear of the effects of any radical changes to African state boundaries to produce a state of atrophy and stagnation in the continent and alienation from Africa's illustrious past. Ordinarily, it would have been expected that the first task for the newly "independent" African states would be to undo the egregious injustice and structural deformities created by the colonial mutilation of African nations and peoples.

It is hardly in doubt that the teeming population of Africans, particularly those border citizens with kith and kin separated by the Berlin-designed borders, do not share the same enthusiasm for the artificial states of Africa.[110] Consequently, some radical African scholars have called for a new cartography for Africa, both in terms of the actual redrawing of modern

African political boundaries and a normative content of social and economic justice guaranteed by law.[111] Some of these factors have led some scholars[112] to conclude that the colonial mutilation of African nations, the erosion of African self-esteem, and the negation of economic, social, and cultural rights of the African populace generate internal conflicts.[113] In addition, these factors encourage the internationalization of internal conflicts in Africa.

Added to the complications of contrived citizenry in African states, it must be noted that the nascent African states were hardly ready for the demands of Eurocentric statehood. In most African states, the departing colonialists barely created or sustained those institutions necessary to support a modern state as construed under the dominant Eurocentric paradigm. More worrisome, the colonialist era left a legacy of state brutality and impunity that the postcolonial officers easily inherited. Some historical factors may explain this phenomenon.

First, the juridical categorization of humanity on racial grounds suffered a quick and deadly blow after the Allied triumph over Nazi Germany. In other words, formal European colonization of Africa ended earlier and faster than the colonial overlords had contemplated or expected. Instead of the proposed centuries of colonization and "enlightenment of the savage," European colonialists were chased out of Africa by an emerging international attitude against colonialism.

In some cases, such as Belgian Congo and French Guinea, departing colonialists deliberately looted and impoverished the colonies in order to spite the local agitators for political independence who were hurrying and harrying them out of Africa. Given that the colonial forms of governments had not yet become a part of the culture of Africans and that emergent states had not yet congealed into nation-states with a common vision, destiny, and identity, there were significant juridical, cultural, and institutional cracks and a vacuum of legitimate authority. Of course, it hardly needs restating that the evolution of common vision, destiny, and identity among people of various ethnic groups is a process that takes centuries, perhaps millennia. Consequently, the mantle of leadership fell on the few native elites who, in the absence of the requisite culture, institutions, and national cohesion, largely appropriated the vestiges and cultural imprints of colonial power for themselves.

Second, it ought to be borne in mind that the principal objective of the colonial enterprise was the economic exploitation of African peoples and resources. Instead of producing food for the populace, African agricultural methods, energies, and resources were radically altered and channelled towards producing agricultural raw materials for European factories. Tea, coffee, sisal, cocoa, cotton, rubber, gum arabic, and the like replaced food crops such as maize, rice, beans, cassava, and so on. Ironically, Africans have little domestic use or need for those industrial crops. Even in modern times, famine afflicts some African states as they sell tea, coffee, and cocoa. In effect, Africa became a continent famous for producing what it does not consume and consuming what it does not produce.

The colonial powers were preoccupied with the exploitation of their colonies rather than with their avowed messianic and civilizing mission to the African continent. Thus, there was a vacuum of viable political and economic structures for the good governance of the colonized peoples and the promotion of accountability. In many cases, the colonial bureaucracy was designed as a mechanism to facilitate the economic exploitation of natives and their resources in such tasks as mining, logging, tax collection, and the production of industrial raw materials for the cosmopolitan imperial cities. The machinery of government thus became a tool for legalized extortion of the people, allocation and transfer of wealth, and cronyism, and a pipe through which local wealth was funnelled abroad to the metropolis of Europe. For efficient exploitation of the natives, the colonialist officers and regime operated outside the pale of the minimum requirements of due process of law and legitimacy of governance; if the need arose, violence was liberally employed.

In Kenya, for example, Harvard professor Caroline Elkins's recent investigations show that over 50,000 native Kenyans were killed by British security forces in the colonial occupation of that state. According to the report, "new evidence has been unearthed alleging British atrocities, on such a scale that it will require the rewriting of British imperial history."[114] Given the prevalent practice of horrific tortures and murders imposed on anticolonialist elements in African states, colonial Africa was practically a slave labour camp. The African state was thus a law unto itself and unaccountable to the local inhabitants of the territories. The semblance of order it maintained was substantially devoted towards the exploitation of local resources, protection of the colonial elite, and intimidation of local citizenry. Rarely was the colonial overlord subjected to a regime of equality with the natives under the law. Consequently, the governments and cultural imprints inherited by the new African elite were deliberately designed to be impervious to social needs and public accountability. It is not a coincidence that many emergent African states, acting out the scripts already prepared in the colonial age, continued to be engines of terror and acted with impunity.

Rather than engage in a fundamental deconstruction and reconstruction of the postcolonial Africa polity, these direct and uncritical successors of the colonialist contraptions insisted on absolute loyalty to a fictitious nation-state. As Hansen laments, "though they were African themselves, the leaders ignored African identities, territories, and boundaries in favour of a European-defined one."[115] Ever since, African states have spent more time, money, and blood than all other continents grappling with dysfunctional and collapsing states. Far less time is devoted to the actual governance of the beleaguered peoples and nations of Africa. Consequently, postcolonial African states have the most bloated bureaucracies in the world and spend an overwhelming part of their annual incomes on oiling the wheels of government. For example, Nigeria spends nearly 80 percent of its annual budget on political officers and institutions that are largely designed to pacify representatives of restive nationalities or potentially disruptive elites.[116]

In the attempt to enforce "state unity" at all costs among ethnic groups with vastly different political values and institutions,[117] the African state thus became the greatest institution of patronage and the subject of "intense distributional conflicts."[118] In addition, some newly independent African states engaged in the populist but ill-advised nationalization of foreign industries. This merely provided more avenues for the opportunistic power holders and ruling cliques to dispense patronage to a few cronies, ethnic jingoists, and representatives of powerful or restive ethnic nationalities. Citizenship suffered, and prostituted loyalty to the government of the day (otherwise known in Nigerian parlance as Any-Government-in-Power [AGIP]) became the norm. As another observer noted, officeholders appropriated state resources to consolidate their power bases and reward their network of clients. State interests were subordinated to the interests of politicians and their supporters, who viewed public office as private property. Consequently, the age of clientelism, what Basil Davidson has referred to as the African equivalent of New York's infamous "Tammany Hall" conception of governance, took root in postcolonial Africa.

Hence, power in Africa was, and to a large extent still is, maintained by a convenient play of the "ethnic card,"[119] and governance, as instituted by the colonial overlords, degenerated into intricate ways of "sharing the national cake" among a narrow band of alienated elite. This is a system of mobilizing dubious ethnic sentiments to obfuscate important issues and deprive them of objectivity. For instance, a call for constitutional reform or reappraisal of the postcolonial state may be portrayed by government propaganda as a call by the proponent's ethnic group for dismemberment of the state in order to give political advantage to another group. These perversions weakened the internal legitimacy of the African states, rendering them excessively vulnerable to external forces.

In effect, rather than becoming an effective mechanism for the articulation of the means and framework in which life, liberty, and happiness may be enjoyed by its citizens, the African state, from its conception by the Europeans and its checkered life thereafter, has largely been a hostage of manufactured history, foreign or disconnected elitism, and clientelism. In this paradigm, Samuel Doe construed criticisms against his government as attempts by other ethnic groups to unseat his own ethnic group from power. He purported to be the champion of the Krahn ethnic group, and was so perceived by members of the other ethnic groups. To sustain himself in power, he mobilized his ethnic group by giving them preference over other groups. The loss of power by a leader like Doe constituted a credible threat to the viability of his ethnic group.[120]

Hence, like most other dictators of his ilk, he maintained his power by divide-and-rule tactics, pitting one ethnic group or set of vested interests against other ethnic groups or sets of vested interests. In the course of the subsequent crisis, the factions themselves naturally split along the lines of elitist cliques and, more importantly, ethnic lines, which of course ran deep into the territories of other neighbouring states. When coercion and appeasement failed, brute force was resorted to. In effect, the unity of several West African states such as Liberia has been sustained on a peculiar mixture of force, ethnic patronage, dysfunctional governments founded on clientelism, uncritical fidelity to colonial boundaries, and the prevailing international morality on the notions of sovereignty. The consent and informed participation of the governed have been of little relevance. These inequities and iniquities in African states were largely ignored for at least three reasons.

First, the new African states were creatures of a world order fashioned on the Westphalian paradigm, with its excessive deference to the canons of non-intervention in the internal affairs of other states. Second, the notion of statehood being largely juridical in the Eurocentric sense, and thus of marginal relevance to African history and experience, threw up empty shells and incongruous entities like Chad and Niger emerged as states. These sparsely populated territories with little or no cohesive structure of governance and cultural affinity between the constitutive nations over their arid and expansive territories, attained recognition as juridical states.[121] Third, prior to the end of the Cold War, the notion of collective security did not encompass "the development of human dignity and basic rights."[122] Although it was embedded in the United Nations Charter, peace and collective security were interchangeable with the absence of war. The Cold War/Westphalian notions of state sovereignty ensured that whatever went on within the borders of such countries was not the legitimate subject for external concern.

For African rulers who had inherited the colonial and artificial fiefdoms with their notorious indifference to the well-being of the citizenry, it was a licence to pillage the state and oppress their peoples as Cold War imperatives afforded both a shield and distraction. In effect, most of those juridical states, regardless of their absence or poverty of internal legitimacy in governance, survived as a result of the indifference of global power machinations to substantive justice in African states. The Westphalian doctrine of *cuius regio, eius religio* was, in Africa, read to mean that the prince (= president) was free to do as he or she liked within the boundaries of the artificial states. Like the colonial African states, the immediate postcolonial states were hostages of the new ruling cliques: postcolonial fiefdoms complete with the chicanery of illegitimate governance and rule by whim.

Hence, most African states became synonymous with the persona of those who ruled them. The examples are legion: Doe's Liberia, Nkrumah's Ghana, Kenyatta's Kenya, Banda's Malawi, Eyadema's Togo, Boigny's Côte d'Ivoire, Mobutu's Zaire, Selassie's/Mengistu's Ethiopia, Keita's Mali, Kerekou's Benin, Sekou Toure's Guinea, Nyerere's Tanzania, Kaunda's Zambia. The juridical state in Africa was merged and became synonymous with its ruler. The crisis of legitimacy in governance was occasionally resisted by boiling popular discontent, riots, strikes, and popular demonstrations, but violent forms of discontent, ethno-nationalism, quest for self-determination, and warlordism remained largely subdued. This state of affairs spanning what has been referred to as the lost three decades survived because of the bipolarization of global politics, the resolute fidelity of the African ruling elite to the colonial boundaries, and an uncritical narrative and praxis of the doctrine of sovereignty of states at international law.

In addition, Cold War politics enabled some African states to assert a misconceived notion of geopolitical relevance. They could obtain funds and arms from their superpower sponsors without questions about domestic political and economic accountability. Thus, rulers of states like Liberia, Zaire, and Somalia (among others), being of strategic geopolitical importance to the United States and the Soviet Union, survived on American or Soviet patronage and protection. It is here that the global community is indicted for its complicity in the reign of terror and bastardization of governance inflicted on the people of Africa, and indeed on all African nations.

Under the old regime, those who had effective control over the capital cities of the African countries and who possessed the keys to the presidential villas were feted, feasted, and hugged in the Kremlin, Bonn, the White House, the Elysée, and other centres of global power and legitimation. According to Clapham, this was the regime of "letter-box sovereignty."[123] Whoever happened to be the occupant of the presidential mansion was entitled to regard himself as the head of state of that country. It helped a lot if that occupant served an economic or geopolitical purpose agreeable to any of the contending superpowers. Their means of occupation and sustenance of that occupation were internal matters that their oppressed peoples should sort out by themselves. This was the classical age of the politics of patrimony and disconnected elitism in Africa.

Thus, by an adroit mixture of coercion and corruption of the domestic order and deft manipulation of the international security paradigm, a host of African rulers held sway in their respective presidential mansions for decades.[124] The notion of collective security excluded an activist, progressive, and cosmopolitan perception of justice and respect for substantive human rights in the plenitude of its contemporary expanding ramifications. In this withered conception of collective security and preoccupation with the conspiracies of the Cold War, Mobutu of Zaire, who fronted as a bulwark against communism, with the support of the United States, ruled and ruined Zaire with an iron fist for thirty-two years.[125]

Remarkably, the great powers often dispatched troops to save Mobutu each time an attempt was made to forcibly unseat him. However, Mobutu's political relevance to the US, France, and Belgium expired with the end of the Cold War, and he soon fell from power, died in exile in Morocco, and left his country embroiled in a chronic civil war. His personal fortune in European banks was estimated in 1982 at about $5 billion, the equivalent of Zaire's external debt.[126] Bernard Kouchner, the French Minister for Humanitarian Affairs and co-founder of Médecins Sans Frontières, scornfully described Mobutu as a "walking bank account in a Leopard skin hat."[127] When he was in power, however, he was most welcome at the Elysée.

Similarly, Mengistu Haile Mariam of Ethiopia and Mohammed Siad Barre of Somalia spouted communistic slogans and in return received Soviet military and economic support, which allowed them to tyrannize their countries for seventeen and twenty-two years, respectively.[128] According to Kofi Quashigah, "in their [the superpowers'] relationships with the African nations other determinants, such as morality and justice often played very minimal roles. The human rights implications of their policies in Africa were not often of prime consideration in the policies of the developed nations."[129] As events such as the Liberian crisis indicate, this regime undermined the emergence in Africa of legitimate systems of governance that would probably have avoided the internecine conflicts threatening the collective security of the entire continent.

Another aspect of the Cold War rivalry in Africa that impacted heavily on global collective security was the massive export of weapons to Africa, which the archetypal authoritarian regimes used to prop themselves up. To maintain the balance of terror all over the world, governments in Africa, irrespective of their degrees of illegitimacy, were substantially bolstered by arms from the superpowers in preparation for any eventual global showdown. Liberia alone received well over $500 million in military aid. In a country that had never engaged in an inter-state conflict and that had reasonably good relationships with its immediate neighbours, those guns and bombs could not but have been used on Liberians. This point was corroborated by

Congressman Ted Weiss in his speech on the Liberian crisis in the US Congress.[130] According to Weiss, "the United States certainly did not cause the current crisis in Liberia; this is a conflict between Liberian people over Liberian grievances. But as a result of the Administration's long silence, the United States must share some of the responsibility. Our Government failed to publicly demonstrate a commitment to protect human rights in Liberia. More importantly, we turned a blind eye to the aspirations of the Liberian people themselves, who should have been able to depend on the United States to speak out in defense of democracy and human rights."[131]

However, the regime of internal illegitimacy and external indifference was not to last forever. The end of the Cold War inspired in the West a self-serving movement towards a questionable regime of political and economic accountability in Africa. This movement, which has been hailed in some quarters as the dawn of a "Grotian moment," a juridical revolution,[132] is still unfolding, and its impact on the collective security and stability of West African states deserves some close consideration.

Orphaned by the end of the Cold War, these types of governments whose geopolitical relevance had just expired were confronted with the imperatives of legitimizing themselves with their people and grappling with the inconsistencies of the artificial state. It was a demand and necessity strange to them. Some of them who had used the universal preoccupation with the Cold War as a shield to cover atrocities perpetrated against their own people were faced with the challenges of a collapsing artifice: the artificial African state mired in moral, juridical, and structural disorientation. The people hitherto oppressed not only sought economic and political liberation but in some cases craved vengeance.

The demand for this historical indebtedness, in the form of state failure and consequent warlordism and other forms of militaristic dissent, came at a critical time. The Soviet Union's *Perestroika* and *Glasnost* and the United States' domestic problems did not warrant superpower concern in Africa's perennial conflict. Accordingly, most of the African governments had few resources or even the political will and courage needed to address the root causes of the conflicts and douse the flames of discontent. Support at international forums and the flow of military and economic aid were no longer to be taken for granted merely because the affected regime espoused capitalist or communist doctrines or served a geopolitical purpose. In the new fad of "human rights," it is significant that "foreign aid" was conditioned on economic policies or political changes. In the latter case, neoliberal prescriptions such as periodic elections, privatization of public utilities, multiparty politics, and other manifestations of Western preoccupation with political and civil rights (while understating the radical importance of economic, social, and cultural rights) became fashionable. Again, the erroneous conception of Africa as a monolithic entity devoid of history held sway as virtually all the international financial institutions and their sponsor governments uncritically prescribed the same solution for fifty-three different African states peopled by societies that speak more than 400 different languages in the world's second largest continent.

Indeed, what is more disturbing is the insistence on the mainstream ideology of human rights and excessive emphasis on periodic elections without a fundamental appraisal and reconstruction of the African state as presently constituted and governed. This attitude is reductionist and simplistic as a solution to the crises that afflict most postcolonial African states. To construe human rights and democracy within the stifling and narrow context of periodic elections in a multiparty system without seriously redressing historical inequities in the polity and economy, and without proper regard for African value systems of social and economic justice and dignity, minority rights, and self-determination of peoples, is itself a travesty of human rights.[133]

The post–Cold War embrace of this abridged and expedient concept of human rights, which came to be christened the "La Boulle Doctrine,"[134] apparently gave vent to diverse forces within the polity of many African countries and is partly the cause of the ubiquitous "democratic" changes sprouting up in African states. It was in this context that President Doe contrived a "democratic" election in 1986. Similar events took place in Kenya, Benin, Zambia, Tanzania, Malawi, and Côte d'Ivoire, to mention a few.[135] The one-party states yielded to multiparty politics, and these hollow rituals satisfied Western prescriptions of democracy. Needless to add, the ceremonies were too often window dressing and a sham. No sooner are "elections" held under the "supervision" of Western political figures and civil society organizations than another crisis unfolds.

As already noted, a considerable number of these democratizations were pathetic travesties, merely designed to satisfy the rhetoric and ideological prescriptions of Western financial institutions, "human rights activists," and uncritical government officials in the West. It was therefore not surprising that in the absence of a fundamental rethinking and restructuring of the postcolonial African state, trouble loomed. In some cases, this took the form of militaristic rebellion and warlordism. In this context, Liberia was the epitome of governmental dysfunction, political chicanery, and the expediency of international politics. It is also in the recognition of the consequences of the Berlin Conference borders that the anxiety of Liberia's neighbouring states may be appreciated. The era of overbearing illegitimate governments sustained by fictional respect for juridical statehood stood in grave danger, but more worrisome was the nature of the replacement. The challenge was not welcomed by the old order.[136]

Furthermore, the growing marginalization of Africa in the post–Cold War era has created a vacuum of leadership that economically stronger states like Nigeria,[137] South Africa, and Zimbabwe have sought to fill in those crises that ostensibly threatened regional security. As this shift in power unravelled some African countries,[138] its consequences became more pronounced for two reasons. The first relates to Africa's chronic political instability,[139] and the second is a function of the Berlin Conference partitioning of Africa and the complications of cross-border ethno-nationalism.[140] Accordingly, the success of a militaristic challenge to the old order is not limited to the particular municipal forum where its success has been recorded but extends to neighbouring states sharing identical ethnic origins.

In addition, successful rebellions provide a strong precedent for similar ideas and sentiments in neighbouring states. As the saying in West Africa goes, "when Ghana sneezes, Nigeria catches cold." Hence, President Jawara of Gambia lamented (three months before he was removed by a coup d'état) that "if Charles Taylor with the support of what I may call mercenaries from other countries of the sub-region were to come into power, one can imagine the implications it would have for regional stability."[141] During the Biafran secession bid in Nigeria, the leaders of the Ewe nation (straddling Ghana and Togo) indicated their readiness to declare their statehood if the Biafrans succeeded or if the Biafrans were supported by the Ghanaian government.[142] The combination of these factors in the Liberian crisis created an explosive mix capable of destabilizing other governments in the subregion.[143] It is in this context that the argument by the West African states that the Liberian crisis posed a danger to their territorial integrity rings politically and historically true.

At this point, it is important to comment on the questionable role of some West African states in encouraging and fuelling the rebellion by Charles Taylor. Although the Liberian conflict has been depicted as a Liberian affair, there is some evidence to support the opinion that from the conception of the rebellion to its execution, it was more than that. For various reasons, the neighbouring states were hardly disinterested observers. First, the original batch of twenty-four NPFL rebels had some sprinkling of Gambian, Ghanaian, and Sierra Leonean nationals. It is remarkable that among them was Foday Sankoh, the head of the rebel movement that nearly destroyed Sierra Leone.

The pertinent question is why these people of disparate nationalities should have banded together. While some sit-tight West African leaders such as Dauda Jawara of Gambia and Mathew Kerekou of Benin, who have between them spent nearly fifty years in office, were content to dismiss the rebels as mercenaries, it seems that money was not the only factor. Some of them were ideologues and disgruntled elites disgusted with the political decadence and drift in West Africa, as symbolized by the Doe regime in Liberia. In their view, the rebellion led by Charles Taylor was a "revolution" against the old order represented by Doe.[144] Second, it has to be reiterated that the

African colonial state was designed to be a site for the allocation and transfer of indigenous loot and local resources extorted or obtained from the natives. In effect, successful control of the apparatus of state has its material rewards in Africa. Hence, those dissidents had ample precedent, stretching from the colonial overlords to their domestic apprentices, for believing that their success would translate into economically lucrative political offices.

Prior to the invasion, however, Taylor travelled within the West African subregion organizing dissidents and exiles from Doe's tyranny.[145] Taylor's personal charisma and superb abilities as a fundraiser and organizer produced results. Doe's tyranny had created many enemies, particularly in the displaced ruling clique, and previous attempts to unseat him by coups d'état and democratic elections had been ruthlessly crushed. Doe had become a pariah in regional political circles, with the notable exception of Nigeria under General Babangida. Liberia's relevance in the Cold War had expired, increasing Doe's isolation. Thus, the new international order, regional ostracism, Doe's appalling record, and the conviction that only an armed invasion could rid Liberia of him were decisive factors favouring the rebellion.

Although externally funded armed invasions of African states have been recorded, Kwesi Aning observes that the "Liberian instance represents an entirely new dimension. For the first time neighbouring states advanced patronage to a well-orchestrated act of insurrection with strong support among the states of the region."[146] Similar observations have been made by Emeka Nwokedi, who notes that the Liberian conflict marked "the first large-scale and sustained civilian campaign from an extra-territorial base against a government in West Africa."[147] Regarding Ghana, Doe's coup of April 1980 and its excesses had strained relations between Ghana and Liberia. Repeated Liberian allegations of subversion by Ghana led to the occasional mutual recall of ambassadors.[148] There is no doubt that Ghana initially extended some degree of patronage to Charles Taylor when the latter was planning the rebellion against Doe. It appeared, however, that this romance did not last long, as Taylor's recruitment of rebels in Ghana became a security concern for Ghanaian authorities, and he was consequently detained twice. Taylor had become a problem. Quoting a Ghanaian intelligence officer, Aning notes that "there were a number of Ghanaian dissidents willing to fight alongside Taylor in Liberia."[149]

It was not only Ghana that inadvertently or otherwise contributed to the creation of the NPFL. Byron Tarr asserts that "in 1987, Taylor approached the embassy of Burkina Faso in Accra and requested assistance to overthrow Doe ... Madame Mamouna Quattara, a client of Captain Blaise Compaore [the Burkinabe President] received Taylor's written proposal."[150] Taylor eventually gained access to the Burkinabes and thence to Ghaddafi of Libya, who had financed the Thomas Sankara/Compaore revolution in Burkina Faso. Stedman is thus correct in his argument that Burkina Faso, Côte d'Ivoire, and Libya provided military assistance to Charles Taylor's forces in Liberia. It is equally instructive that the Burkinabe government, at the Twenty-Seventh Summit of the Organization of African Unity in Abuja, Nigeria, gave assurances to the "Interim Government in Liberia that Mr. Taylor would no longer enjoy their support."[151]

At the start of the rebellion, the government of Burkina Faso dispatched 400 of its troops to Charles Taylor and justified this as "moral support."[152] According to Mark Huband, "in early 1991, the Nigerians confirmed that Taylor visited the Burkina Faso capital of Ougadougou and was developing plans to train mercenaries at the Po military base south of the city. The force included nationals from Liberia, Burkina Faso, Ivory Coast and Guinea and was being trained as new weapons were transported across Ivory Coast into Liberia."[153]

As for Libya, its attempts to influence sub-Saharan African affairs is well known.[154] A significant number of the first batch of the NPFL rebels were Burkinabe and or trained in Burkina Faso and in Libyan military camps.[155] Indeed, one of the reasons given by Yormie Johnson for splitting with the NPFL to found the INPFL was that there were improprieties in disbursing Libyan finances. He also alleged excessive Libyan influence over the NPFL. Similarly, in February 1992, Liberian Interim President Amos Sawyer led a delegation to the Libyan leader, Muammar Ghaddafi, in an effort to persuade him to stop supporting Taylor's NPFL. According to Sawyer, "Ghaddafi told me that he made a mistake in supporting Charles Taylor because he [Taylor] was now a tool of French imperialism, to whom he had stopped supplying weapons in December 1991."[156]

This welter of evidence was confirmed by Herman Cohen, then US Assistant Secretary of State for African Affairs. In his testimony before the US Congress, he asserted that "we do have some evidence that about 50 of those people (the NPFL) rebels were trained in Libya and armed by Libya."[157] The Burkinabe/Libyan/Ivorian support for the NPFL was further evidenced by their initial strong refusal to contribute forces to ECOMOG. In addition, they persuaded some West African states not to support the intervention. During the crisis, ECOMOG jet bombers strafed the supply lines linking the rebels to their supply bases in Burkina Faso and Côte d'Ivoire. The support for the NPFL by some states and individuals had economic, ideological, military, ethnic, and personal motives.[158] As Croft and Treacher note, "Liberia was the stage for a bitter struggle for dominance within the ECOWAS; the organization was fissured along Anglophone and Francophone lines. The Peace process was subsumed by the respective regional interests and the personal ambitions of the political leaders. Each state had a different agenda for the Liberian crisis. Above all, Nigeria saw the war as a test of what it perceived to be its regional hegemony, for it was determined that

Liberia would not succumb to the NPFL and then join the francophone bloc inside ECOWAS."[159]

Nigerian support for the Doe regime has never been substantially rebutted by that country. Nigeria took over the repayment of the $50 million African Development Bank debt owed by Liberia in May 1990, and it was widely alleged that the embattled President Doe, during his visit to Nigeria, asked for 2,000 Nigerian troops to counter the NPFL rebellion. It was common knowledge that the Nigerian government headed by General Babangida was particularly close to or at least sympathized with Doe's regime in Liberia. The Nigerian factor was crucial and decisive in influencing the Liberian crisis. In addition, it marked the height of the competition for influence between France and Nigeria.[160]

Another international aspect of the Liberian conflict is discernible from the hostage-taking policies of the rebel groups. These policies were adopted for various reasons. While the NPFL targeted Nigerians, Guineans, and Ghanaians and kidnapped and killed them because of their governments' support for ECOMOG, Yormie Johnson's INPFL justified its preference for American, British, Lebanese, and Indian civilians in order to provoke international intervention in the crisis. This strategy worked in varying degrees and eventually elicited some response from the international community.

It is equally pertinent that the field of conflict was not restricted to Liberian territory, quite apart from the traditional support that rebel movements usually get from some neighbouring countries or ethnic groups sympathetic to their struggle. For instance, the NPFL rebels on 23 March 1991 attacked two towns in Sierra Leone, killing two senior military officers and eleven civilians. This invasion, which enabled the rebels to secure transit for the flow of arms into Liberia, ultimately led to the downfall of the government of President Joseph Saidu Momoh. In addition, one of the Sierra Leoneans trained in Libya for the NPFL invasion of Liberia, Corporal Foday Sankoh, founded the Revolutionary United Front (RUF), which waged a fratricidal war in Sierra Leone. Indeed, the Sierra Leone conflict is probably unmatched in its savagery and wickedness. Children as young as two months were regularly hacked to death and often had their limbs cut off by the "Cut Hands Commando" units of the rebels. By the end of the Sierra Leone conflict in May 2002, the RUF rebellion had killed 50,000 Sierra Leoneans, mutilated over 100,000, pushed over 1 million into neighbouring states as refugees, and internally displaced over 2 million (half of the population).[161] At the inception of the crisis, the Secretary-General of the Commonwealth warned that:

> Sierra Leone faces a tragedy unprecedented in its history and horrendous even by the standards of a world increasingly inured to the brutalities of

> war. The entire population of Sierra Leone, without exception, is at the mercy of a murderous rebel war machine which makes no distinction between women and children on the one hand and combatants on the other. The escalation in the amputation of limbs and other bestialities, to say nothing of the almost random mass killings of defenceless civilians, point to a Dark Age threatening to overtake Sierra Leone. The vaunted scorched-earth policy launched by the RUF has left Sierra Leone's infrastructure in ruins and thousands of homes in Freetown and elsewhere in the country burnt and razed to the ground ... in Sierra Leone, no less than in Kosovo, the sentience of the world community faces its sternest test.[162]

The impact of the Liberian crisis on Sierra Leone formed the substance of the belated deliberations of the United Nations General Assembly at its eighty-sixth plenary meeting held on 21 December 1993.[163] The subsequent resolution passed by that body included the following findings:

- that the spillover effect of the Liberian crisis had caused serious destruction and devastation of the productive areas of the territory of Sierra Leone and of its economy as a whole
- that the conflict in Liberia had "devastated lives and properties in the eastern and southern provinces of Sierra Leone, causing massive outflows of refugees and displaced persons."[164]

These factors exacted an astronomical cost on the government of Sierra Leone, which had to battle to protect its territory and people from the spillover effect of the conflict in Liberia. For a country that was included by the General Assembly in its Resolution 37/133 of 17 December 1982 as one of the least industrialized countries in the world, the tragedy was and still remains harrowing. What is more disturbing about the global response or lack thereof to the Sierra Leone conflict is that such a tragedy, which United Nations Human Rights Commissioner Mary Robinson acknowledged was twenty-five times more horrendous than the Kosovo tragedy, elicited little or no early response from the great powers. According to the BBC's Mark Doyle, who closely followed the events surrounding the West's response to the conflict, "it is not an exaggeration to suggest, just tentatively, that the international reaction to Sierra Leone might have been very different if all those people with their limbs chopped off had been white."[165]

Be that as it may, it was not only Sierra Leone that bore the brunt of the spreading conflict. Taylor's forces also plundered parts of Guinea, and the war spilled over into Côte d'Ivoire as well.[166] Scholars are divided on the motives for this internationalization of the Liberian conflict, especially with respect to Sierra Leone. According to William Reno, the NPFL invaded the diamond mines of Sierra Leone to finance its rebellion. This allegation is credible, particularly in light of the fact that the United Nations Security Council unanimously passed a resolution on 7 March 2001 prohibiting arms sales to Liberia for its subversive role in the so-called conflict diamonds of Sierra Leone.[167]

Apart from the economic motivation, however, political-cum-military significance has been read into the NPFL invasion of Sierra Leone, more so as the NPFL invasion "sparked off another civil war in Sierra Leone."[168] The civil war in that country as provoked and sustained by Taylor's NPFL has thus been construed as Taylor's "punishment for Sierra Leone's participation in the ECOWAS led intervention in Liberia."[169] Whatever the motives, the reality is that after the NPFL rebellion in Liberia sparked the rebellion in Sierra Leone, that country became one of the most dangerous places in the world, with a mounting refugee crisis threatening to destabilize the subregion.[170]

Similarly, some of the rebel groups in Liberia, such as the United Liberation Movement for Democracy in Liberia (ULIMO) and the Lofa Defence Force (LDF), were formed in Sierra Leone and Guinea, and it was for these reasons that the United Nations Security Council unequivocally determined that the deteriorating situation in Liberia constituted "a threat to international peace and security, particularly West Africa as a whole."[171] Another aspect that probably lends credence to the destabilizing ability of the Liberian crisis was the ease of the arms flow within the subregion, which has been acknowledged as the root of the intractable nature of the ongoing civil war in Sierra Leone. As Stedman noted, "Africa's wars have created a booming cross-border traffic in small arms. This leads to political instability in several ways. The availability of arms and the porousness of borders will intensify civil conflicts in several African states where dictators have fanned ethnic hatred in order to stay in power. Countries that are trying to manage democratic transitions find that disgruntled groups have access to weapons and can challenge the viability of new governments."[172] In an ostensible attempt to curtail this ugly trend, the United Nations Security Council, in Resolution 788 of 1992, imposed a complete arms embargo on Liberia and called on all member states to exercise self-restraint in their relations with all parties to the Liberian conflict and to refrain from taking any action that would be inimical to the peace process. Apparently this exhortation fell on deaf ears. According to the United Nations Report for 1995, "factions continued to acquire arms across the borders," and this was attributed to the inability of ECOMOG to deploy troops at the major points across the borders of Liberia in accordance with the Cotonou Accord.

The Security Council was thus compelled to note with concern that "in violation of Resolution 788 of 1992, arms continue to be imported into Liberia, exacerbating the conflict."[173] Besides reaffirming the embargo on the supply of arms to the rebels, the Security Council took a further step by establishing an arms-monitoring committee of the Council to seek from all states, and in particular all neighbouring states, information on action taken by them concerning the effective implementation of the arms embargo. In addition, the committee was to recommend appropriate measures in response to violations of the arms embargo.

Having examined the internal contradictions and weaknesses in the Liberia polity that rendered it very vulnerable to external factors fuelling the rebellion, I must draw some conclusions. First, the absence of real states in which autochthonous forms of legitimate governance could be practised was a situation fraught with grave risks to African stability. African alienation from its original history was a project fraught with immense risks. Second, the global world order's view of collective security and peace as the absence of war was ruinously shortsighted. Third, the illegitimacy of governance lasted so long principally because the prevailing international order tolerated, and in some cases supported and sustained, domestic political anomie in the contrived states.

On the other hand, the redefinition of collective security to include concepts hitherto excluded imposed a severe strain on most illegitimate regimes, which were in any case an endangered species. West African states connived at the creation of and in some cases collaborated with, different factions, ethnic groups, and camps in Liberia, and this had an impact on the duration and spread of the crisis. While the complicity of some West African states in the Liberian crisis may not meet the austere standards set by the International Court of Justice in the *Nicaragua Case* regarding state responsibility for support of rebellions (with which I shall deal later), the facts of the Liberian crisis at least show that they (the West African states) were not innocent or disinterested bystanders.

Furthermore, the resulting refugee crisis was a threat to the collective security of the subregion. According to Michael Brown, "at a minimum, refugees impose heavy economic burdens on host states, and they pose political and security problems as well."[174] In the Rwandan crisis, 250,000 Rwandans fled into Tanzania in a single day.[175] In the Liberian crisis, over 1.7 million people out of its estimated population of 2 million were internally and externally displaced.

The important normative point here is that until recently, internal conflicts that created large numbers of internally displaced persons have been largely ignored by the international community and were not necessarily construed as threats to international peace. In contrast, by articulating the contemporary features of the notion of collective security, the Security Council determined that the Liberian crisis was a threat to international peace and security. This metamorphosis of the concept and scope of collective security poses immense challenges to the emerging global regime on peace and security. After the events of 11 September 2001, it now seems clear that the degeneration of one state may no longer be considered a benign event to other states, no matter how widely separated they are by geographic distance.

As the distance between states shrinks in the age of globalization, new security issues emerge. Consequently, the concept of collective security is more likely to assume modern meanings not contemplated by the original jurisprudence of the United Nations Charter. Whether the reconfigured and changing meanings of collective security will act as a cloak for the international projection of the self-interest of powerful states is an open question. However, a deeper appreciation of the possible future directions of the concept of collective security requires careful consideration of the history and development of this concept, particularly in the modern context of groups of states or "coalitions of the willing" evincing a willingness to unilaterally respond to circumstances considered by them to be threats to global security. These issues are examined in the next chapter.

2
Collective Security and the Liberian Conflict

The concept of collective security and the notion that events in Liberia constituted a threat to regional peace and security formed the rationale for the intervention by West African states in the Liberian crisis. It is equally significant that in responding to the conflict, the United Nations Security Council came to the conclusion that the collapse of Liberia had degenerated into a threat to international peace and security. Both conceptions of the Liberian crisis raise considerable questions regarding (1) when the nature and scope of events in a state may be determined to be, or may be construed as, a threat to international peace, (2) who may legitimately make such a determination, and (3) the appropriate agency or institution that may respond to that threat.

The reason why these questions are of grave import is that the answers constitute the trigger mechanism or threshold for the use of force in international law outside the narrow confines of self-defence. The nature of internal anomie in a state, the juridical status of the institution making the determination that a state of affairs in a state is so anomalous as to constitute a threat to international peace, and the appropriate institution authorized to respond accordingly are indispensable criteria in determining the lawful use of force in international law. In the post 11 September 2001 era and the current "war on terror," and with the increasing threat of unilateral use of force by some states, the response of the Economic Community of West African States (ECOWAS) to the Liberian crisis becomes a disturbing precedent. This is so because it was one of those rare cases where a group of states practically usurped the function and role of the Security Council by using force to resolve an apparently domestic crisis that they perceived to constitute a threat to international peace and security.

The Classical Notion of Collective Security

> *Domestic interests are no longer defined as belonging to a sphere separate from that of international interests; rather, they are seen as*

> *existing in relation to transnational, regional and global spheres. The space of international law is becoming increasingly international, as opposed to inter-statal, and the state is no longer capable of serving as the sole locus of international law's legitimacy.*[1]
>
> – *Jaye Ellis*

In spite of the ubiquitous character of the notion of collective security and its common currency in international law, collective security is in fact one of the most elusive ideas in the regulation of use of force in international relations. Consider, for instance, the United Nations. It is supposed to be the manifestation and realization of the immensity of the doctrine of collective security, yet nowhere in its Charter does the term "collective security" appear. It is not only in this type of great omission that the concept of collective security betrays its elusiveness; teachings by publicists and the behaviour of states have not lent much clarity to its precepts.

This state of affairs is perhaps traceable to the intrinsically fluid and organic nature of the concept of collective security, and also to the confusion of its earliest proponents. They battled with the political realities of the day, and thus propounded a doctrine heavily dependent on the expediencies of perceived national interests. Where the political wind blew affected politicians' perception and conception of the doctrine. Thus, President Woodrow Wilson, reputed to be the father of collective security, was himself steeped in confusion on the issue. From his first idea of a "universal government of all states," which is central to the concept of collective security, he tumbled into the slippery and parochial doctrine of balance of power.[2] In fairness to him, however, at the Paris Peace Conference of 1919 convened shortly after the First World War, he persuaded the Conference to accept that "collective security requires the creation of a global apparatus capable of giving institutional expression to its basic principles."[3]

In spite of this impressive intention to actualize collective security in its purity, President Wilson could not sell the idea to the American Congress, especially the Senate. The Senate refused to ratify the Covenant of the League of Nations, and the United States never joined the League. Thus, the ideal yielded to a cruder version of the convenient and expedient. Like the Concert of Europe, the truncation of the concept of collective security and the halfhearted attempts to enforce its diluted version sounded its death knell. Through the mealy-mouthed response of the great powers to the Japanese aggression in Manchuria and the halfhearted reaction to Mussolini's grave pretensions in Ethiopia, the concept of collective security stumbled and wobbled into disrepute.

It was not only President Wilson who engaged in conceptual somersaults on the question of collective security. In 1936, when Italian troops invaded Ethiopia and thereby exposed the impotence of the League of Nations and its dubious relevance to global security, Canadian Prime Minister Mackenzie King dismissed calls for a collective restraint of Italy. In his view, the concept of collective security was "a hypothetical argument, bearing no relation to the actualities of the day."[4] It was probably safe for him to say so, since Canada was not facing any direct threat from Mussolini's dangerous escapades in Ethiopia. Three years later, when Mussolini, in collaboration with the awesome Nazi war machine, was mowing down Western civilization and knocking on Canadian doors, Prime Minister King changed his mind. In an ideological reversal, he lamented that "if Britain goes down, if France goes down, the whole business of isolation will prove to have been a myth."[5]

With the concept of collective security hostage to swinging Euro-American states' interests, it took a combination of Adolf Hitler's monstrous policies of a German *lebensraum* and "final solution" and the American explosion of two nuclear devices in Japan for parts of the world to perceive collective security as a global issue. Purporting to have learned profound lessons from the disaster of the Second World War, humanity denounced aggression and embraced an enhanced concept of collective security.[6] With this new lease on life, the concept emerged in postwar discourse as the Holy Grail of perpetual peace. In ways reminiscent of global outrage against the dastardly events of 11 September 2001 in the United States, politicians extolled the virtues of interdependence, multilateralism, and collective security as irreplaceable virtues and the path to global peace and security.

The concept of collective security is premised on the theory that peace is universal and indivisible.[7] This notion, it seems, attains its greatest popularity among states after the dissipation of blood and life in expensive warfare or, as in recent times, in the aftermath of growing acts of international terrorism. In its classical theory, the concept of collective security thrives on the practical supposition that "a world wide combination of all states against all potential aggressors would create a global system of collective security."[8] Indeed, the history of inter-state relationships confirms the abiding notion that states find security in combining with other states that on the whole share some of their values and most of their interests.[9] No state has yet admitted that peace is not a universally shared value. It is upon this seemingly trite principle that the whole edifice of global collective security encompassing the elaborateness of the United Nations and the ubiquitous nature of its agencies is built. As a doctrine, collective security assumes that any aberrant aggression in the face of communal devotion to peace and unanimity of strength would be unprofitable, if not suicidal. It affirms that human societies (here identified as states) are not suicide clubs.[10] As such, no state would be inclined towards aggression knowing that such a course of action would ultimately lead to its defeat and possible destruction. Kelsen compared the rationale for collective security to individual experiences at municipal law. He argued that just as individualistic attempts at security in municipal law are futile, so are individual state attempts at international law. In his words, "security can only be collective, security is a pleonastic term."[11]

Scholars such as Otto and Critchley have asked the question that strikes at the very root of the principle of collective security. In their view, if peace is manifestly desirable, an absolute good, and of universal value, why do we need collective institutionalization and maximization of the means of coercion to secure it? Henry Kissinger offers a rather pragmatic answer. In his view, in spite of the touted rationality of humanity, the practice of states in the course of history confirms that where peace is premised upon mere gentle persuasions of its inherent goodness, humanity has always been at the mercy of the most ruthless dictator in the international community.[12] Collective security affirms the inherent rationality of humanity but does close its eyes to human nature and history.

While there is merit in Otto and Critchley's argument, there is a danger in assuming that collective security depends solely on maximum unification of the international means of coercion. First, collective security is not about military alliances per se, or sabre rattling. Just as the coercive instrument in the state goes beyond the police and other awesome institutions of force and enforced obedience, the concept of collective security goes beyond global machinery for enforced compliance with international law. Collective security includes the knowledge and consciousness that acts of states that disturb international peace are prohibited in the conduct of inter-state relations, save where justified at international law. It confesses the existence of certain universal values that states are obliged to obey, not necessarily by compulsion or force but by a recognition of the legitimacy, justice, and rationality of such norms. It invokes normativity and reasonableness in the behaviour of states, and rewards them accordingly. Towards this end, collective security includes the spirit or notion of legitimacy in international justice and rule of law. It acknowledges that the internal stability of states and global security interact continuously.

In practice, collective security has not always been the exemplar of global consensus and rationality. This inconsistency is apparent in post–Second World War theory and state practice. The theoretical dissonance is to be examined first. Some scholars, such as Hans Kelsen, argue that the concept of collective security may be compatible with devolution of the mechanism of international coercion to regional bodies. Others, such as M.V. Naidu and Inis Claude,[13] argue otherwise. Claude and Naidu prefer the more idealistic and classical view of collective security. In their view, universal collectivity is the means and security is the end – that is, security of all states, by all states, and for all states. In this context, absolute centralization and universalization of Western notions of morality and means of coercion are the fundamental characteristics of collective security. Unlike Kelsen's compromise, there are no half measures: there is either a universal and centralized security system or nothing. In this pure theory of collective security, which approximates to a world government, there is no "aggression" by states per se, as there is a world order. Delicts by states will thus rank as illegal use of force necessitating global police action.

The intellectual rigour and purity posited by Claude and Naidu is a far cry from state practice at international law. In spite of the clamour for the ideal, the practice of states since the end of the Second World War until the late 1980s shows a bifurcation of the world order along the lines of the Soviet- and American-led race for arms supremacy. In effect, universality lost out and the concept of collective security became a pawn of Cold War politics and intrigue. Although the development of security alliances (fashioned along the lines of the Cold War attrition) as the active engine room for the maintenance of international peace is hardly unprecedented,[14] its consequences are no less worrying.[15] Some scholars blame the origin and spread of the practice of regional security outfits in the postwar era on Soviet hegemonic tendencies.[16]

This tendency was enhanced by auspicious circumstances and Russia's keen awareness of the lessons of its own history. The Teutonic invasions of the thirteenth century, the Polish/Lithuanian attack of the seventeenth century, the Swedish invasion of 1812, and Hitler's Operation Barbarossa had all combined to persuade the Russians that their survival depended on the security of their European borders. Ideologically, the doctrines of Marxism had predicted an inevitable showdown between capitalism and communism. Hence, the Soviet-Russian position on collective security grew out of a combination of historical and ideological concerns. As the now-defunct Soviet Union imposed its will in East Europe in apparent preparation for the Marxist-prophesied showdown between capitalism and socialism, the Western world took note and responded accordingly. The Soviet Union, yielding to its historical concern with securing its problematic European flank, proceeded to establish satellite states.

In response, the United States encouraged the immediate rearming of the Federal Republic of Germany and the creation of the North Atlantic Treaty Organization (NATO).[17] In a counter-response, the Soviet Union and its client states of Poland, the German Democratic Republic, Czechoslovakia, Romania, Bulgaria, Hungary, and Albania formed a formal regional security arrangement under the Treaty of Friendship, Cooperation, and Mutual Assistance signed in Warsaw, Poland.[18] With these arrangements, the arms race between both systems/regions began. In this race, the obvious loser was the cosmopolitan definition of collective security.

However, with the proliferation and optimization of the dreadful capabilities of thermonuclear devices, it probably dawned on all[19] that no one, including the comradely communist and the profit-seeking capitalist, would survive a thermonuclear holocaust.[20] To the contrary, such a conflict would wipe out all of humanity several times over. Such was the complete triumph of the truncated version of collective security that for nearly fifty years after the end of the Second World War, the globe was preoccupied with the intrigues, machinations, and politics of the Cold War.[21] Peace and collective security thus became negatively defined and circumscribed as the absence of war. While this truncated concept of collective security, evidenced by the rise of regional security arrangements and the peace of the graveyard, may have marked a triumph for superpower politics, Quincy Wright opines that it was a loss to international law.[22] He argues that while the trend probably produced a balance of power, it failed to create a legally restrained world community. In the harsher judgment of Naidu, the trend was "a diffused and demented version of the collective security envisaged by the United Nations Charter."[23] In his view, such regionalism runs counter to collective security as it means security for some and not for all. However, such arrangements as represented by the NATO and Warsaw Pact alliances are distinguishable from the Protocol on Mutual Assistance on Defence (PMAD) of ECOWAS.[24] The difference is that, unlike NATO and similar organizations, which are aimed at deterring inter-state aggression, the PMAD encompasses intra-state conflicts that threaten regional security.

From the foregoing analysis, it can be said that the notion of collective security was primarily focused on peace and the avoidance of war. In recent times, however, the concept of collective security has assumed a more globalized content and anthropocentric, if not environmental, bias. Collective security now includes legitimate concerns for the security implications of such diverse issues as nuclear weapons,[25] environmental degradation, mass migration, democratization of states, sea and water pollution, ozone layer depletion, and myriad issues hitherto construed as being within the exclusive domain of state sovereignty. It is therefore important at this stage to comment on the changing content of collective security vis-à-vis state sovereignty.

The Westphalian notion of state sovereignty acknowledges the boundaries of the state as that sphere of a peopled territory with an effective government within which the institutions of governance are not accountable or answerable to external entities.[26] In the relationship of one state with another, the idea of statehood, the juridical means of its attainment, and its overall features, a strong preference for pragmatism in its jurisprudence was manifest.[27] This regime emerged from the decay and collapse of papal authority in temporal matters and the supplanting of the church in political matters by the emergent states of Europe. Anxious to blunt the edges of extreme nationalism, the inherent inequality of states, and the dangers of absolute sovereignty, the nascent Christian, European states at the famous Peace of Westphalia (1648) evolved a policy of juridical equality of all states and qualified state sovereignty in the domestic terrain. It was this emerging order, especially the central role of states in the new dispensation, that Hugo Grotius ably foretold and articulated in his groundbreaking work entitled *De Jure Belli ac Pacis*.[28]

The emergent Grotian age, as it came to be known, was marked by a system of balance of power, settlement of disputes by mediation, growth of diplomacy, restraint on the use of force, and development of international law premised on Christian/Eurocentric values and philosophies.[29] The Westphalian[30] and Grotian conceptions of sovereignty hinged on the equality of states and the supremacy of the sovereign in the state. Although the sovereign in states, most often the royalty, had near-absolute discretion in fixing the boundaries for the expression of human interests in their domain, state sovereignty has never been absolute but always qualified. For example, the Treaty of Onasbruck and similar international agreements provided for the humane treatment of minorities within states.

However, the basic unit of international discourse and interaction was the state, and the regime of collective security and the means for securing it were through the restraint of inter-state aggression and by the promotion of diplomacy. More importantly, the state was distrusted and its ability for mischief was virtually a given. The state having been construed as a potential vampire, a savage, and innately inclined to excesses,[31] particularly at the international level, it was imperative to create juridical and institutional measures to restrain and check its power. Regrettably, great emphasis was placed on the state's external savagery and potential for regional or continental mischief. The internal (il)legitimacy of the state and its apparatus was often given short shrift. In effect, collective security meant the absence of international war, and whoever held the mantle of power in the state and maintained peace, even if it was the peace of the graveyard, was the recognized head of that country.

Apparently, the carnage of the Second World War contributed to further entrenchment of the view that peace was the mere absence of war. However, the UN Charter acknowledged respect for human dignity, particularly within the narrower paradigm of political and civil rights, as basic to collective security. The overall earth space was grandly conceived as the turf for collective security, but this noble vision was to remain obscured by the politics and intrigues of the Cold War. Abuses of human rights and mutilation of the economic and social aspirations of peoples were routinely dismissed, especially in colonial and postcolonial Africa, as matters within the domestic competence of states that other states had no legitimate right to address.

It was under this regime that most states with what Obiora Okafor has aptly termed chronic municipal "legitimacy deficits"[32] relied on the international order fashioned on a "law and order" paradigm to engage in serial and systemic abuses of human rights.

Given the legacy of illegitimacy of colonial governments and the withered jurisdiction of internal legal systems, domestic courts too reflected the values of this regime of near-absolute state sovereignty and the narrow conception of legitimacy in governance vis-à-vis collective security. Thus, the Privy Council in the case of *Mitchell and Others* v. *D.P.P.* held that "the issue as to whether *de jure* recognition was to be given to a revolutionary regime was a matter of municipal law in the state, and not international law."[33] This deplorable regime continued until late into the 1980s.[34] However, the concept of collective security has shown resilience, and there now seems to be a disposition to import wider concerns such as social justice, environmentalism, refugees and mass migration, self-determination of peoples, nuclear weaponry and arms races, substantive democratization, and so on.[35] This template shift, which has been occurring since the end of the Cold War, has wrought changes on our contemporary understanding of the limits of state sovereignty, environmental aspects of global security, and the cultural contingency of human rights discourse.[36] By the recurrent nature of both international discourse on these issues and the number of states participating in the conferences that yield these conventions and declarations, the emergence of a holistic yet culturally nuanced conception of collective security cannot be denied. Needless to say, these conventions and similar developments evidence a normative shift in the conception of collective security.

As the International Court of Justice observed in the *Nuclear Weapons Case,* even though some of the resolutions of the UN General Assembly on these issues may not be binding, depending on their circumstances, they do have some normative value. In the context of an emerging holistic concept of collective security, the series of international declarations and conferences drawing a direct link between democratization, sustainable use of the environment, population control, refugee problems, and terrorism, for example, to collective security show an evolving global consensus on the point.[37] In this age of transnational terrorism, the expansion of the notion of collective security and the celebrated move towards an international society[38] may not be so much an affirmation of our common humanity as a pragmatic recognition that some supposedly state problems know no artificial boundaries.[39] For example, a dysfunctional state such as Afghanistan became a haven for terrorists. In effect, some apparently domestic problems simply do not respect the boundaries between states and could have devastating consequences for other states. This emerging trend may arguably be moving from the North of the globe to the South. Hence, an emerging school of critical African scholars such as Makau Wa Mutua, James Thuo Gathi, Obiora Okafor, and Kofi Quashigah have queried whether the phenomenon is really a case of genuine globalization of common human values or, in fact, a "globalization" of Western concerns, anxieties, and ideology.[40]

According to Quashigah, the emerging order "is definitely not due to a change in moral or humanistic values of the Western states in their relation to the south, it is simply a change in security interests brought about by the break up of the Soviet Union."[41] Be that as it may, threats to global collective security posed by issues outside the actual existence of warfare and answers thereto are matters that can hardly be pursued from a statist or unilateralist viewpoint. They are global problems and accordingly must be resolved by a global approach.

As noted earlier, it is not completely correct to assert that the emerging holistic approach to collective security is a purely recent phenomenon. On the contrary, it is also rooted in the provisions of the United Nations Charter.[42] As the focal point[43] of state practice at international law, the Charter, in spite of its state-centric perception of collective security and its means of securement, contains a cluster of values of human rights and the seeds of an expansive concept of collective security. The symbiotic linkage among democracy, human rights, and peace[44] finds anchor in the Charter. Its eloquent preamble speaks of the determination to "establish conditions under which justice and respect for the obligations arising from treaties and other sources of international law can be maintained."[45] It also reaffirms its faith in fundamental human rights and promotion of social progress and better standards of life in larger freedom. Its Article 1 affirms the interrelationship of enlarged human freedom to global peace and collective security, and Article 103 makes the pre-eminence of the Charter obligations clear. While these auspicious aspects of international law were almost subsumed in the Cold War intrigues, recent multilateral treaties, conventions, and declarations reaffirm a holistic conception of collective security and accord it priority.

The Conference on Security and Cooperation in Europe (CSCE), at its Conference on the Human Dimension of Security held in Geneva in early 1991, unanimously declared that "issues concerning national minorities, as well as compliance with international obligations and commitments concerning the rights of persons belonging to them, are matters of legitimate international concern and consequently do not constitute exclusively an internal affair of the respective state."[46] This confirmation of a cosmopolitan nature of collective security[47] is further buttressed by the Santiago Commitment to Democracy, adopted by the General Assembly of the Organization of American States (OAS) in June 1991.[48] This declaration re-echoes the CSCE commitment stated above. The CSCE declaration was further elaborated in its Copenhagen Meeting on the Human Dimension of the Conference on Security and Cooperation.[49] The importance of these developments, as the International Court of Justice noted in the *Libya/Malta Continental Shelf Case,* is that they "have an important role to play in recording and defining rules deriving therefrom, or indeed in developing them."[50]

Although these developments are inspired from the Western part of the globe and bear the cultural imprints of their origins, their impacts have been felt in Africa, a continent that inherited and still practices a rigid and stifling insistence on the near-absolute principles of state sovereignty. However, the Secretary-General of the OAU, Salim A. Salim, in applauding the ECOWAS action in Liberia, rejected the claim that it constituted a violation of the OAU Charter prohibition on intervention in the internal affairs of other countries. In his words:

> Non-interference should not be taken to mean indifference ... For an African Government to have the right to kill its citizens or let its citizens be killed, I believe there is no clause in the Charter that allows this ... To tell the truth, the Charter was created to preserve the humanity, dignity, and the rights of the African. You cannot use a clause of the Charter to oppress the African and say that you are implementing the OAU Charter. What has happened is that people have interpreted the Charter as if to mean that what happens in the next house is not one's concern. This does not accord with the reality of the world.[51]

It seems that part of the tragedy of political instability in postcolonial Africa lies in the OAU's skewed interpretation and application of the principle of self-determination of peoples and its impact on collective security. It is amazing that while most African states fashioned from the blue pencils of European colonialists have resolutely defended and espoused the rights of oppressed Africans to self-determination and freedom from racist and colonial rule, the African ruling cliques of the immediate postcolonial era equivocated on the rights of self-determination of African peoples and nations boxed into or split across African states. The outcome of the petition filed with the African Commission on Human and Peoples Rights by Gerald Moke of the Katangese Peoples Congress of Zaire raises interesting questions. In its ruling, the commission held that while it was obliged to recognize the sovereignty and territorial integrity of Zaire, it also believed that a variant of self-determination was attainable for the Katangese within the confines of the borders of Zaire drawn up by Europeans.[52] It is yet to be seen how this paradox can be resolved, particularly for nationalities split into two or more states by the Berlin Conference boundaries. It is arguable that African ruling elites are caught in a dangerous dilemma of either unravelling the colonial artifices or continuing with the anomalies of the mutilation of precolonial African nations and peoples.

More significantly, African states have shown greater willingness to recognize the security implications of the global toleration of the colonization of African territories by Europeans. For example, the Harare Declaration[53] on the situation in South Africa elaborated and affirmed the notion that decolonization of South Africa was imperative for regional peace. In the fifth paragraph of its preamble, African states avowed that they understood the reality that permanent peace and stability in Southern Africa could only be achieved when the system of apartheid in South Africa had been liquidated and South Africa transformed into a united, democratic, and nonracial country. While this paragraph purported to recognize a direct relationship between regional security and the formal decolonization of South Africa, African states have been remarkably afraid of making similar connections between the rickety boundaries of African states vis-à-vis the right to self-determination of peoples in African states that are no longer under formal colonialism.

It is equally significant that the Harare Declaration demonstrates that the inequities and iniquities in South Africa were a threat to peace in Southern Africa, and not merely in South Africa. In paragraph 9 of the Declaration, African states affirmed their continued support, politically and militarily, for all those fighting apartheid in South Africa. No such support has ever been made publicly for African nations or peoples struggling for self-determination from or within the artifices of European-constructed African states. In other words, European denial of self-determination to African peoples is unacceptable to African ruling elites, but denial or abridgment of the same rights by African rulers is tolerable. It would thus seem that African elites and ruling cliques have always felt better condemning oppression and denial of the right of self-determination if perpetrated by an external, European or Western power. In this twisted logic, it is tolerable for black Africans in power in African states to deny fellow Africans an absolute right to self-determination, for fear that it would lead to the fragmentation of the continent. Within this expedient conception of the right to self-determination and collective security, African state practice reflects an unfortunate timidity that often finds expression in explosive elitist squabbling capable of throwing an entire region or continent into a conflagration and orgy of violence. Such was the case with Liberia.

The Liberian conflict, as has been noted, caused the death of over 200,000 people and exiled over a million to various countries in the subregion. Given the interlocking nature of the ethnic configuration of Liberia with that of its neighbours and the inherent and unavoidable ethnicization of the conflict, the field of conflict rapidly spread to neighbouring states. In view of these factors, it cannot be seriously argued that the Liberian conflict, on its face and in the overall context of the emerging holistic concept of collective security, was not a matter of legitimate concern for neighbouring countries.

In a region like West Africa, where ethnic groups traverse the frontiers of state boundaries, such a conflict is intrinsically international. Given the events in Sierra Leone and Haiti,[54] where foreign interventions were ostensibly undertaken to remove illegitimate governments that were disturbing the tranquillity of neighbouring states, a change in the concept of state sovereignty and recognition of the relationship between illegitimate governance and collective security can hardly be denied. Agreement is possible with Kampelman, who has argued that "there is a shifting dividing line between internal affairs to be protected against intervention and the responsibility of the international community to intervene in order to preserve peace and important human values."[55]

Clearly, the Liberian civil war constituted, *prima facie,* a legitimate subject of concern to neighbouring states. However, this fact does not mean that neighbouring states could have joined the fray or intervened militarily in the character of knights errant. On the contrary, the pertinent questions should have been who ought to have made the determination that the events in Liberia were a threat to international peace, the scope of action that ECOWAS could lawfully have taken in arresting the situation in Liberia, the legality of the invitation by President Doe to ECOWAS to intervene, and the legality of the Security Council's ratification of the measures taken by ECOWAS.

ECOWAS, Liberia, and Collective Security

At the thirteenth ECOWAS summit in Banjul, Gambia, the (ECOWAS) Standing Mediation Committee[56] decided to establish an ECOWAS Cease-fire Monitoring Group (ECOMOG) with the mandate to "keep peace, restore law and order and ensure that a cease-fire agreed to by the warring factions in Liberia was respected."[57] This unprecedented action was anchored, among other things, on the ECOWAS findings that:

> The failure of the warring parties to cease hostilities has led to the massive destruction of property and the massacre by all the parties of thousands of innocent civilians including foreign nationals, women and children, some of whom had sought sanctuary in churches, hospitals, diplomatic missions and under Red Cross protection, contrary to all civilized behaviour ... the civil war has also trapped thousands of foreign nationals, including ECOWAS citizens without any means of escape or protection ... the result of all this is a state of anarchy and the total breakdown of law and order in Liberia. Presently, there is a government in Liberia which cannot govern and contending factions which are holding the entire population as hostage, depriving them of food, health facilities and other basic necessities of life ... these developments have traumatized the Liberian population and greatly shocked the people of the sub-region and the rest of the international

> community. They have also led to hundreds of thousands of Liberians being displaced and made refugees in neighbouring countries, and the spilling of hostilities into neighbouring countries.[58]

With this broad mandate, 3,000 ECOMOG troops arrived in Liberia on 25 August 1990.[59] Prior to this bold initiative, ECOWAS had adopted a diplomatic approach in which representatives of the major rebel group, the National Patriotic Front of Liberia (NPFL), had held discussions on a peaceful settlement of the conflict. These diplomatic efforts failed, as neither the Doe regime nor the rebels were willing to yield on the question of how and when Doe should step down as president of Liberia.

It is important at this stage to examine the juridical basis and structure of ECOWAS. The Economic Community of West African States is a regional alliance of sixteen states.[60] Geographically, the West African subregion is conventionally delimited as the area bounded by the Atlantic and lying south of the Sahara and west of Cameroon. Between 1844 and 1966, the entire area save for Liberia was subject to French, British, Portuguese, and German rule. The treaty establishing the organization[61] makes it clear that ECOWAS was originally designed to accelerate regional economic development and integration.[62] This ambition was not novel. Prior to the appearance on the global scene of the West African states with the Berlin Conference boundaries, close economic activities (and internecine rivalries) had existed among the various peoples of the region.[63]

Although the formation process of ECOWAS was long and checkered,[64] its formation has been acknowledged as the most significant West African effort at integration. It is also ironic that the idea of an economic entity in the nature of ECOWAS was first suggested by President Tolbert of Liberia.[65] Following his suggestion, a series of meetings and negotiations led to the launching of the organization by Nigeria's General Yakubu Gowon in Lome, Togo, in April 1972.[66] The ECOWAS Treaty was adopted by a ministerial meeting and signed by the original fifteen members in Lagos, Nigeria, on 28 May 1975.

The creation of ECOWAS was a diplomatic feat for states in a region notorious for colonially induced inter-state rivalry, suspicion, and hostility. According to Julius Okolo, ECOWAS was created out of the teeth of "the perennial frontier disputes between Ivory Coast and Ghana and between Benin and Nigeria ... the irredentist movement among Ghana's Ewes; Togo's suspicions of Ghana since the assassination of President Sylvanus Olympio in 1963, the long standing suspicion of Nigeria by Ivory Coast ... the rivalry between Senegal and Mali."[67] The recurrent suspicion of Nigerian motives in the subregion is as old as the history of colonialism in that region and deserves some consideration.

Following the colonization of Africa and its partition at the Berlin Conference of 1884-85, British Nigeria was an outstanding possession. First, the territory called Nigeria had (and still has) a population larger than all other West African states combined. Its southern state of Lagos (Nigeria has thirty-six states) has a population of over 12 million people, twice that of the Republic of Benin and greater than the combined population of the French-speaking republics of Togo and Benin.[68] Similarly, the population of Nigeria's northern city of Kano is greater than the combined population of the French-speaking republics of Niger and Chad bordering it to the north. Nigeria has half of the entire West African economic market. In addition, it is the richest country in the subregion, accounting for a sixth of the entire global supply of crude oil.

Although these riches and immense human resources have been largely squandered as a result of chronic corrupt military rule, the consciousness of its wealth and its huge and mobile population imbue Nigeria's citizenry and government with what some commentators aptly call a sense of manifest destiny in the continent of Africa. This is the feeling that the country is destined to lead the West African region, indeed, the entire African continent. This attitude raises serious doubts about its real motives whenever Nigeria dabbles in regional politics. The disparity in wealth and size between anglophone West Africa led by Nigeria and the relatively less endowed French-speaking countries in the subregion has been observed by some publicists as fuelling French suspicion of Nigeria in West Africa. Interestingly, France has a long history of a policy of construing its freed colonies as cultural heirs of mainland France. Accordingly, France is always perceived as sabotaging British West African dominance of the subregion by its encouragement of divisions and dissent within ECOWAS. During talks leading to the formation of ECOWAS (which dragged on for fifteen years), French President Georges Pompidou counselled French West Africa to boycott the British West African–led proposal for ECOWAS and form a French West African economic alliance to isolate and weaken rival influences such as Ghana and Nigeria.[69]

This division was manifested in the nature of support by ECOWAS countries for the various factions in the Liberian conflict and in the overall French attitude towards the Nigerian-led attempt to resolve the crisis. While most of the French West African countries supported or at least were indifferent to the rebellion by Charles Taylor, the anglophone countries were vocal and active in their condemnation of the rebellion and in their support for the ECOMOG effort.

It is pertinent to address the question of the constitutional structure of ECOWAS. ECOWAS has several organs engaged in the daily running of the organization. The organs established by the organization's charter are the

Authority of Heads of States and Governments, the Council of Ministers, the Executive Secretariat, a Tribunal, and several technical and specialized commissions. The Authority of Heads of States and Governments, which is established by Article 5 of the ECOWAS Treaty, is the principal governing institution of the organization. It is made up of the various leaders of the member states. It meets at least once a year, and directs and controls all the executive functions of ECOWAS; its decisions are "binding on all institutions" of the West African Community.[70] It may delegate its functions to a group of members chosen from its fold. It did this in the Liberian case when it constituted a Standing Mediation Committee to fashion ways of dealing with the Liberian problem. The Authority of Heads of States and Governments acts on the advice of the Council of Ministers. A careful reading of the entire treaty, however, leaves no doubt that no organ of the organization has any powers to intervene in matters solely within the domestic competence of a member state.

The Council of Ministers consists of two representatives from each member state. Its responsibility includes giving directions to all other subordinate institutions of the organization.[71] It also advises the Authority of Heads of States and Governments on matters of policy aimed at achieving the goals of the organization. As with the Authority of Heads of States and Governments, its decisions are binding on the other organs of the organization subordinate to it. The bureaucratic hub of the organization is the Executive Secretariat, headquartered in Abuja, the capital of Nigeria. This organ is charged with the actual implementation of decisions reached by the Authority of Heads of States and Governments or the Council of Ministers.[72] Article 15 of the ECOWAS Treaty provides for a judicial tribunal that would ensure the observance of law and justice in interpreting the provisions of the ECOWAS Treaty. Besides the organs mentioned above, the ECOWAS Treaty provides for the creation of specialized commissions to deal with such diverse issues as trade, customs, immigration, industry, transport, telecommunications, and so on. The ECOWAS Treaty empowers the Authority of Heads of States and Governments to establish other commissions from time to time as needed.

In recognition of the indispensability of peace and security to the attainment of its economic goals, ECOWAS expanded the scope of its competence beyond the confines of commerce and economic integration. The extra-economic character of ECOWAS is discernible from the organization's Protocol on Non-Aggression, concluded on 22 April 1978.[73] The ECOWAS Non-Aggression Pact obliges all member states to uphold international norms forbidding the resort to military settlement of disputes. In addition, it imposes a duty on member states to desist from subverting, or allowing foreign elements to use their territories to subvert, the authority of member states. This is one fundamental difference between the ECOWAS Non-

Aggression Pact and other collective security pacts such as NATO[74] and the defunct Warsaw Pact.[75] The Protocol on Non-Aggression was subsequently supplemented by the 1981 Protocol on Mutual Assistance on Defence (PMAD). The latter protocol, with a contextualized view on collective security, is remarkable for its adaptive response to conflicts of peculiarly African character.[76] It is arguable that the PMAD was primarily aimed at plugging loopholes in the Non-Aggression Pact. Unlike the Non-Aggression Pact, it has provisions for deterring and dealing with "external aggression and externally supported domestic insurrection and revolt which constitute major threats to stability in the community."[77]

In spite of these provisions, the question has been raised as to whether ECOWAS is a regional body as contemplated by the United Nations Charter.[78] Scholars such as Hans Kelsen[79] and M.V. Naidu[80] have proposed some tests for determining when a grouping of states may, for the purposes of Chapter 8 of the United Nations Charter, be considered a regional body. These tests must be cumulatively answered in the affirmative: (a) its membership includes almost all the states within the region, (b) it has a permanent and centralized authority, and (c) it guarantees the security of one state against another.[81]

The preamble of the ECOWAS Treaty and the provisions of the PMAD show that ECOWAS is a regional body. Its membership encompasses all the states in the subregion and it has a permanent and centralized authority. It also has assurances of mutual and collective security. It is equally significant that Resolution 813 of 1993 passed by the Security Council[82] and other Security Council resolutions on the Liberian crisis were made pursuant to Chapters 7 and 8 of the United Nations Charter. These contain provisions for regulating the relationship between regional bodies and the Security Council in the maintenance of global peace. Based on the foregoing, it follows that ECOWAS is a regional organization.

As a regional organization, however, its role in the conflict is controversial.[83] More importantly, the ECOWAS intervention on grounds of both altruistic humanitarianism and self-interest[84] raise some controversial points of international law. On the issue of self-interest, several rationales and justifications centred on the collective security of the region have been advanced by ECOWAS for its action in Liberia. General Ibrahim Babangida, then president of Nigeria, justified the ECOWAS action on the grounds that the Liberian conflict "had a destabilizing effect on the West African subregion."[85] In his words, "if events are such that have the potential to threaten the stability, peace and security in this sub-region, Nigeria in collaboration with others in this sub-region, was duty bound to react or respond in appropriate manner necessary to either avert the disaster or to take adequate measures to ensure peace, tranquility and security."[86] As this argument appeared unconvincing to critics of the intervention, he queried on humanitarian grounds whether "Nigeria and other responsible countries in this sub-region [should] stand by and watch the whole of Liberia turned into one mass graveyard?"[87]

From New York, the head of Nigerian legation at the United Nations, Ibrahim Gambari, in a letter to the Security Council argued that ECOWAS stepped in "to prevent the situation in Liberia degenerating into a situation likely to constitute a real threat to international peace and security and that the goals of the community had received endorsement from all the leaders of the West African sub-region as well as from the OAU."[88] Further, the Secretary-General of ECOWAS contended that the intervention was in "collective self defence" of the subregion. President Babangida, who at that time was the chairperson of ECOWAS and the moving spirit behind the intervention, offered yet another legal justification. He argued: "We have heard of the legality of the intervention ... people who raise the issue of legality should promptly look at Article 52 of the Charter of the United Nations for the appropriate and expected role of the ECOMOG and other sub-regional organizations world-wide."[89] In sum, the intervening members of ECOWAS declared unequivocally that "the reasons for our dynamic but positive action in the Liberian crisis are not mysterious ... they are to ensure collective security ... of our peoples."[90]

The justifications tendered by ECOWAS have not blunted the edge of criticisms against the intervention, which have contended that it flouted norms of international law forbidding intervention in domestic conflicts. It is important to summarize the case of the critics before examining its merits in international law and as it relates to the issue of collective security in the subregion.[91] Critics of the ECOWAS action invoke the customary international law principle of non-intervention[92] in the internal affairs of a sovereign state. This principle of non-intervention is well established in customary international law and confirmed by treaty law, at least since the Treaty of Westphalia. In modern times, the rule against intervention is so sacrosanct that even the UN Charter, in Article 2(7), forbids the UN itself from intervening "in matters that are essentially within the domestic jurisdiction of any state."[93] However, it has also been argued that no state can insist on the right of non-intervention if restraint from intervention would cause disproportionate injury to the community of nations.

Notwithstanding such arguments, non-intervention is a fundamental principle of customary international law and is also affirmed and reiterated in the UN Charter and in international conventions and treaties. It is also evidenced by state practice and espoused in judicial decisions and various UN declarations.[94] These varied manifestations of international law undoubtedly reflect and restate its fundamental character as a basic component of state sovereignty. As a corollary to the prohibition on the use of force by states, which is a rule of *ius cogens,* its radical character is hardly debatable, and it is on this formidable pillar that the criticism against the ECOWAS action in Liberia partly rests.

The case of the critics is also anchored on subsidiary sources of international law, such as the opinion of writers. Similarly, decisions of the International Court of Justice in the *Nicaragua Case*[95] and the *Corfu Channel Case*[96] on use of force by states and the doctrine of non-intervention have been called in aid. These arguments are apparently well founded. In the *Nicaragua Case,* the Court reiterated that the prohibition on military intervention without valid invitation is a necessary and constitutive part of every state's right to sovereignty, territorial integrity, and political independence. Similarly, virtually every multilateral treaty of importance on inter-state concourse provides for the right of non-intervention. The critics conclude on this point that the existence of the principle of non-intervention in the *opinio juris* of states is backed by substantial and established state practice.[97]

There is hardly any doubt that international law in its primary and subsidiary manifestations forbids the intervention by one state or a group of states in the internal affairs of another state, militarily or otherwise. To avoid doubt, the "internal affairs" forming the subject of state sovereignty in which other states are barred from intervening are those matters that each state is permitted, by the principles of state sovereignty, to decide freely on. Implicit in this observation is that state sovereignty and the principle of non-intervention are not absolute rights or principles. As subsequent analysis will show, states may not in their insistence on sovereignty menace other states or the international community by engaging in acts that constitute a threat to other states, even if such acts or omissions are perpetrated within the borders of the state claiming protection under the doctrine of non-intervention.[98]

More important, the doctrine of non-intervention presupposes the existence of a state and that the state asserting the right is engaged in acts that states are permitted by international law to decide freely on. Given the advances in global technologies and the interconnectedness of the world, the domestic scope of state prerogatives seems to be shrinking, and it is within this context that the nature of what constitutes domestic subject matter has to be addressed. Hence, issues such as environmental pollution and the unlawful possession of or quest for nuclear or other weapons of mass destruction fall within the modern rubric of global concern. In effect, the notion of what constitutes domestic sovereignty in international law is not cast in stone. However, it has to be conceded that there is grave danger in permitting undue flexibility in the limits of domestic sovereignty.

Critics of the intervention in Liberia have made the important distinction that the ECOWAS action would have been lawful if the effective government of Liberia had invited ECOWAS to intervene in the conflict. In effect, the critics concede that at international law, a state or a group of states may be exempted from the prohibition on external intervention in the domestic affairs of a sovereign state if the effective government in the troubled state invites the intervention. This is a very interesting point, especially as the critics of the intervention further opine that ECOWAS ought to have assembled the various heads of the warring factions to obtain their consent before intervening in Liberia. With this golden rod, as it were, the waters of (il)legality in external interventions are parted. Thus, in the absence of a collective consent by the warlords, the critics argue that the proper intervening body is the UN. On this second aspect, the critics argue that only the United Nations has the legal mandate to receive and act upon an invitation for intervention from a troubled incumbent government.

Such criticisms have thus likened the ECOWAS intervention in Liberia to the unilateral intervention of the United States in the tiny Caribbean republic of Grenada[99] and Soviet intervention in Czechoslovakia,[100] both of which received universal condemnation. These arguments are supported with liberal references to the United Nations General Assembly Declaration on the Definition of Aggression,[101] which arguably defines aggression to include the ECOWAS intervention in Liberia. For the above reasons, the ECOWAS action, the critics argue, constituted "enforcement action" under Chapter 7 of the UN Charter and since it was effected without prior authorization of the Security Council, it was unlawful. Despite a real danger that a liberal construction of the right to enforcement actions would benefit strong states at the expense of the weak, there is an equal danger in the position adopted by critics of the intervention. Arguably, the postulations of the critics are steeped in denial of African historical realities and of global realpolitik, and thus constitute a purist application of Eurocentric conceptions without sufficient regard for global attitudes towards black Africans in their moments of crisis. The serial neglect by powerful Western states of African massacres in Rwanda, Sierra Leone, Zaire, Burundi, Sudan, Uganda, and so on yield the clear impression that black African lives count for little in the global politics of economic and ideological pre-eminence.

Historically, the concept of non-intervention is no stranger to imprecision, cultural affinity, and regional sensibilities.[102] This state of affairs is probably a function of the manifold aspects of intervention in domestic affairs of other states.[103] Oppenheim has defined intervention in terms of a "dictatorial interference by a state in the affairs of another state for the purpose of maintaining or altering the actual condition of things."[104] This is an important definition, but in the context of the subject of this book, it should be restricted to military interventions[105] in African postcolonial experience.

Although the doctrine of non-intervention is a well-established principle of international law, it did not spring full-blown. Rather, its contemporary features have their roots deeply embedded in the practice of European, Christian states spanning five centuries.[106] To locate the earliest scholarly articulation of its norms, historians of international law have referred to the writings of Wolff and Vattel. According to the latter, "to intermediate in the domestic affairs of another nation or to undertake to restrain its councils is to do it an injury." [107] These writings probably afforded intellectual clarity for the dissonant practice of European states on the issue. Reasons for this historical practice range from the genuine fear of internal conflicts destabilizing an entire region to the reactionary escapades of fatally threatened regimes, such as the Holy Alliance.

In 1823, England, France, and Russia intervened militarily in Greece on the ostensible grounds that the Greek civil war threatened the security of Europe.[108] Similarly, between 1875 and 1876, Europe was upset by the recurrent Turkish outrages, which threatened European security, and intervened by force of arms. Again, Russia and Saxony had by their armed intervention in Poland in 1733-63 placed the Saxon king on the throne of Poland. Further, the revolts in Bosnia and Herzegovina against Turkish misrule and atrocities persuaded the imperial courts in Russia and Austria to adopt the Berlin Memorandum of May 1875.

The Berlin Memorandum of May 1875 and the Constantinople Conference of December 1876 were international efforts that imposed certain obligations on Turkey regarding the administration of her tottering empire. Needless to say, this was a clear act of intervention in a domestic problem. Although Britain did not accede to the Memorandum, France, Italy, and Russia did. When the Turks could not prevent their empire from imploding and threatening European continental security, Russia, purporting to act on behalf of Europe, intervened militarily. These cases show that it was not unusual for European states to agree to put a disintegrating European state in order. It appears, however, that the intervening states were obliged to show that the problem in the troubled state was of such magnitude and character as to endanger the general security of the region or of neighbouring states. In other words, cultural and ethnic sympathies often influenced the stability of European states; hence, when they threatened the collective security of Europe, intervention could occur. More important, there must be a clear and present danger that non-intervention would result in disproportionate injury to the neighbouring states.

However, not every outrage or conflict in neighbouring states rose to the level of threat to the security of the region, and therefore an acceptable basis for collective military action. For instance, although the trouble in Belgrade in 1903[109] shocked Europe and was wholly condemned, it was not enough to compel the European states to intervene. On the night of 10 June 1903, a military uprising against the royal house in Belgrade earned the King forty stab wounds and the Queen sixty-five. Other members of the royal house and ruling class suffered similar acts of savagery. The atrocities outraged all of Europe, and left in their wake very severe diplomatic consequences for the usurpers in Belgrade. As Admiral Morin of Italy observed, however, "though this feeling dominates all other impressions in the presence of this terrible tragedy, the government must remember that the events which took place at Belgrade relate to internal affairs."[110] Similarly, the British condemned the intervention by the Holy Alliance in the republican uprising in Naples that had deposed the monarchy and instituted a popular parliament in 1820. The British foreign minister argued that such an intervention could be justified only if dangers from such internal affairs constituted clear, grave, imminent and actual danger, military in character, to neighbouring states.

In spite of this restraint and rationalization, which was to distinguish collective actions for collective security from unilateral interventions, the Holy Alliance[111] stretched the emerging state practice. Notwithstanding its grand name, the Holy Alliance was a rather reactionary group of monarchists determined to crush by force of arms the rising wave of republicanism in Europe. Thus, these European monarchies from Austria, Prussia, and Russia, on their way to obsolescence hastened by the rising wave of republicanism, did not yield without a struggle. The monarchists saw the wave of republicanism as a spreading contagion that must be stopped. The Holy Alliance under Metternich attempted to enforce this "contagion theory" by militarily suppressing revolutionary movements in the European states that had overthrown their monarchies.

The monarchists argued that the spread of republicanism was a raging conflagration that would consume and destroy Europe. Thus, in the preliminary Protocol of Troppau dated 8 December 1820, the Holy Alliance declared that in "states which have undergone a change of government due to revolution, the result of which threatens other states, the Princes bind themselves by peaceful means or if need be by arms to bring back the guilty state into the bosom" of the Holy Alliance. The spread of republicanism in Europe, which the blue-blooded princes of the Holy Alliance construed as a "conflagration" was roundly rebutted by a witty Frenchwoman who reminded the agitated royalty that "what you believe to be a conflagration is only an illumination."[112] As the conflagration or illumination swept Europe, the Holy Alliance was persuaded to intervene and contain the spreading "contagion of revolution." In addition to the contempt with which most states in Europe held the objectives of the Holy Alliance, the contagion doctrine and its variants were devoid of respect among publicists.[113] Westlake, Hall, Stowell, and other pre-eminent publicists of the day flatly rejected the contagion doctrine.

At the Conference of Verona in 1822, British opposition to the presumptions of the Holy Alliance was brushed aside when the Alliance authorized Imperial France to intervene militarily in Spain to restore the deposed King Ferdinand VII to the throne. Spanish monarchical institutions were successfully restored. Great Britain, speaking through George Canning, argued in vain that "no proof was produced ... on the part of Spanish government to invade the territory of France ... or any project to undermine her political institutions; and so long as the troubles and disturbances of Spain should be confined within her own territory, they could not be admitted by the British Government to afford a plea for foreign interference."[114]

In arguing against the Holy Alliance's intervention in Spain, Britain further rationalized its earlier intervention in the French polity. According to Lord Castlereagh, British intervention in Napoleonic France (unlike the Spanish case) came about because France "attempted to propagate first her principles and then her domain [of Europe] by the sword."[115] Thus, contrary to the presumptions of the Holy Alliance, there was an emerging opinion among European states that the mere existence of a pernicious institution in a neighbouring state does not warrant or justify external intervention. There must be proof of actual danger. Here, it seems that the crux of the matter turned on finding the test with which "illuminations" may be distinguished from "conflagrations." While "illuminations" were strictly out of bounds for foreign states, it was emerging as acceptable and admissible in international law that states that had a centralized and objective framework for determining the existence of raging "conflagrations" might act collectively to put out the inferno without breaching the norm on interventions. The latter came to be known as "collective actions"[116] under the enforcement jurisdiction of the United Nations Security Council.

Regarding this modern regime on collective security, it was writers such as Von Martens who distilled from the practice of states coherent principles for determining the legality of multilateral actions.[117] During the days of the Holy Alliance and long thereafter, the determination of the legality or otherwise of multilateral military interventions largely depended on third-party perception of the motive of the interveners. As Winfield observed, the non-intervention rule appeared to be a patent consequence of independence with a host of disorderly exceptions fastened upon it. Arguing further, he lamented the vagueness of the doctrine of non-intervention. In his despair, he made the criticism that "we are told it is a right; that it is a crime; that it is the exception; that it is never permissible at all. A reader after perusing Phillimore's chapter upon intervention, might close the book with the impression that intervention might be anything from a speech of Lord Palmerston's in the House of Commons to the partition of Poland."[118] Other publicists, such as Gericke,[119] subsequently clarified the position and articulated customary international law on the subject.

Shortly before the emergence of the UN Charter, the following factors and tests distinguished collective actions from unilateral interventions. According to the findings of the Inter-American Juridical Committee,[120] the distinctions include the fact that collective actions, unlike unilateral interventions, are usually undertaken by states in a treaty-based or clearly defined relationship. Second, while unilateral interventions disregard the fundamental rights of states, collective action always tends to restore the violated right. Third, while unilateral intervention is arbitrary and is for certain interests, collective action defends all the member states of the organization. Fourth, while intervention signifies an attitude that exceeds the competence of a state, collective action is exercised within the framework of the multilateral body.

Sir Ivor Jennings has acknowledged the work of Murdoch[121] on the subject as being decisive.[122] It is equally interesting to note that Murdoch's conclusions are similar to those of the Inter-American Jurists. However, the pre-Charter regime, marked by its reliance on ad hoc conferences[123] for the maintenance of collective security, has been superseded by the provisions of the UN Charter.[124] Under the Charter regime, external intervention on the grounds of internal anomie is severely circumscribed. For example, on 29 April 1946, a subcommittee of the Security Council rejected a Polish proposal "to apply Article 41 to Spain on the ground that the internal regime in Franco Spain did not come within those terms."[125] However, the Council clearly acknowledged that there may be circumstances in which the events in an internal regime may indeed constitute a threat to international peace and security.

The Liberian crisis is probably a "hard case,"[126] as it questions an intervention by a regional organization and the implications for the UN Charter, which is primarily designed to regulate inter-state conflicts and limit the use of force in international relations.[127] Is there room for adaptation of the concept of non-intervention in internal domestic dysfunction when such domestic state failure would seem to constitute a threat to international peace?[128] Given that the provisions of the Charter on enforcement actions refer mainly to inter-state aggression, it seems that recent changes in global security, such as the rash of civil wars in Africa, international terrorism, and collapsed states constituting redoubts for international criminals, challenge the assumptions and templates of the UN Charter. The importance of this is further underscored by the increasing number of state failures in Africa and the induced civil wars, a phenomenon that Luard aptly notes as "unique in history."[129] Given that drafters of the UN Charter hardly contemplated these hybrid and modern forms of danger to global security, what roles, if any, would the principles of collective self-defence and invitation of external forces by beleaguered governments play in the emerging dispensation in the post–Cold War era? It is to these issues that the next chapter turns.

3
The Liberian Conflict and International Law on Foreign Intervention in Domestic Conflicts

The primary challenge posed to international law by the Economic Community of West African States (ECOWAS) intervention in Liberia's imminent collapse and attendant threat to regional security is its apparent legitimization of the unilateral use of force by Nigeria and allied states in the region. Although a lot of good was done and millions of lives were saved, certain hard questions must be asked concerning the normative significance of that intervention and its implications for global peace and security. It can hardly be denied that if Nigeria and allied states had not intervened in Liberia, the horrendous acts of genocide committed in Rwanda would have occurred there. Considering the observation by many observers that there are undertones of racial affinity, if not racism, in the calculations of the great powers as to where and when they should intervene in troubled regions of the world, the legitimacy of the ECOWAS intervention deserves sophisticated analysis.

It is within this context that the tenets of international law on intervention, use of force to enforce restraint, collective security, and multilateral actions must be examined. A sterile, doctrinaire evaluation that closes its eyes to the peculiarities of the African continent and its place in the global scheme must be eschewed. In this chapter, I examine how these principles of international law influenced, and were in turn impacted upon by, the ECOWAS intervention in Liberia.

Intervention at the Invitation of a Government

Some of the critics of the ECOWAS intervention, particularly Kufour and Ofodile,[1] have made the distinction that the ECOWAS action would have been lawful at international law had it been at the invitation of the effective government of Liberia. They have also argued that President Samuel Doe lacked effectiveness and that, under the circumstances, the proper intervening body was the UN. On the foregoing grounds, the ECOWAS intervention in Liberia has been likened to the intervention of the United States in the tiny Caribbean republic of Grenada and the Soviet intervention in Czechoslovakia.[2] The critics have also argued that the ECOWAS intervention constituted "enforcement action" under Chapter 8 of the United Nations Charter, and that without the prior authorization of the Security Council, it was unlawful.

Kufour and Ofodile have further argued that once a conflict such as the Liberian crisis degenerates into a civil war, intervention is illegal without the consent of the warring parties. On the first leg, it has also been urged that the intervention by ECOWAS without the unanimous consent and invitation of the warring factions in Liberia was not only a violation of the sovereignty of Liberia but an unlawful abridgment of the right of Liberian peoples to self-determination.[3] Kufour has further argued that the ECOWAS intervention lacked legitimacy because it was "not based on a consensus amongst the member states of the Community."[4] In effect, since the ECOWAS Treaty adopts the "unanimity rule"[5] in arriving at its decisions, intervention taken in the teeth of opposition by two member states[6] was fatally defective. These critics therefore query whether the decision to intervene was one by the Community itself or rather by a number of member states acting under the guise of the Community's authority.[7]

The question of the legal validity of military intervention by invitation of the government is one that may be answered by specific reference to two interlinked issues.[8] The first consists of the relevant international norms. The second, which is an application of the first issue, refers to the factual scenario on the effectiveness of the incumbent regime at the material time an invitation to intervene is made. In the context of the Liberian crisis, the issues may be framed as follows: (1) whether, having regard to the material circumstances in Liberia, President Doe had the authority to invite ECOWAS intervention, and (2) whether ECOWAS had the legal capacity to act on the invitation by Doe. The third issue deals with the extent of the powers of ECOWAS in responding to the invitation.

International law recognizes the validity of a state or a group of states sending troops to another state upon invitation for a certain limited operation. Indeed, Article 3 of General Assembly Resolution 3314, Definition of Aggression,[9] albeit negatively, exempts invited military intervention from its definition of what constitutes international acts of aggression. Such limited operations have been recognized to include the use of peacekeeping forces that do not become involved in the internal affairs of the state, certain rescue missions, and quelling of minor internal disturbances.[10] When a government is in effective control of most of the state, this principle also affords "a clear alternative to Security Council authorization as a basis for justifying external intervention."[11] Provided the consent to external intervention is clear, voluntary, and from the effective authority in the state, its legal validity is hardly a matter of controversy.[12]

According to Roberto Ago (then Special Rapporteur of the International Law Commission on State Responsibility), the rationale for this is that consent to intervention acts as a form of bilateral agreement between the intervening and consenting states, and this suspends the normal operation of the legal rules that would otherwise govern their relationship.[13] Moreover, it is an expression of a state's sovereign right to choose its mode of bilateral or multilateral relations with other states within the bounds of international law. Often this finds expression in treaties on mutual defence, but is not limited to that.

Although states are abstract entities, international law presumes that when a government exercises effective control over the territory and its population, the government of that state possesses the exclusive authority to express the will of the state. This is borne out by the consistent practice of states. As Farer observes, there is a virtual "uniform practice in international relations of treating any group of nationals in effective control of their state as constituting its legitimate government."[14] This supposition has little reference to how that group of persons in effective control of their state acquired the power, and is probably derived from both practical and theoretical considerations.

States thus accept this position as the only viable means of conducting their relations, and by extension accord legitimacy to interventions at the invitation of the effective regime. However, the legality of the invitation becomes questionable when it is tainted with certain vitiating elements, such as error, fraud, violence, or corruption. Similarly, the presumption of effectiveness of governments and the right to invite intervention becomes problematic when the government is very shaky.

The question may revolve on who is entitled to express the will of the state in inviting external intervention.[15] This scenario arises when the government's authority to represent the state is at issue. The global outrage over the Soviet intervention in Hungary (1956), Czechoslovakia (1968), and Afghanistan (1979) are cases in point.[16] Similar disapproval greeted American intervention in Grenada (1983) and the Dominican Republic (1965). In those cases, what was questioned was not the validity of the principle of the legality of intervention by invitation but the validity of the purported invitations themselves. The Cold War created a situation of near-absolute state sovereignty, and this was in turn translated to mean unabridged support for "effective" governments fighting for their lives.[17] In many cases, control of the capital city and the presidential mansion seemed enough to create the right for a president of a state to speak for the state and request external intervention when necessary. Even when such beleaguered governments suffered legitimacy deficits in governance, they could lawfully invite external aid to assert their wounded authority.[18] Conversely, even if the opposing or rebelling forces espoused freedom and respect for human dignity, aid to them was perceived as a violation of the principle of non-intervention.

The rationale for this regime was not difficult to appreciate. As the International Court of Justice noted in the *Nicaragua Case,* the principle of non-intervention "would certainly lose its effectiveness ... if intervention were to be justified by a mere request for assistance by an opposition group in another state."[19] Accordingly, in that case, aid by the US Government to rebels seeking the overthrow of the effective Nicaraguan government was held illegal.[20] In addition, the Court reaffirmed unequivocally that intervention is generally permissible at the request of the government of a state.

Subsidiary sources of international law, such as the writings of publicists,[21] confirm the legality of an effective government inviting external intervention in the domestic polity. According to Henkin, "upon authentic invitation, a state may introduce military forces into the territory of another to assist the government for various purposes, including maintaining internal order."[22] A caveat must be entered here. That is, an "effective government may not authorize external intervention against a national liberation movement opposing racist or colonial domination."[23] This is a direct application of the general principle that a state may not lawfully authorize another state to take any action that would be illegal under international law if undertaken by the authorizing state itself. Since the prohibition on racial discrimination and the right to self-determination of peoples under colonial rule have the character of *ius cogens,*[24] which are nonderogable rights save when altered by a principle of similar character,[25] this exception appears to strengthen the rule.[26]

The practice of states confirms that an incumbent government, even when it has lost control of a substantial portion of the state, may lawfully invite external intervention, provided it retains control over the capital city and is not in immediate danger of collapse. Similarly, states and international organizations are slow to withdraw recognition from an incumbent government, even when the government has lost control of much of the state.[27] Premature withdrawal of recognition may even be construed as illicit support for the rebels. The disposition to lawfully aid the beleaguered government is further strengthened when it is obvious that the opposing forces are receiving substantial aid and assistance from third states. In the circumstances, aid to the incumbent may be perceived as counter-intervention,[28] if not an exercise of the right of collective self-defence. Given the austere conditions required for a valid exercise of the right of collective self-defence as espoused in the *Nicaragua Case,* and the surreptitious and secretive nature of third-state support for insurrections, the latter claim of right may be more difficult to sustain.

It is interesting to note, however, that this regime, especially during the Cold War era, worked in favour of incumbents who acted as though they had a virtually unlimited right to obtain help from third states in seeking to suppress internal rebellions. Save for the exceptional cases of Hungary, the

Dominican Republic, Afghanistan, and Grenada, the legality of a request for external intervention by beleaguered regimes has been surprisingly consistent at customary international law. Indeed, Security Council Resolution 387 of 1976 reaffirms this principle by acknowledging the inherent and lawful right of every state, in the exercise of its sovereignty, to request assistance from any other state or group of states. The invitation of the UN in 1958 by the beleaguered government in Lebanon, which had control of a part of the capital city and small pieces of the remaining territory is a case in point. In addition, invited external interventions in Oman in 1957 and in Chad, Zambia, Ethiopia, and other countries at the behest of beleaguered regimes bears out this customary international law.[29]

Notwithstanding the formidable array of opinion in favour of the right of a beleaguered government to invite external intervention, scholars like William Hall, Ann and Aaron Thomas, and Quincy Wright have forcefully argued to the contrary.[30] In their view, the existence of widespread rebellion against a government is evidence of its loss of de facto control, and hence of the right to invite external intervention. This aspect of their argument is indeed profound because it demonstrates the complexity of the question and shows that the right to invite external intervention, as in the cases of Kuwait, Haiti, and Sierra Leone, may indeed remain, notwithstanding the contrary pretensions of the usurpers. On the other hand, Hall, Thomas and Thomas, and Wright further argue that such a state of affairs as widespread rebellion against incumbent governments would ultimately abridge the right to self-determination if the right to invite external intervention were held to be subsisting under the circumstances. This connection of their argument to the right to self-determination is formidable, since the right is anchored in *ius cogens*.

The right to self-determination of peoples probably finds its most eloquent exposition in the United Nations General Assembly Declaration on Principles of International Law Concerning Friendly Relations and Cooperation Amongst States. Paragraph 7 of the elaboration of the Declaration stipulates that every state has the duty to refrain from any forcible action that deprives peoples referred to in the elaboration of the principle on equal rights and self-determination of their right to self-determination and freedom and independence. Although Higgins has alluded to the doubt in some quarters over which "self" the right of self-determination applies to,[31] the norms of the right to self-determination, as summarized below, may allow for such doubts in the circumstances of the Liberian conflict.[32]

First, the Liberian case may not be regarded as one of self-determination because African states have construed international law on the issue[33] as applicable only to those struggles against "colonial and alien" occupation and racist regimes. The Liberian crisis was not such a type of conflict. It was neither a secessionist war of independence nor a struggle by the Liberian peoples against colonial and alien domination; nor was it a struggle for the self-determination of any of the constituent Liberian nations. Second, unlike in the case of recognized "national" liberation movements, there was no duty on the international community not to intervene in Liberia because what happened there was a fractious struggle for power among warring Liberian factions rather than between a liberation movement and the government.

In this context, the law on belligerency may be explored briefly. This is not an easy regime to apply to the Liberian case. In the first place, the status of belligerency that obligates third states to be neutral in cases of civil wars is not attained merely by the spread of violence in a civil war but upon the fulfillment of four conditions: the existence of war and hostilities, occupation and a measure of orderly administration of a substantial part of the national territory by the insurgents, observance of the rules of warfare on the part of the insurgents, and a practical necessity for third states to define their attitude. While the warring factions in Liberia may have scaled the first two hurdles, they would probably fail the last two tests.

Further, in according a rebel organization recognition as a belligerent force, international law seeks to bring the conduct of parties to the conflict within the ambit of the laws of war. Thus, by Article 3 of the 1949 Geneva Conventions and Protocol 2 concluded in Geneva in 1977,[34] belligerent forces are obliged to uphold certain humanitarian rules of war. Before coming to a definitive view on the legality of Doe's invitation to ECOWAS and whether the warring factions were recognized as belligerent forces, however, it is useful to recapitulate the facts surrounding Doe's invitation and the means and methods adopted by the warring factions in their prosecution of the rebellion.

The initial impression created by the Liberian government in international circles was that the rebellion was a thwarted coup d'état[35] that had been brought under control. This was far from the truth. Indeed, within one week of the rebellion, over 10,000 Liberian refugees had fled to neighbouring Côte d'Ivoire and government troops (dominated by Doe's ethnic Krahn) sent to Nimba County to quell the rebellion were engaged in genocide[36] of the Dan/Gio in that county. The atrocities by the government troops further polarized the Liberian polity and pushed the Dan/Gio to support the rebellion.[37] As Doe's control waned, his futile plea to Liberians to get their cutlasses and single-barrelled guns and set out into the bush in pursuit of the rebels fell on deaf ears.

It was at this point that ECOWAS, realizing the immensity of the problem, set up a Standing Mediation Committee to look into the Liberian crisis. The rampaging rebels seized over 70 percent of Liberian territory. Doe's supporters and cronies were deserting him and fleeing the country. Foreign nationals in Liberia were also leaving in droves. On 6 June 1990, the embattled Doe wrote US President George Bush, asking for assistance to crush the rebels. As the rebels advanced on Monrovia, they called for Doe's resignation. According to the chief negotiator of the rebel National Patriotic Front of Liberia (NPFL), Tom Woewiyu, "Doe is the source of all problems in Liberia ... We are not calling for the total dissolution of the Liberian government but for the resignation of Doe."[38] As the rebels negotiated with the Liberian government, Doe declared his readiness to welcome any peacekeeping force from the US, the Organization of African Unity (OAU), ECOWAS, or the UN. Meanwhile, Yormie Johnson, alleging excessive Libyan control over the NPFL and financial irregularities, broke away from the NPFL and formed his own rebel group with the objective of stopping Taylor's NPFL from taking Monrovia and Taylor himself from becoming president of Liberia.

Government forces were "greatly reduced due to desertion and losses ... down to about 1,000 men to defend Monrovia."[39] In the pithy words of Congressman Dan Burton of the United States, "he [Charles Taylor] has got the guy [Doe] by the short hair right now."[40] Within Monrovia, opposition parties and professionals mobilized civil demands for Doe's immediate resignation. The situation got more desperate.[41] As Wippman notes, not only had Doe's government lost control of a substantial portion of the state but the "government's international (formal) legitimacy was otherwise subject to doubt."[42] However, the capital city refused to yield to the NPFL rebels. This was because the breakaway Independent National Patriotic Front of Liberia (INPFL) and Doe's truncated Armed Forces of Liberia (AFL) maintained their vicelike grip on Monrovia and the presidential palace. The result was a deadlock. In the words of Wippman: "Although most observers assumed the rebel forces would quickly vanquish the AFL and drive Doe from his fortified mansion, the rebels proved unable to do so. The conflict settled into a military stalemate. The result was anarchy. Each warring faction exercised a slight measure of 'de facto executive and judicial power' in its particular area of control, but for the most part, all semblance of civilian authority was gone."[43] The atrocities against the Liberian civilian populace continued. It was at this stage that the beleaguered Doe extended an invitation to ECOWAS, asking that organization to intervene in Liberia:

> It is with profound appreciation that I convey to your Excellencies compliments and goodwill of the Government and people of Liberia ... As you may no doubt be aware, since the crisis in our country, I have done everything possible to resolve the situation and restore peace to our motherland ... I wish to bring to your attention that our iterative accession to peaceful process has only been rewarded by continuing positions of intransigence and bellicosity on the part of Mr. Taylor and the NPFL ... They (the NPFL)

> continue to create more turmoil and tension in the people of Liberia. Right now in the suburbs of Monrovia thousands have been displaced by the NPFL forces, homes have been destroyed, hundreds slaughtered, even before their victory is achieved. I am therefore concerned that the fighting could accelerate in Monrovia and thus inflame the suffering of the people of Liberia. Consistent with my oath of office to protect and defend the Government and people of Liberia, I cannot countenance Taylor's continued mission to destroy Liberia and its inhabitants because of his inordinate greed to become President ... any attempt to subvert the process of democracy by displacing the Constitution through force of arms would lead to an endless succession of armed insurrection, bring more deaths and destruction, as well as disrupt the socio-political and economic tranquility not only of Liberia, but also the sub-region of the ECOWAS as a whole ... to avert the wanton destruction of lives and properties ... It would seem most expedient at this time to introduce an ECOWAS Peace-keeping Force into Liberia to forestall increasing terror and tension and to assure a peaceful transitional environment. While assuring you of my fullest co-operation, I remain ...
>
> Samuel Kanyon Doe (President of Liberia)[44]

ECOWAS, weighing the regional dimensions of the crisis, drew the attention of the OAU to the crisis and considered imposing a mandatory ceasefire in Liberia to stop the carnage.[45] The Liberian representative at the United Nations tried unsuccessfully to place the crisis on the agenda of the Security Council,[46] and at the ECOWAS meeting in Banjul, Gambia, ECOWAS decided to intervene.[47] The facts presented above depict the circumstances under which Doe invited ECOWAS, and it is with this background that the legality of the invitation should be examined.

In examining the legality of Doe's invitation to ECOWAS, it has to be reaffirmed that state practice strongly supports the right of an effective government to invite external intervention in the event of an uprising in the state.[48] In the absence of vitiating elements, including fraud and coercion, the test of the legality of such an invitation is a function of the effectiveness of the government making the invitation. The human rights record of the effective regime does not affect the strict legality of the invitation, but may influence the scope and quality of the international response. Strictly speaking, if prevalent state practice is a guide, Doe's miserable deficiency in legitimacy and good governance are of little consequence in examining his capacity to invite external intervention. The facts of the Liberian case show that his government was, at least formally, the *de jure* government of Liberia and in appreciable control of the capital city and the presidential mansion. All insignia and paraphernalia of office were still with President Doe at the moment he made the invitation.

The argument that the Liberians were fighting for self-determination may not withstand criticism.[49] In light of state practice, particularly in Africa, the Liberian crisis was neither a war against a racist regime nor an anticolonial struggle nor a war against alien domination, which characterizes struggles for self-determination as construed and applied by African states.[50] More important, although it wore ethnic coloration, the conflict itself was never characterized by the warring factions as a struggle for self-determination of the constitutive nations trapped in the Liberian state. Essentially, it was a brutal and personalized struggle for power by disgruntled elites ruthlessly exploiting the excesses of a decadent polity foisted on an ill-structured state. What is more disturbing is that the orgy of elitist indulgence, political anomie, ethnic demagoguery, and chauvinism was tolerated for too long by an indifferent global security order.

On the question of belligerency, none of the warring factions in Liberia, unlike recognized movements for national liberation of oppressed peoples, possessed legal personality and recognition at international law. Second, virtually all the resolutions passed by the United Nations on the Liberian situation clearly identified them as warring factions pursuing the narrow agendas of their respective leaders at the expense of the average Liberian and members of the constitutive ethnic groups of the Liberian state. They were thus not accorded recognition as belligerent forces. Accordingly, the contention that the rebels' consent was necessary for the ECOWAS intervention to be legal is at best a matter of prudence, not international law. According to Christine Gray, "the consent of other parties involved in the conflict is important as a matter of practical necessity. The peacekeeping force would not be able to function without the cooperation of the parties on the ground."[51] As a matter of law, the Liberian rebels need not have consented to the ECOWAS action in Liberia.

Returning to the question of whether the rebels could have attained the status of belligerency, it is noteworthy that they had no respect for established international norms on armed conflicts. According to US Assistant Secretary of State for African Affairs Herman Cohen, "when we talk of troops (rebels), we are talking of young kids, 14 to 17 years of age, who are running around with Kalashnikovs."[52] The prevalence of child-soldiers in the Liberian crisis is a notorious fact. According to a United Nations report:

> Of the approximately 1.4 million children now living in Liberia, it is believed that 15,000 served as child soldiers in the civil war. The majority of fighters demobilized at the end of the war were between fifteen and twenty-eight years old. Of those aged seventeen and under, the majority – 69 percent – were fifteen to seventeen years old, and had served an average of four years. 27 per cent of the remaining fighters under 17 were between the ages of twelve and fourteen years old ... Many of these children were forced to

> become soldiers by combatants desperate for able bodies of any age to augment their ranks ... Some became practiced killers, and most were exposed to atrocities on a daily basis ... The youngest combatants were six years.[53]

According to the testimony of one of the child-soldiers, "I was given pills that made me crazy. I beat people and hurt them until they bled."[54] These atrocities were committed by all the warring factions. Acts of mass killing carried out by the various factions probably reached their height with the massacre of over 600 Dan/Gios seeking refuge in a church. According to one of the few survivors of that war crime, "over 600 people were killed. There are still blood stains on the altar; they had placed small children there and made them scream, 'there is no God,' as they [the rebels] cut their throats."[55]

A woman telling of how rebel troops at roadblocks would take bets on the sex of an unborn child lamented that they would slice women open and pull out the fetus with a bayonet to find out who had won the bet. In the words of Lori Damrosch, "the savagery of Liberia's civil war is almost unimaginable."[56] Only the splinter rebel group that hacked off thousands of limbs of children in Sierra Leone was more egregious and abominable in its abuses than the Liberian rebel groups. This is hardly the kind of behaviour capable of encouraging third-state recognition of the Liberian rebels as belligerent forces and imposing on third states the obligation to remain neutral in the conflict. What is even more shocking is that the international community, obsessed as it was with the rituals of multiparty democracy after the 1989-96 conflict, never brought any of the rebel leaders who perpetrated these atrocities and war crimes to justice or even trial. Rather, they were appeased with plum political appointments. Once again, impunity trumped the imperatives of justice.

It is equally important to note that even though Doe had the right to invite ECOWAS or any other external state or organization to intervene, ECOWAS intervention was not necessarily to his advantage. ECOWAS did not intervene for Doe.[57] In addition, because of the interference of several states in the Liberian conflict, ECOWAS intervention may also be construed as counter-intervention. Although probative proof of external interference in the Liberian conflict may not meet the austere requirements articulated in the *Nicaragua Case,* I have shown earlier that most states in the subregion had interests in the conflict. Similarly, the conflict had spread beyond the borders of Liberia as some of the warring factions, for diverse reasons, attacked countries like Sierra Leone (necessitating the Security Council's intervention), Guinea, and Côte d'Ivoire. Hence, the facts show that the Liberian crisis was, potentially and in reality, a regional tragedy.

Furthermore, as invitations for external intervention to restore "democracy"[58] (when the incumbent government has lost effective control of the government[59]) gain uncritical universal support, it is difficult to deny that Doe, a *de jure* president with control of a substantial part of the capital city and the presidential mansion, could invite external intervention. Although this trend may support earlier arguments regarding the increasingly self-serving application of doctrines of human rights[60] and collective security, it equally supports the view that a *de jure* regime may still invite external intervention even when its effectiveness hangs in the balance.[61] In both the Sierra Leone and Haiti cases, the inviting incumbents had lost effectiveness.[62]

It has also been argued that the scope of activities and measures undertaken by ECOWAS was illegal and for a peacekeeping body *ultra vires*. The complaint here is that the ECOWAS Cease-fire Monitoring Group (ECOMOG) went too far in constituting an interim government for Liberia, organizing and overseeing elections to various political offices in Liberia, and reorganizing the Liberian army and police. This is an important issue necessitating further analysis. The practice of peacekeeping is a contemporary phenomenon. It is a distinctive innovation by the United Nations and, indeed, the Charter does not mention it at all. Peacekeeping originated during the United Nations intervention in the Greek civil war in 1947 and has usually been employed in maintaining ceasefires, assisting in the withdrawal of troops, and providing a buffer zone between opposing forces. Peacekeeping operations are usually temporary and not really engaged in the settlement of conflicts, but are used to provide auspicious conditions for peaceful resolution of conflicts.

In effect, peacekeeping operations are not necessarily, as the International Court of Justice held in the *Certain Expenses of the United Nations Case,*[63] enforcement actions. In accomplishing their missions, however, peacekeeping forces may have both military and civilian components necessary for the aforementioned tasks and the provision of humanitarian services. Although they are characterized by the absence of enforcement capabilities, they may use military force in self-defence. Contemporary events have shown the pragmatic character of peacekeeping operations. In Namibia, Lebanon, Yugoslavia, Liberia, and Cambodia, they have engaged in roles hardly consistent with mere separation of warring forces and facilitation of humanitarian services in crisis situations. This is particularly true of those operations sanctioned by the UN Security Council. Accordingly, the absence of consent of warring parties in such UN-sanctioned peacekeeping operations appears to pose little impediment to the dispatch of peacekeeping forces to trouble spots. Similarly, the scope of their operations appears to be tailored to the peculiarities of each crisis. As the Secretary-General of the United Nations confirmed in his report to the General Assembly entitled *Supplement to the Agenda for Peace,* "three aspects of recent mandates, in particular, have led peacekeeping operations to forfeit the consent of parties, to behave in a way that was not perceived of or to use force other than in self defence. These were the task of *protecting humanitarian operations during fighting,* the *protection of civilian populations in safe areas, and pressing parties to accept national reconciliation at a pace faster than they were ready to accept.*"[64]

As Berdal has pointedly noted, the volatile, complex, and dangerous nature of internal conflicts, which often inflict fatalities on peacekeepers, [65] has given rise to the contemporary practice whereby host-state consent and traditional peacekeeping have yielded to what is now known as "robust peacekeeping."[66] There are other cases evidencing a noticeable trend in contemporary international law where traditional peacekeeping yields occasionally to peace enforcement or other roles not wholly compatible with traditional notions of peacekeeping.[67] For instance, in 1989-90 the United Nations set up the UN Transition Assistance Group (UNTAG) to supervise the electoral process in Namibia.[68] This task was clearly outside the traditional task of monitoring a ceasefire or supervising the withdrawal of belligerent forces. In another instance, in 1991 and 1992 the UN set up the United Nations Advance Mission in Cambodia (UNTAMIC) and the United Nations Temporary Authority in Cambodia (UNTAC) to supervise government functions and eventual elections while rebuilding Cambodia and disarming the factions.

This second-generation peacekeeping is closer to conflict management and peace enforcement than mere separation of warring parties. The new thinking and practice that peacekeeping should move "beyond the Sheriff's posse"[69] probably reflects pragmatism[70] and evidence of what international society considers to be prudent and necessary in the contemporary circumstances. Given that measures taken by the ECOMOG peacekeepers were undertaken in active conjunction with the United Nations Observer Mission in Liberia (UNOMIL) and were sanctioned and/or ratified by the Security Council, the objections by Kufour and Ofodile on the point are misconceived.[71] Second, the invitation by Doe did not delimit the scope of measures that ECOMOG could adopt to bring the crisis under control. Third, the ECOMOG mandate was not limited to merely separating the Liberian warlords.

On the issue that the ECOWAS decision to intervene was made without compliance with the necessary rules contained in the ECOWAS Protocol on Mutual Assistance on Defence (PMAD) embodying its principles on collective security, it is pertinent to examine the doctrine of collective self-defence as applied to the Liberian crisis.

Collective Self-Defence and the Liberian Crisis

> *World peace, like war, has tended to become indivisible.*[72]
>
> – *R.A. Akindele*

The ECOWAS argument on collective self-defence has been flayed on the grounds that the rebellion did not constitute an armed attack on Liberia as envisaged by the doctrine of collective self-defence. In addition, the applicability or otherwise of the PMAD to the Liberian case has been questioned. It has been further argued that even if the PMAD had been applicable, the necessary procedural mechanism for invocation of the right of collective self-defence was not followed by ECOWAS. Therefore, the critics contend, the ECOWAS intervention was unlawful at international law. Since these arguments turn on very important principles of international law regarding the use of force, it is pertinent to start from the historical origins of the principle of collective self-defence.

The right of collective self-defence, like most legal principles, is distilled from practical experience. It is probably in this context that Grotius argued that it is a right rooted in nature. However, the scope of the exercise of the right of self-defence is delimited by positive law.[73] As the name suggests, self-defence is the defence of self. It is different from necessity as it "arises when a wrong has been done."[74] Second, unlike a reprisal, it is not an enforcement of perceived legal rights, which is a preserve of the state.[75] Third, unlike a reprisal, it is invoked at a moment of imminent danger that is of such character that waiting on regular agencies of law enforcement for protection would be fatal to the potential victim of the attack. According to Kelsen, "between the moment the illegal attack starts and the moment the centralized machinery of collective security is put into action, there is even in case of perfectly prompt functioning, a space of time, an interval which may be disastrous to the victim."[76]

Max Sorensen has argued that the principles governing self-defence by states in international law are analogous to and derived from municipal laws on self-defence.[77] If this argument is accepted, it follows, as McDougal and Feliciano affirm, that the principles governing recourse to self-defence in a collective arrangement in international law are themselves similar to those rules applicable in the individual context.[78] Self-defence is tempered by the conditions of necessity, immediacy, and proportionality, and these elements combine to afford justification.[79] Contrary to Vattel's argument that self-defence is a "sacred duty"[80] that a state must exercise, international law merely recognizes the rightful option of recourse to self-defence and imposes no duty to exercise it. As Dinstein has shrewdly noted, "a prudent state may decline to exercise this right on the ground that a political compromise is preferable to a clash of arms. The indubitable military supremacy of the adversary may have a sobering effect on the target state, inhibiting it from steps that would transmute a theoretical right into a practical disaster. The idea that a state must sacrifice realism at the altar of conceptualism and risk defeat while prodded on by a 'sacred duty' is incongruous."[81]

One of the theoretical conundrums surrounding the concept of collective self-defence is whether it in fact means the defence of others or a defence of a theoretical "comprehensive self."[82] In addition to these complexities,[83] the concept of self-defence is often compounded by the dishonesty of its assertion by states.[84] Victims of aggression may therefore dispute assertions of the right by the presumed aggressor. This ambiguity compounds the theoretical and practical difficulties in evaluating the concept. [85]

In examining the applicability of the principles of collective self-defence to the ECOWAS intervention in Liberia, reference must be made to customary international law as evidenced by the practice of states, ECOWAS PMAD, and subsidiary sources of international law such as judicial decisions and the opinion of writers. The analysis will, however, be made within the context of the collective security peculiarities of West Africa. It is perhaps useful to start off with the practice and principles of the doctrine of collective self-defence under customary international law.

Contrary to the argument of Judge Oda in the celebrated *Nicaragua Case* that the right of collective self-defence is of contemporary origin, scholars such as Georg Schwarzenberger[86] have traced the practice to the provisions of the Perpetual League (1291) between the Swiss tribal communities and the Union of Utrecht (1579) between Great Britain and France, treaties that acknowledged the concept of collective self-defence.[87] Thus, before the civil war in Spain in 1936-38 (where there was an express agreement by states not to aid the parties in the conflict), there existed alliances for collective self-defence in medieval Europe. Therefore, the doctrine of collective self-defence predates the UN Charter provisions of Article 51.

It is probable that the right of collective self-defence attained refinement as a rule of customary international law in Europe and Latin America during the nineteenth century and early twentieth century. In this period, Europe and particularly Latin America were the foci of the exercise of the right. It literally formed the theoretical basis for continental and regional arrangements for security. It was entrenched in the Inter-American Treaty of Reciprocal Assistance concluded on 2 September 1947[88] (see Article 3 of that treaty). During the negotiations for the United Nations Charter, the Latin American countries insisted that they would not sacrifice this right at the altar of the nascent United Nations.[89] The right of collective self-defence was also recognized by the United States policy in the famous Monroe Doctrine. It was further articulated in the "Declaration of Lima" by the Eighth International Conference of American States, 24 December 1938, and probably influenced the letter of Article 51 of the UN Charter. This historical flavour influenced the International Court of Justice's interpretation of the customary right of collective self-defence in the *Nicaragua Case*.

It was not only the US that affirmed the existence of the right as state practice and adopted it as a state policy, particularly in the age of colonialism and empire. States such as Great Britain claimed to act in collective self-defence with colonies as far away and as diverse as Persia, Egypt, and Afghanistan.[90] Thus, in connection with the Kellogg-Briand Treaty for the Renunciation of War of 1928, Britain warned that "there are certain regions of the world, the welfare and integrity of which constitute special and vital interest to our peace ... their protection against attack is to the British empire a measure of self defense."[91] It was this expansive, perhaps hubristic, construction of the right that publicists have theoretically construed as the notion of a comprehensive self. This concept will be examined shortly.

However, the liberal construction of the right of collective self-defence in the guise of a virtually unlimited notion of comprehensive self was rejected by most publicists. To Hans Wehberg, a leading publicist of the last century, the British claim was sheer imperialistic excess that "diminished the significance of the *Kellogg Pact* to a considerable degree."[92] To D.W. Bowett, it was sheer greed for territorial expansion and colonial indulgence.[93] Similar Japanese pronouncements with respect to China were equally rebuffed by scholars. Notwithstanding this critique from international law scholars, state practice, which reflected European customary international law on the question, permitted a liberal notion that states may act collectively to repel aggression against one state.

Thus, the claims by those powerful states characterized their conception of what they considered to be their spheres of influence. It is therefore safe to say that at customary international law, especially before the wind of anticolonialism shrank the frontiers of those states and delegitimated cravings for empire, the right of collective self-defence was exercised on the basis of a common regional security arrangement or where recognizable "vital interests" founded on imperialism and colonialism were threatened by state aggression. The concept of vital interest and similar linkages of interests or interconnectivity of security, which scholars redefined as the notion of a comprehensive self, was a wide umbrella covering diverse notions, including geographic and imperialistic assumptions. Often, however, it tended to involve states in a proximate or contiguous relationship.[94] From his analysis of state practice, Dinstein has argued that the doctrine of self-interest or vital interest is sufficient to warrant an invocation of the right of collective self-defence at customary international law.[95] A caveat has been entered here, however, to wit: the security of states acting in collective self-defence must be closely interwoven to warrant the invocation of that right. The clearest interwoven security interest is usually the existence of a mutual treaty on collective self-defence. In effect, an attack on one such member state would constitute an attack on the other states so as to warrant their intervention in exercise of the right of collective self-defence.

These principles have not drowned out loud theoretical and practical complaints about the nature of what constitutes a comprehensive self, or about whether a state that is contiguous to an attacked state but not itself the direct victim of the aggression may lawfully invoke the doctrine of collective self-defence under customary international law, or about whether a state far away from the field of original aggression but possessing some vital interest there may purport to be acting in collective self-defence with the initial victim. McDougal and Feliciano have articulated state practice in this regard, and their explanation accords with customary international law on the matter. According to them, "a claim of collective self-defence arises whenever a number of traditional bodies-politic asserting certain demands for security as well as common expectations that such security can be achieved only by larger cooperative efforts, and purporting to define their respective identification structures so as to create a common overlap and interlock, confront an opponent, and present themselves to the rest of the general community as one unified group or collectivity for purposes of security and defence."[96] This formulation therefore encompasses the following elements as creating a comprehensive self. There must be first a prior assertion by the relevant states of mutual securities arising from overlapping and interlocking securities, and a public assertion and recognition of the means of securing that interlocking security by collective means. Needless to add, the existence of treaty obligations satisfies these tests.

In the context of West Africa, indeed of postcolonial Africa, the overlapping and interlocking nature of the ethnic groups there, their common assertion of collective security, and assurance of it through collective efforts amounts to a *prima facie* case for the existence of a comprehensive self in the region. At customary international law, however, the existence of a comprehensive self only creates a right of collective self-defence, and does not impose a duty to act in collective self-defence.[97] Furthermore, for states in the region to assert the right of collective self-defence, the attack on one must constitute a clear and present danger to the interlocking security of the entire region. Having regard to the dangers of abuse and hegemonic tendencies, the threshold of security must of necessity remain high if the right is not to be a cloak for the ulterior interests of powerful states purporting to assist in collective self-defence.

The exercise of collective self-defence is naturally premised upon a confrontation with immediate danger, and this raises the issue of who construes or determines what danger or aggression is "clear and present" to that comprehensive self so as to warrant an exercise of the right of collective self-defence. Customary international law allowed for "auto interpretation"[98] of what constituted clear and imminent danger short of armed attack.[99] In consequence, not only was the exercise of collective self-defence probable in the absence of actual armed attack but members of the comprehensive self were at liberty to determine by themselves the existence or otherwise of an imminent armed attack. However, as McDougal and Feliciano insist, "imminence of attack of such high degree as to preclude effective resort by the intended victim to non-violent modalities of response has always been recognized as sufficient justification."[100]

Oppenheim supports this view and cites several historical instances, such as: (1) the British pre-emptive shelling in 1807 of the Danish fleet at Copenhagen to frustrate the secret pact between Denmark and Napoleonic France,[101] (2) the Amelia Islands invasion by the United States in 1817 to flush out pirates on the Spanish island, (3) the German invasion of Luxembourg and Belgium in 1914, (4) the sinking of the French fleet at Oran in 1940, and (5) the Anglo-Soviet pre-emptive collective self-defensive occupation of Iran in 1941. In construing the 1928 Kellogg-Briand Treaty for the Renunciation of War, France and the United States declared that a state purporting to be exercising the right of self-defence "was alone competent to decide whether circumstances require recourse to war in self defence."[102]

This contention has drawn considerable disagreement from some scholars of international law. Lauterpacht contends that "such a claim is self contradictory as it purports to be based on legal right and at the same time, it dissociates itself from regulation and evaluation of the law."[103] During the Nuremberg trials, the tribunal reasoned in a similar vein[104] and held that "whether action taken under the claim of self defence was in fact aggressive or defensive must ultimately be subject to investigation or adjudication if international law is ever to be enforced."[105] In conclusion, it may be said that at customary international law, the principle of auto-interpretation[106] is permitted but the claim is justiciable.[107]

Another element of the right of collective self-defence is immediacy of the response to the danger or peril constituted by the initial unlawful attack. On this question, it seems that regard is had to the means and readiness of articulating a response by the comprehensive self to the danger at issue. The difficulty here is that a belated response could confuse an exercise of the right of collective self-defence with acts of reprisal. Save for cases of continuing aggression, the repulsion of the initial aggression has to be executed with relative dispatch and under circumstances where such response is the only option to secure a return to lawful norms. As American Secretary of State Daniel Webster argued in his correspondence in the *Caroline Case* of 1842,[108] for the United Kingdom to avail of the right, it should "show a necessity of self defence, instant, overwhelming, leaving no choice of means, and no moment for deliberation and the action must involve nothing unreasonable or excessive; since the act justified by the necessity of self defence, must be limited by that necessity and kept clearly within it."[109] Webster's test largely remains the classical summation of the right individually or in the collective context under customary international law. Similarly, the response was to be limited "in intensity and magnitude to what was reasonably necessary promptly to secure the permissible objectives of self defence under the conditions of necessity."[110]

The twin essential elements of necessity and proportionality in the exercise of collective self-defence at customary international law was recently reaffirmed by the International Court of Justice in the *Nuclear Weapons Case* and in the *Nicaragua Case*. A summary of the elements of customary international law on collective self-defence may be stated as follows:

- There must be an unlawful armed attack, or at least an imminent unlawful armed attack.
- The attack or imminence thereof must be of such character that there cannot be a reasonable expectation by the victim of a recourse to pacific settlement.
- Save for "continuing aggression," the response to the attack or the imminent armed attack must be of an immediate character, regard being had to the nature of the attack or threat and the means of its removal.
- The response must be reasonable and proportionate to the threat or the unlawful aggression.
- The states acting collectively must have some acceptable degree of proximate relationship between them, and must have given adequate notice to the international community of the existence thereof.

As an aside, it is clear that on the basis of these entrenched principles of international law, recent events that indicate an enthusiasm on the part of the United States and possibly the United Kingdom to use force on some states, such as Iraq, outside the constraints of customary international law on pre-emptive collective self-defence is unjustifiable. Before applying these principles to the ECOWAS intervention in Liberia, it is pertinent to examine the impact of the UN Charter on the customary international law regime on collective self-defence.

Collective Self-Defence and the UN Charter

Article 51 of the United Nations Charter provides as follows:

> Nothing in the present charter shall impair the inherent right of individual or collective self defense if an armed attack occurs against a member of the United Nations until the Security Council has taken the measures necessary to maintain international peace and security. Measures taken by members in the exercise of this right of self defense shall be immediately reported to the Security Council and shall not in any way affect the authority and responsibility of the Security Council under the present Charter to take at

any time such action as it deems necessary in order to maintain or restore international peace and security.

The true meaning of these words in the application of the principles of collective self-defence has been problematic. While some publicists argue that the right of collective self-defence in customary international law has been tempered by and subsumed under Article 51, another school of thought maintains that the right exists in its classical state untouched by Charter provisions.[111] There are two parallel regimes on the right of collective self-defence.

The salient issue here is that in considering the extent to which the UN Charter has limited the scope of customary international law on collective self defence, it has to be borne in mind that the fundamental objective of the Charter is to substitute unilateral actions with a deliberative international machinery. This is the essential contribution of the Charter to the global regime on use of force by states. The corollary question, therefore, is the extent, if any, of the influence on customary international law of the spirit and letter of Article 51. Without pre-empting the arguments that will appear below, it seems that the question of whether the practice of states has been qualified by Article 51 betrays an expectation that Article 51 of the Charter ought to curtail the rather liberal regime of collective self-defence under customary international law. The question may well be asked whether state practice should be read subject to the Charter.

Having regard to the circumstances under which the Charter was negotiated, drawn up, and agreed to by member states, and to its raison d'être, there is a discernible attitude and disposition against the use of force by states in their dealings with one another. Article 2(4) expressly reinforces this teleological disposition. The provisions of Articles 25 and 28 further confirm this view as they seek to confer a monopoly on the use of force in international law on the Security Council. In other words, the object of the Charter is to constrain states in their ability to have recourse to force in the resolution of disputes. Under the circumstances, the modern machinery and substance of international law is a juridical and normative constraint rather than a facilitator of violence and armed engagements. Consequently, recourse to collective self-defence should be a last resort by states and is justiciable under Article 51.

Scholars like Kelsen,[112] Jessup,[113] and Henkin[114] have argued that under Article 51 the right of collective self-defence is conditional upon the occurrence of an armed attack. In the rather blunt words of Henkin, the argument on anticipatory collective self-defence under the Charter regime "is unfounded, its reasoning fallacious and its doctrine pernicious."[115] On the other hand, another formidable school of thought represented by Dinstein[116] and by Myers McDougal and Feliciano[117] has made a persuasive case for anticipatory self-defence under Article 51. Although the Court in the *Nicaragua Case* did not express a view on this issue, because it was decided under the normative regime of customary international law, the Court did affirm that under customary law, "the exercise of this right is conditional on armed attack."[118] Be that as it may, when Article 51 is read in the overall context of the Charter's intent to avoid and reduce the frequency and scope of armed conflicts, the better view would be that exercise of the right of collective self-defence under Article 51 is limited to cases of actual armed attack. Clearly, under the Charter, there is no room for the doctrine of anticipatory or preemptive strikes by a state or a group of states purporting to be acting in collective self-defence.

What, then, is an armed attack, and who determines when it has occurred? The consensus of writers is that this is a privilege of the victim of the armed attack. However, as under customary international law, this privilege is clearly justiciable. What is the meaning of "armed attack"? It seems that the International Court of Justice and a majority of international law scholars have no disagreement with the definition offered by Article 3(g) of the Definition of Aggression annexed to General Assembly Resolution 3314 of 14 December 1974. Thus, in addition to the sending of regular forces across an international border, "the sending by or on behalf of a state of armed bands, groups, irregulars, or mercenaries, which carry out acts of armed force against another state of such gravity as to amount to ... armed attack if carried out by regular forces constitutes armed attack for the purposes of Article 51."[119]

It is remarkable that the Court adopted a rather restrictive interpretation of this phrase. This again affirms the teleological intention of the Charter to restrain and constrain states from easy and enthusiastic recourse to armed force. Although the dissenting view of Judge Jennings may appear to serve the expedient or perceived realities of a world currently grappling with international terrorism, it potentially opens the door to a liberal recourse to further violence and destruction of the multilateral basis of the world legal order regulating the use or threat of the use of force. Moreover, the role of the law is not to follow the perceived realities or expediencies of the day but to regulate reality itself in a coherent and predictable manner. Thus, an expedient, unprincipled, and unilateralist recourse to force in international relations is more likely to unravel global legal order in a violent world rather than remedy the perceived dangers of the hour.

The question of who may lawfully act in collective self-defence has not been any less controversial under Article 51 than under its customary international law counterpart. In this context, the Court in the *Nicaragua Case* indirectly considered the concept of a comprehensive self. The facts of the case as found by the Court were that after the collapse of the Somoza regime and its replacement by the junta led by Daniel Ortega, the Ortega regime reneged on its promises to the United States. It did so by adopting socialist policies and also by refusing to "democratize." Further, the junta became very friendly with the communist regime of Fidel Castro in Cuba and with other members of the communist bloc. The US then began aiding neighbouring countries in the hemisphere, such as Honduras, El Salvador, and Costa Rica, to subvert the Ortega regime. It also funded and assisted a band of Nicaraguan rebels dedicated to the overthrow of the Ortega regime, and mined Nicaraguan ports. As a result of these activities, the Nicaraguan government filed a claim in the Court against the United States.

On the question of whether the US could maintain a claim of collective self-defence with El Salvador for acts of aggression allegedly carried out by the Ortega government some four to five years before the US-aided subversion of Nicaragua, the Court had cause to address the notion of collectivity of interest and the alleged requirement that a victim state must request third-state help before a claim of collective self-defence would be admissible. For the reasons stated below, this aspect of the Court's decision is difficult to reconcile with customary international law and the UN Charter. First, the condition of formal request for help is novel and of dubious validity. No such requirement is evident on the face of Article 51. Second, it seems that the Court's position misapprehends the philosophy of the right of collective self-defence. Collective self-defence is not necessarily the defence of another state but the defence of self on the principle that an aggression on another state constitutes (for reasons tied to mutual security and interdependence, as evidenced in a treaty) a direct attack on a comprehensive self. The assisting state in effect defends itself. It is not a champion of the primary victim of the aggression.

Third, the Court was probably unduly influenced by the Inter-American Treaty of Reciprocal Assistance, 19 September 1947, otherwise known as the Rio Treaty, of which Article 3(2) makes the exercise of the right of collective self-defence conditional upon a request by the primary victim.[120] It is difficult to understand why the Court imposed this limitation on the right of collective self-defence, especially as it purported to be applying customary international law and not the provisions of the Rio Declaration.[121] Even if the Court was motivated by the understandable need to restrict the scope of the right of collective self-defence, its interpretation of that right was unwarranted.

Regarding the question of parties who may partake in collective self-defence under the UN Charter, Kunz has argued that in the absence of any treaty obligation, collective self-defence is only a right and not a duty, but this hardly answers the question.[122] In the *Nicaragua Case,* the Court did not specifically address this issue, as none of the parties raised it.[123] However, it appears that there is no strict requirement for the existence of a formal defence pact between states before they can have recourse to the right of collective self-defence under Article 51.[124] Dinstein shares this view,[125] and in the absence of any provision to the contrary on the face of Article 51, it seems literally correct. It may therefore be said that in theory, where the security of states are closely interwoven and such a circumstance is brought to the knowledge of third states or is reasonably apparent to them, an attack on one state, even in the absence of treaty obligations, may constitute an attack on the other states. Accordingly, the right of collective self-defence under Article 51 may be invoked. But this interpretation flies in the face of the clear and overall intent of the Charter to severely circumscribe the conditions under which states may resort to force. Therefore, it would be unhelpful to read Article 51 as if it were an independent provision.

Bowett has therefore argued that having regard to the preparatory work of the Charter and Article 51, the exercise of the right of collective self-defence is limited to states in a defence pact or in a regional arrangement for mutual security.[126] This argument is more persuasive and compelling, because although the right of collective self-defence antedated Latin American state practice, the *travaux préparatoires* of the Charter at the Dumbarton Oaks Conference clearly show that Article 51 was tailored after Latin American state practice. It is well to remember that the Latin American experience was not necessarily reflective of the practice of states across the globe, as it was a continental practice rather than a universal phenomenon. However, its norms are compelling, and in a world teeming with violent groups and perceived threats to the national security of different states, the threshold of connectivity of collective security must remain high if the right of collective self-defence is not to be a cloak for aggression, regional hegemony, and external meddling in purely domestic affairs.

Regarding the question of the acceptable time span between the act of aggression and the exercise of the right of self-defence, it appears that Article 51 maintains the customary international law rule that it should be relatively contemporaneous with the attack. On the issue of the requirement that states resorting to collective self-defence should immediately report measures taken in the exercise of the right to the Security Council, some publicists like Kelsen have argued that this is mandatory.

Who determines whether the measures taken by the Security Council are necessary to restore the peace? Kelsen has argued that this is a responsibility of the Security Council.[127] On the other hand, scholars like Greig have argued that the requirement to report to the Security Council on measures ostensibly taken in collective self-defence is directory, exhortatory, and not mandatory. His argument is that doing otherwise does not invalidate the exercise of the right.[128] However, the better view, and as further confirmed by the Court in the *Nuclear Weapons Case,* is that the assisting state must report the steps taken by it to the Security Council as it substantially reflects on the *bona fides* of the belief in the right. This view is consistent with the disposition of the Charter to restrain the use of force by states, and it also enhances the justiciability of the assertion of the right.

Turning to the question of the scope of the right of collective self defence when the Security Council intervenes, it seems that the obligation to cease acting in collective self defence would arise only when the steps taken by the Security Council are by themselves capable of removing the attack giving rise to the resort to collective self-defence. A rather extreme view contends that states exercising the right of collective self-defence have the right to pursue collective self-defence to a logical conclusion by defeating the aggressor and imposing a peace treaty on the vanquished aggressor.[129] This view is problematic as it introduces alien elements of reprisals, punishment, and self-help. It seems that in this context, the right is not at large and must be measured on the standard bar of what is reasonable and proportionate to the initial aggression.

In summary, the principles governing the exercise of collective self-defence under the UN Charter may be stated as follows:

- There must be an armed attack, and the determination of its occurrence is the responsibility of the victim or comprehensive self, but this claim remains justiciable and is subject to the scrutiny of the Security Council.
- There must be a strong mutual security relationship and treaty nexus between the victim and the assisting state constituting a comprehensive self, and the initial aggression must constitute a clear and present danger to the security of the comprehensive self.
- Save for cases of continuing aggression, the response by the comprehensive self must be immediate, regard being had to the nature of the aggression and the reasonable time it would take to assess the manner and the nature of the response to be adopted.
- The victim of the armed attack is obliged to report all measures taken in collective self-defence to the Security Council.
- Parties to the conflict are to hold their peace once the Security Council has effectively intervened to restore peace.

When the principles of collective self-defence under the regime of the UN Charter are compared with customary international law, it is clear that the Charter regime is narrower and more consistent with its avowed intent of limiting the use or threat of use of force by states in their relations.

Justification of the ECOWAS Intervention as Collective Self-Defence

As already noted in the preceding pages, the threshold for the invocation of the right of collective self-defence is the occurrence of an armed attack. The question now is whether the NPFL invasion of Liberia and its support by some third states rose to the level of an armed attack as contemplated by Article 51. The Definition of Aggression contained in the General Assembly Resolution 3314 of December 1974 contains binding normative definitions of what constitutes armed attack. This has been further articulated and reiterated by the International Court of Justice in both the *Nicaragua Case* and the *Nuclear Weapons Case.*[130]

Article 3(g) of the Definition of Aggression defines armed attack as including "the sending by or on behalf of a state of armed bands, groups, irregulars, or mercenaries, which carry out acts of armed force against another state of such gravity as to amount to ... armed attack." This definition would suffice for the purposes of this analysis. Being a declaration of the United Nations adopted with substantial support by states, it is evidence of international law on the matter. The issue to be resolved is whether the facts of the rebellion and the ostensible third-state support for it constitute armed attack for the purposes of Article 51 and customary international law on collective self-defence.

The alleged support given to the rebels by various states within and around the West African subregion has already been documented in the preceding chapters. While a repetition of those allegations is hardly helpful, for the purposes of elucidating the arguments here, some of the more pertinent instances will be revisited and their legal implications addressed. I have already commented on the training of some of the NPFL rebels in Libya. The Libyan motive is rather controversial. Some commentators, such as Mark Huband, who interviewed some of the ex-NPFL rebels, contend that Ghaddafi wanted a beachhead in West Africa and control of the sophisticated American Omega Relay satellite in Liberia.[131] Other reasons include his alleged desire to use the NPFL rebels to seize the relatively large number of Americans in Liberia. Be that as it may, the crucial question here is whether the alleged support of the various factions by diverse states is sufficiently attributable to those states, and whether such support constitutes armed attack.

It is not in doubt that the NPFL rebels launched the rebellion from Côte d'Ivoire and allegedly received extensive support from both the Ivorian government and the government of Burkina Faso. Given the occurrence of similar events in Afghanistan and the notion that the defunct Taliban regime worked hand in glove with or allegedly permitted Osama bin Laden's al-Qaeda to use Afghan territory to plot attacks on a sovereign state, these acts or omissions have profound implications for the discourse on global security. The critical test here is whether the governments of Côte d'Ivoire and Burkina Faso, or Afghanistan, for that matter, merely neglected to safeguard their territories from being used by the rebels/al-Qaeda or whether they voluntarily placed their territories at the disposal of the rebels/al-Qaeda.

In the former case, it would be a delict at international law. While speculations on the nature of cooperation between outlaw elements and "rogue states" may seem difficult to resolve, they bear heavily on the legality or otherwise of the use of force by states to deal with such problematic situations. As the International Court of Justice pertinently noted in the *Corfu Channel Case,* "it cannot be concluded from the mere fact of the control exercised by a State over its territory and waters that that state necessarily knew, or ought to have known, of any unlawful act perpetrated therein, nor yet that it necessarily knew, or should have known, the authors. This fact, by itself and apart from other circumstances, neither involves prima facie responsibility nor shifts the burden of proof."[132] Thus, the use of a state's territory by a rebel or terrorist organization group does not necessarily amount to armed attack but may constitute subversion of the victim state.

In addition, support of the warring factions by some states does not necessarily make them the agents of their benefactors. As the Court held in the *Nicaragua Case,* it must be shown not only that the warring factions were created by those states financing their campaign but also that they were under their control. At international law, a state's offering of logistical support and finances to a rebel group or to a terrorist organization such as the al-Qaeda may not be not enough to justify another state's recourse to use of force in self-defence. The element of control is critical. In the absence of probative proof that Côte d'Ivoire, Burkina Faso, and Libya created and controlled the warring factions, the question of the existence or not of an armed attack under this heading does not arise. But this is not the end of the matter, as the sending of 400 troops by the Burkina Faso government to Liberia to fight alongside the NPFL rebels is a different issue.

As I have already indicated, the government of Burkina Faso acknowledged sending over 400 troops to the NPFL rebels, which it justified as "moral support" for the rebels.[133] The legal significance of this fact is critical. The decision of the International Court of Justice in the *Nicaragua Case*[134] leaves little doubt that the Burkinabe government action took the matter out of the rubric of indirect aggression[135] to one of actual direct aggression constituting armed attack. According to the Court in the *Nicaragua Case,* "in particular, it may be considered to be agreed that an armed attack must be understood as including, not merely action by regular armed forces across an international border, but also the *sending* [emphasis added] by or on behalf of a state of armed bands, groups, irregulars or mercenaries, which carry out acts of armed force against another state of such gravity as to amount to *inter alia* an armed attack conducted by regular forces, or its substantial involvement therein."[136]

Although these remarks were made with respect to the customary law regime, they apply with equal force to the Charter regime on collective self-defence. Accordingly, the action of the Burkinabe government constituted an armed attack against Liberia. The existence of a civil war in Liberia at the material time does not excuse the armed attack. As the Court held in the *Nicaragua Case,* state sovereignty and the doctrine of non-intervention "would certainly lose its effectiveness ... if intervention were to be justified by a mere request for assistance by an opposition group in another state."[137] Consequently, the unlawful dispatch of troops by Burkina Faso to help in the rebellion against President Doe violated international law and constituted a potential trigger of any agreement on collective self-defence affecting Liberia.

The threshold on collective self-defence having been crossed, the second test is whether ECOWAS and its constitutive states were a "comprehensive self" warranting intervention by ECOWAS. In answering this question, the crucial test ought to be the substantiality of the new comprehensive self created by public assertions of an interconnectedness of securities by the affected states. In the Liberian case, ECOWAS's collective security arrangement in its Protocol on Mutual Assistance on Defence was sufficient to create and assert its comprehensiveness of self. The preamble to the PMAD and its substantive provisions leave no doubt about the existence of a comprehensive self. The preamble not only recognizes that member states belong to the same geographical area but also affirms the consciousness of ECOWAS that regional security can best be achieved by pooling their resources within a common agency. Thus, in addition to the shared economic interests of the ECOWAS member states, there exists an understanding and public affirmation in the subregion of the interlocking and interdependent nature of their interdependent securities.

This understanding finds ample expression in the substantive provisions of the PMAD and the ECOWAS Protocol on Non-Aggression. Some of the pertinent provisions of these protocols are as follows.

Article 2 of the Protocol on Non-Aggression states: "Each member shall refrain from committing, encouraging or condoning acts of subversion, hostility or aggression against the territorial integrity or political independence of the other member states."[138] The provisions of Articles 3 and 4 impose a positive duty on member states to ensure that their territories are not used for acts of regional and inter-state subversion.

Article 3 of the PMAD states: "Each member state shall undertake to prevent foreigners on its territory from committing the acts referred to in Article 2 above against the sovereignty and territorial integrity of other member states."[139] Article 4 of the PMAD states: "Each member state shall undertake to prevent non-resident foreigners from using its territory as a base for committing the acts referred to in Article 2 above against the sovereignty and territorial integrity of member states."[140] In addition, the PMAD articulates ECOWAS's explicit approval of the doctrine of collective self-defence within the region, as Article 2 provides that "member states declare and accept that any armed attack or aggression directed against any member state shall constitute a threat or aggression against the entire Community."[141] Members of ECOWAS are, by virtue of Article 3 of the PMAD, obliged to give mutual aid and assistance for defence against any armed threat or aggression. This objective is to be achieved through the instrumentality of an Allied Armed Forces of the Community (AAFC) to be composed of nationals from existing armed forces of the Community earmarked for that purpose and placed at the disposal of the Community in cases of any "armed intervention."[142] The phrase "armed intervention" seems to have a contextualized meaning with regard to the provisions of Article 15(1), which provides that "intervention by AAFC [the Community's Allied Armed Forces] shall in all cases be justified by the legitimate defence of the community." However, ECOWAS shall not employ this provision to intervene "if the conflict remains purely internal."[143]

It is very pertinent to note that by virtue of Article 18 of the PMAD, a conflict is not internal if, as in the Liberian case, it is "actively maintained and sustained from the outside."[144] Nor would it still be construed as an internal matter when it actually spilled over into Sierra Leone with catastrophic consequences. The impact of the Liberian crisis on Sierra Leone formed the substance of the deliberations of the United Nations General Assembly at its eighty-sixth plenary meeting held on 21 December 1993.[145] The subsequent resolution passed by that body contained the following findings:

- that the spillover effect of the Liberian crisis had caused serious destruction to and devastation of the productive areas of the territory of Sierra Leone and of its economy as a whole[146]
- that the conflict in Liberia had "devastated lives and properties in the eastern and southern provinces of Sierra Leone, causing massive outflows of refugees and displaced persons."[147]

On the foregoing grounds, it is clear that in addition to the treaty obligations imposed on member states by the ECOWAS Protocol on Non-Aggression and the PMAD, there existed the collectivity of interest and a comprehensive self justifying the assertion of a right of collective self-defence by ECOWAS.

It has been argued by critics of the intervention that the decision to intervene via the framework of the PMAD was flawed and invalid because of alleged noncompliance with the provisions of the PMAD and the ECOWAS Treaty.[148] This argument is apparently formidable, and Article 6 of the PMAD has been invoked in support of it. The Article provides that "the Authority[149] shall decide on the expediency of military action and entrust its execution to the Force Commander of the Allied Armed Forces of the

Community (AAFC)."[150] Since the decision to intervene militarily was taken by the Standing Mediation Committee, a delegate of the ECOWAS Authority of Heads of States and Governments[151] as provided above, the decision to intervene, it has been argued, was invalid. It has to be recalled that the Authority of Heads of States and Governments met on 30 May 1990 in Gambia and established the Standing Mediation Committee.[152]

This body, made up of four members of the ECOWAS Authority itself, was appointed by that organ and chaired by the chairperson of ECOWAS. Its mandate was to suggest and explore amicable ways of settling disputes in the subregion and report to the full Authority.[153] It was the Standing Mediation Committee that recommended the dispatch of peacekeeping troops to Liberia. The argument that the decision to intervene taken by the Standing Mediation Committee instead of the full body of the Authority of Heads of States and Governments was illegal is erroneous and ignores subsequent developments on the issue.

At the extraordinary summit of the Authority convened at Bamako, Mali, on 27-28 November 1990, "the Authority expressed its appreciation to the members of the Mediation Committee for the initiatives taken in finding a peaceful resolution to the crisis in Liberia" and, moreover, "ratified the ECOWAS peace plan for Liberia as embodied in the Banjul Communiqué and Decisions of the Standing Mediation Committee adopted on 7 August 1990."[154] Although this clear ratification of the decision to intervene taken by the Standing Mediation Committee was *ex post facto,* arguments on the purported incompetence of the decision to intervene are not well founded.

The other condition for justification under collective self-defence is whether the response by the West African states was necessary, timely, and proportionate to the threat posed by the conflict. In evaluating this aspect of the right of collective self-defence, regard should be given to the complexities of the civil war in Liberia, its impact on the countries in the subregion, the relative difficulties in raising the necessary military response, and, finally, the most reasonable solution to the problem. I have already dealt with the impact of the Liberian conflict on Liberians, the region, and the international community. It has already been noted that six weeks after the rebellion, the neighbouring countries were already feeling the pain of the conflict as the rate of inflow of refugees was already stretching the capacity and security of those states. Meanwhile, both the OAU and the UN, beyond platitudes and homilies on peaceful coexistence and amicable settlement of conflicts, ignored the spreading disaster. The crisis had recorded numerous atrocities and was becoming increasingly ethnicized, a phenomenon that, given the problems of the Berlin Conference partitioning of Africa, was bound to draw the conflict as it did beyond the artificial frontiers of Liberia. Considering these factors, the ECOWAS response was necessary.

On the question of the timeliness of response and reporting to the Security Council of measures taken under Article 51 of the UN Charter, it is important to recall that President Doe's letter inviting ECOWAS to intervene in the anarchy in Liberia was addressed to that body on 14 July 1990.[155] Three weeks later, on 7 August 1990, the ECOWAS Standing Mediation Committee, acting on behalf of the ECOWAS Authority of Heads of States and Governments, did the following:

- established an ECOWAS Cease-fire Monitoring Group (ECOMOG)
- ordered a ceasefire in Liberia
- ordered all combatants in the conflict to surrender all arms to ECOMOG
- ordered all parties to the conflict to refrain from the importation of arms and ammunition into Liberia
- proposed the establishment of a democratically elected government in Liberia
- proposed the establishment of an interim government for Liberia.[156]

These far-reaching decisions, made shortly after Doe's intimation to ECOWAS about the crisis in Liberia, can hardly be said to have been belated; moreover, the crisis was in the nature of a continuing aggression. It is thus clear that the ECOWAS response was very timely, especially in the context of the efforts necessary to convene sixteen different states to agree on a common agenda.

Some commentators have argued that the ECOWAS response that ultimately led to a seeming resolution of the crisis and the installation of a "democratically" elected government in Liberia was not proportionate to the threat posed by the Liberian crisis. This argument, attractive as it seems on the surface, makes a profound mistake. As Louis Henkin noted, any inquiry into the role of law "must take into account the state of 'the system' – the character of international society and of the law at a given time."[157] This is not to mean that scholars or international lawyers are at liberty to torture legal rules to yield particularly pliable and amenable interpretations and justifications. Far from that; the issue here is that to the extent that argument on this aspect of the question fails to take into consideration the prevailing conditions and the intrinsic nature of the issues at hand, the objection remains suspect and disconnected from reality.

It is well to recall the earlier arguments on the emergence of a pragmatic instead of a doctrinaire approach to peacekeeping or collective self-defence, as the case may be. As earlier noted, a study of multilateral responses to civil strife with international repercussions shows that peacekeeping measures are more or less a necessary demand of the nature of the crisis. Peacekeeping bodies intervening in intra-state conflicts increasingly insist on "universally observed elections" in resolving those conflicts. While grave suspicions may be entertained about the touted benefits of foreign-induced periodic multiparty elections that fail to address the root causes of state failure in Africa, it can hardly be denied that modern state practice in Africa and indeed all over the world has accepted the supervision of domestic elections as part of the resolution of conflicts by peacekeepers.

In addition to undue simplification wrought by this attitude, the prodding from ideologically driven human rights activists and institutions for a "democratic" Africa and "democratic elections" supervised or overseen by "international observers" has become an unfortunate yardstick for measuring the success of modern peacekeeping in troubled states, particularly in Africa. To the extent, therefore, that ECOWAS created and sustained an environment whereby the warring factions were disarmed and "democratic elections" held, the ECOWAS response was proportionate to the threat posed by the civil war. Of course, this does not mean that such "democratization" exercises constitute a cure for chronic state failure in Africa. Indeed, there is mounting evidence, even from post–civil war Liberia, that such elections and democratization that neither deal with the fundamental causes of the conflicts nor punish egregious abuses of human rights perpetrated in such conflicts are mere window dressing. Be that as it may, the measures taken by ECOWAS enabled most of the neighbouring member states to maintain a semblance of their threatened sovereignty and did not go beyond the ECOMOG mandate; nor were they limited by Doe's original invitation.

The next criterion for justification under collective self-defence under the UN Charter is that parties acting in collective self-defence should speedily report to the Security Council the steps taken by them pursuant to Article 51 of the Charter. Here the ECOWAS action may well be the paragon of scrupulous compliance. The ECOWAS decision to act in collective self-defence was made on 7 August 1990, and it is significant to note that the Security Council was informed of it within forty-eight hours, through a letter dated 9 August 1990 and addressed to the Security Council.[158] The pertinent aspects of the letter read as follows:

> I consider it necessary to invite you to this brief session on the tragic situation in Republic of Liberia and on the efforts at the regional level to restore peace to that country ... the Authority held its first Summit in Banjul from the 6-7 August 1990 and came up with effective steps for ending the Liberian tragedy. Conscious of its responsibility for the maintenance of peace and security in the sub-region, the Committee on behalf of the Authority of ECOWAS Heads of States and Government, decided as follows:
>
> - There shall be an immediate cease-fire. All parties to the conflict shall cease all activities of a military and paramilitary nature as well as all acts of violence.

- Under the authority of Chairman of ECOWAS, a Cease-fire Monitoring Group (ECOMOG), was set up; it comprises military contingents from member states of the ECOWAS Standing Mediation Committee, as well as Guinea and Sierra Leone, Liberia's neighbours.
- ECOMOG shall assist the Committee in supervising the implementation and ensuring strict compliance of the cease-fire by all the parties to the conflict.
- That a broad-based Interim National Government shall be set up in the Republic of Liberia to administer that country and organize free and fair elections, leading to a democratically elected government. The composition of the Interim Government shall be determined by all parties to the conflict, including political parties and other interest groups.
- None of the leaders of the warring parties shall head the Interim Government.
- For the purposes of carrying out a peacekeeping role and monitoring the peace process in Liberia, a special emergency fund was established. There shall be voluntary contribution by the member states of ECOWAS, the OAU and other friendly countries to the special fund. A budget of about US$50 million is projected for financing the military operations, and for the immediate humanitarian needs of the Liberian people.[159]

The letter concludes with a statement that the ECOMOG action was not designed to take sides in the conflict, and urged the international community to support ECOWAS in its initiative. The letter dispels any doubt as to whether ECOWAS satisfied this condition for a valid invocation of the right of collective self-defence as provided by Article 51 of the UN Charter.

The last condition is that the states acting in collective self-defence should cease further action in that regard once the Security Council takes effective steps to resolve the conflict. With particular reference to the case of the ECOWAS action in Liberia, it is remarkable that the Security Council not only approved of the actions taken by ECOWAS but within eighteen months after the initial ECOWAS intervention, engaged in an unprecedented alliance with that body. The alliance, in the form of the United Nations Observer Mission in Liberia (UNOMIL), lasted from 1992 to 1997.

In view of the various implications of this novel arrangement and its impact on collective security, and of the provisions of the United Nations Charter relating to regional arrangements, attention ought to be paid to the continuing expansion of the meaning of the phrase "threat to international peace," and to its role as the trigger mechanism for the provisions of Chapter 7 of the UN Charter. State practice shows an untidy and incoherent compliance with the relevant Charter provisions on regional enforcement actions. In most cases, including Liberia, the relationship between regional bodies and the Security Council in the application of Chapter 7 is accidental, ad hoc, and opportunistic. This seems to present the Security Council with the need to "ratify" whatever presumptuous or unauthorized measures are adopted by multilateral security organizations without prior authorization of the Council. The cases of Liberia and Kosovo are examples. One of the grave dangers in this evolving practice is that regional organizations may now proceed to engage in illicit military interventions in the knowledge that, presented with a *fait accompli,* the Security Council would "ratify" such a brazen and dangerous usurpation of a responsibility hitherto reserved exclusively for the Security Council.

4
The UN Charter and the Ratification of the ECOWAS Action by the Security Council: Implications for Global Security

In the Cold War politics of collective security, regional organizations emerged as the main mechanism for articulating responses to perceived threats to member states of regional bodies. This practice marginalized the authority of the Security Council. The relationship between the Council and regional bodies was not always gladiatorial, however. Regionalism often worked alongside universalism. As Pittman Potter pointed out, the principal task of the student of international organizations is "not to waste more time debating over regionalism versus universalism but to study the ways in which, in concrete cases, the two principles can be utilized in combination and the standards to be applied in determining the dosage of each to be adopted."[1]

With reference to the relationship between the Economic Community of West African States (ECOWAS) and the UN Security Council, the latter provided the ECOWAS Cease-fire Monitoring Group (ECOMOG) with various means of ensuring the implementation of the agreements related to the enforcement of restraint in Liberia. For example, the Security Council established a trust fund that enabled African countries to send reinforcements to ECOMOG. These funds were also utilized by ECOMOG for elections and demobilization of the warring factions in Liberia.[2] The implications of this relationship echo the insight of Louis Henkin that in the final quarter of the twentieth century, the character and significance of international law "will be importantly influenced by the Third World."[3]

Regional Enforcement Actions and the UN Charter

It is now common knowledge that the increasing number of internal conflicts of international character imposes a huge strain on the United Nations. This trend has probably resulted in the apparent readiness of the United Nations to welcome regional initiatives in the maintenance of international security or, in some cases, to merely watch from the sidelines when such efforts are undertaken by regional organizations. Witness the cases of the

Organization of American States (OAS) intervention in Haiti, the Organization of Islamic Countries (OIC) and Arab League initiatives in the Somali crisis, the Association of Southeast Asian Nations (ASEAN) efforts in the Cambodian crisis, the Conference on Security and Cooperation in Europe (CSCE) initiatives regarding the new states in the defunct Soviet Union, and the 1999 European Union/NATO bombing of Yugoslavia.

Beyond the apparent abdication of responsibility, a far more disturbing trend in this practice is the implicit racialization that sometimes determines whether or when such interventions, as authorized by the United Nations, would occur. In addition to the subtle politics of race, the political and economic self-interests of powerful veto-wielding members of the Security Council appear to play a role in determining whether and when the Council intervenes in a troubled state or region. Hence, the apparent ease and readiness with which the Council "franchises" the intervention to a regional body. In other words, the realpolitik of racial affinity, geopolitical and economic considerations, and hemispheric concerns heavily influence whether powerful states sitting on the Security Council would intervene in troubled areas. This opportunistic and expedient approach to interventions raises fundamental questions regarding our conceptions of humanity. The most damning evidence of racial affinity or lack thereof underpinning or influencing global indifference or a tardy response to an African crisis is the Rwandan genocide.

In spite of clear, ample, and timely warnings by Canadian Major General Romeo Dallaire, the UN force commander in Rwanda, and a security operative of the Rwandan government that there was a looming genocide of the Tutsis, powerful states on the Security Council, especially the United States under President Bill Clinton, stood by while "800,000 people were put to death in the most unambiguous case of state-sponsored genocide ... since the Nazi Holocaust of the Jews of Europe."[4] This brutal savagery, well planned and fully known to the Security Council in advance, was executed within 100 days, while the US representative to the UN at the time, Madeleine Albright, "actively blocked UN Security Council intervention to stop the killing."[5]

Similar indifference was seen in the case of Zaire, Sierra Leone, Madagascar, and many other so-called Third World countries where non-Caucasians have been affected. Arguably, if Rwandans had been Caucasians, like the Kosovars in Yugoslavia or Zimbabweans of Caucasian extraction who have recently borne the brunt of President Robert Mugabe's land reallocation program, it is most likely that the response from powerful states in the Security Council would have been different. This attitude of selective and racialized intervention, barely concealed economic/political opportunism, and expediency when dealing with states in the Third World must be of concern to scholars of global security and stability. This is not to say that African states or Third

World states need more unilateral Western military interventions. The point here is that interventions must be transparently justifiable on *a priori* rules. Racial considerations or the economic and political self-interests of members of the Security Council must be eschewed in the process of determining when and how the Council is to be moved to intervene.

On the Liberian crisis, the United Nations report on its Observer Mission in Liberia (UNOMIL) acknowledges that "the United Nations, from the beginning of the conflict, supported the efforts of the ECOWAS member states."[6] This sense of support for ECOWAS gradually and eventually yielded to a diminished UN role in Liberia. This subordination of the UN was justified by the Secretary-General of the United Nations as "reaffirming ... commitment to a systematic cooperation between the United Nations and a regional organization," as envisaged in Chapter 8 of the Charter. Besides delivering rhetoric on peace and security, the UN contented itself with giving ECOWAS "assistance" on political reconciliation and humanitarian and electoral issues. It is not surprising that this report and subsequent proceedings and events leading to the unprecedented abdication of responsibility by the UN to a regional organization has engaged the close scrutiny of some scholars. Although the ECOWAS intervention has already been justified on the grounds of collective self-defence and the doctrine of invitation, another critical question here is whether, having regard to the provisions of the UN Charter, a regional body may legitimately proceed to undertake enforcement actions without the prior approval and authorization of the Security Council. The disturbing reality is that such interventions severely challenge global order. In resolving this issue, a problem is the expanded meaning of the phrase "threat to international peace" in its role as the trigger mechanism for the provisions of Chapter 7 of the Charter.

It is perhaps prudent to recall the events in the Gulf War of 1991. The unified response of the Security Council to the Gulf conflict raised the illusory prospect of a "new world order" of global commitment to the maintenance of international law, institutionalization of substantive democracy, and removal of threats to international peace.[7] As subsequent events indicate, the ouster of Saddam Hussein's forces from Kuwait seems to have been designed to sustain oil supply and thus maintain a way of living in the West and elsewhere regardless of the unrepresentative and anachronistic character of the Kuwaiti government. Interestingly, neither human rights activists nor the major powers of the world have sniffed at the Kuwaiti monarchy or required it to become a democracy.

The end of the Second World War had given rise to a resounding determination by states to "save succeeding generations from the scourge of war."[8] The United Nations was set up with the fundamental purpose of maintaining international peace and security. This was to be achieved primarily by taking "effective collective measures for the prevention and removal of threats to the peace."[9] Regrettably, the fond expectation of a world governed by law and of the willingness of great powers to lend their might in defence of justice and international law has since the end of the Second World War been frustrated by the self-serving, provincial, and/or ideological agendas of powerful states.

Although the phrase "threat to international peace" is not defined in the UN Charter, the body capable of making that determination was provided for in Chapter 5. This chapter makes clear provision for the mechanism by which such crucial functions may be exercised. While Article 7 of the Charter establishes the Security Council, Articles 23 and 24 state the responsibility of the Council. Article 24 provides that the members of the United Nations "confer on the Security Council primary responsibility for the maintenance of international peace and security, and agree that in carrying out its duties under this responsibility the Security Council acts on their behalf."

However, the power to maintain international peace is not to be exercised at the whims of the Council. Article 24(2) delimits the scope of this responsibility. It clearly provides that "in discharging these duties the Council shall act in accordance with the Purposes and Principles of the United Nations."[10] To reinforce the supremacy of the Council in the maintenance of international peace, determination of what constitutes a threat to international peace and security is the sole responsibility of the Council. Hence, Article 39 of the Charter provides that "the Security Council *shall determine the existence of any threat to the peace,* breach of the peace, or act of aggression and shall make recommendations or *decide what measures shall be taken* in accordance with Articles 41 and 42, to maintain or *restore* international peace and security."[11]

This regime of supreme and primary responsibility for the maintenance of international peace appears to be tempered by a desire in the Charter to strike a balance between regional imperatives and the need for international collective security. In effect, some of the responsibilities relating to the maintenance of international security need not be discharged by the Council itself but may be discharged on its behalf by regional agencies.[12] Thus, Article 52 provides that "nothing in the present Charter precludes the existence of regional arrangements or agencies for dealing with such matters relating to the maintenance of international peace and security as are appropriate for regional action." This compromise is quickly qualified by the provisions of the Charter that limit this margin of regional initiatives to measures not necessitating what it refers to as "enforcement actions." Thus, while the regional bodies may be used for enforcement actions by the Council, they cannot lawfully seize such initiatives on their own volition. In the express words of Article 53, "the Security Council shall, where appropriate, utilize such regional agencies or arrangements *for enforcement action under its authority.* But no enforcement action shall be taken under regional arrangements or by regional agencies without the authorization of the Security Council."[13]

The foregoing rules mean that if any enforcement action is to be undertaken by any regional agency, it must be with the prior authorization of the Council. For the assessment of the lawfulness of the ECOWAS action in Liberia under the prevailing Charter regime, three issues arise: (1) the meaning of "threat to international peace"; (2) the meaning of enforcement action; and (3) whether, if an enforcement action is undertaken to remove a threat to international peace but without the prior authorization of the Council, such an action may be accorded *ex post facto* ratification. It is upon these three sets of issues that the legality of the ECOWAS action in Liberia and the subsequent UN response will be evaluated.

It must be remembered, however, that the Charter provisions on regional arrangements and initiatives, like other provisions of the Charter, are ostensibly designed for inter-state conflicts.[14] Thus, Article 2(4), which contains the ban on the use of force, and Articles 39, 51, 52, and 53, which contain the exceptions thereto, apply basically to member states in their relations with each other. Be that as it may, the contemporary rash of civil wars has probably resulted in the Council engaging in an ingenious and liberal construction[15] and interpretation of Article 39 of the Charter. This awesome provision confers on the Council the powers to act and, if need be, override the limitations posed by the principle of non-intervention.

It is upon making this determination that the Council may take measures necessary for the removal of such threats to international peace. This duty overrides the prohibition on the Council and states from interfering in matters that are purely "internal" to a state, when the crisis at issue constitutes a clear and present threat to international peace and security. The determination of the existence of a threat to international peace and security is the gateway to enforcement actions and military abridgment of state sovereignty. It is therefore important that the phrase "threat to international peace and security" be properly scrutinized and its boundaries delimited with as much precision and circumspection as possible.

Recent state practice reflecting the gradual evolution of a holistic and global conception of collective security,[16] which I have dealt with earlier, points to the emergence of a rather inconsistent and potentially opportunistic regime on the determination of what constitutes a threat to international peace and security. For example, while Saddam Hussein of Iraq faced enforcement actions by the United States and its allies for his regime's interest in weapons of mass destruction, the possession of such weapons by Israel, Pakistan, India, and possibly North Korea has gone unpunished. Similarly, while the undemocratic nature of the Iraqi government is consistently characterized by some states as a potential threat to world peace, the regressive monarchies and dictatorships in Saudi Arabia, Kuwait, Pakistan, and so on are hardly tarred with the same brush. However, it would seem that the Security Council has been more consistent in characterizing state failures in the industrializing parts of the world as constituting threats to international peace. In this regard, it is interesting to note that the Somali debacle, the Yugoslavian crisis, the Sierra Leonean conflict, and several other civil wars have all been determined by the Council to constitute threats to international peace and security.[17] The obvious implication here is that weak states are more likely to endure interventions by powerful states acting with or without UN Security Council authorization.

The collapse of a government in a civil war, genocide, and refugee crises has been construed in contemporary times as threats to international peace and security and thus beyond the domestic jurisdiction of the affected state. In other words, internally generated crises that physically impact on neighbouring states are being increasingly perceived as threats to international peace warranting the intervention of the Council in the primary zone of crisis. The responses to these threats may vary from one to another, however. This often reflects the self-interests and, sometimes, racial affinity of members of the Security Council vis-à-vis the troubled state.

In effect, the realpolitik of intervention by the Security Council has so far seemed to be a function of racial affinity, political and economic interests, and other self-serving motivations. It is instructive that during the Rwandan genocide, on 8 April 1994, President Clinton addressed the press thus: "I mention it only because there are sizable numbers of Americans there and it is a very tense situation. And I just want to assure the families of those who are there that we are doing everything we possibly can to ensure the safety of our citizens there."[18] Taking the cue from President Clinton, on 9-10 April 1994, "France and Belgium sent troops to rescue their citizens. American civilians are airlifted. No Rwandans are rescued, not even Rwandans employed by Western governments in their embassies, consulates, etc."[19] Nearly a million Rwandans were subsequently massacred. It is equally significant that in the recent state failure in Côte d'Ivoire, the first thing the great powers did was to evacuate their nationals from the country; since then, the Security Council has contented itself with delivering homilies to Côte d'Ivoire on the need for peace. As Ivorians are being killed and displaced, the only significant mention of the crisis is with respect to the impact of that conflict on the price of chocolate in Europe and America – Côte d'Ivoire, after all, is the world's largest producer of cocoa beans and it would be a tragedy if the price of chocolate went up in the industrialized world. Yet the human impact of the Ivorian conflict has been really disastrous.

Besides racial biases, geopolitical and economic concerns play significant roles in determining whether and when powerful states in the Council may prod the organization to intervene in conflicts already determined to be a threat to international peace. Returning to the Rwandan genocide, Philip

Gourevitch notes that "the political calculus from the White House's point of view [was] if they completely did the wrong thing in Rwanda, was there ever going to be a bill to pay for it politically? Probably not ... and even if it would cost them morally, there would be a few people around tabulating that cost and reminding them."[20] Similar cynical calculations influenced US indifference to the atrocities in East Timor. These computations may sometimes be dangerously shortsighted. For example, until Afghanistan became a redoubt for Osama bin Laden's al-Qaeda, it was largely ignored by powerful states, particularly the US. It was only when the events of 11 September 2001 occurred and bin Laden's cave hideouts in Afghanistan were identified by the US as the launching pad for global terrorism that the indivisibility of peace transcended narrow racial, religious, political, and economic considerations. Yet Afghanistan had been a failed state for decades and had been recognized as a threat to international peace. Until 11 September 2001, the Afghan crisis barely featured in global discourse.

As states have, pursuant to Article 25 of the Charter, undertaken to "accept and carry out the decisions of the council in accordance with the Charter," it is beyond doubt that where such determinations have been made, member states are obliged to collectively enforce such decisions.[21] Widespread human rights abuses, the denial of the right to self-determination, extreme violence,[22] civil wars, genocide, and overthrow of "democratic" regimes by force may now be construed as threats to international peace. Where such activities impact on neighbouring states, it would seem that the true criteria affecting the Council's desire to intervene are affected by political, racial, and economic considerations. Accordingly, selective intervention appears to be the norm rather than the exception.[23] Because what constitutes a threat to international peace is the gateway to the use of force by the Council and, by delegation, regional bodies, the need for clarity and objectivity concerning its elements and *a priori* contents can hardly be overstated. The malleability of the concept of threat to international peace appears to be substantially reduced or avoided on the rare occasions when the Council has made such decisions by unanimous votes. However, the practice of the Council indicates an appreciable latitude in its determination of what constitutes such a threat. Needless to say, for the Council to make the determination that a particular crisis is a threat to international peace, it needs the relevant information from those states that are directly confronted by the threat. This is probably the aspect where the "margin of appreciation" possessed by regional bodies becomes very useful.[24]

As McCoubrey and White argue, the elasticity of the concept of threat to international peace is apparent in the extensive and varied use made of it between 1965 and 1968.[25] It is similarly reflected in the contemporary resurgence of civil conflicts.[26] The examples of Iraq,[27] Yugoslavia,[28] Somalia, and Haiti buttress this point. Again, the elasticity of the concept imports less than salutary motives as it gives rise to constructions that may reflect the biases of powerful states or the so-called coalitions of the willing. Why should the crisis in Yugoslavia be construed and dealt with as a threat to international peace when the genocide in Rwanda remained relatively ignored in spite of the atrocities there and the destabilizing impact on neighbouring states? Are the Kurds of Iraq better deserving of protection than the Kurds of Turkey? Are Kuwaitis more deserving of liberation than the Tibetans? These are the questions whose answers expose the ugly underbelly of world realpolitik on global security.

In the case of Liberia, suffice it to note that the Security Council, by Resolution 788 of 1992, made a determination that the violence in that country was a threat to international peace.[29] That threshold having been crossed, the next issue is, what is an "enforcement action"? Article 53 of the Charter and other provisions of the Charter are not helpful, as they do not offer any definition of this all-important phrase.[30] The editors of the *European Commentary on the Charter of the United Nations* are of the view that by virtue of the *travaux preparatoires* of the Charter, all measures under Chapter 8 of the Charter, without exception, are enforcement measures. On the other hand, some North and South American scholars believe that it refers to the use of military force and mandatory sanctions, excluding purely defensive actions.[31] The better view seems to be that it relates to those actions (excluding defensive acts) that ultimately require military coercion or force for their effect. Although there is great doubt regarding the authority of the Security Council to interpret the Charter, it is nonetheless useful to note that the Council decided in the matter of the Dominican Republic that enforcement actions refer to actions undertaken with military force outside the confines of collective or individual self-defence by states.

In that case, the collective measures taken by the OAS against the Dominican Republic that fell short of armed force were implicitly held by the Security Council not to constitute an enforcement action as contemplated by Chapters 7 and 8 of the Charter. The Council's three resolutions merely urged the Council to "take note"[32] of the OAS action. In effect, the economic sanctions by the OAS against the Dominican Republic, as a regional action not requiring the use of armed force for its execution, was construed as not being an enforcement action for the purposes of Article 53. This interpretation by the Council, however, is incompatible with its subsequent reaction to the quarantine of Cuba by United States forces in 1962.[33] Here the Council, by necessary implication, decided that the naval blockade imposed on Cuba by the US/OAS, which obviously required military manoeuvres for its effectiveness, was not an enforcement action requiring the Council's prior authorization.[34]

The hallowed grounds of enforcement action can hardly be defiled by cosmetic use of the term "peacekeeping."[35] As the learned editors of the

European Commentary on the Charter of the United Nations have noted, "it is problematic to state categorically that peacekeeping is not enforcement action because peacekeeping activities can be performed in various guises. It is apparent that some observation missions function as means for peaceful settlement of disputes. But it is difficult to draw a line which will ensure in every particular case, that peacekeeping forces do not resort to coercive measures; especially when the forces are on the initiative of a regional arrangement."[36]

The short point here is that the ECOWAS action in Liberia, being a clear use of military force, albeit for the ostensible good of the region and Liberia, was an enforcement action requiring that prior authorization of the Security Council first be sought and obtained. However, scholars such as Binaifer Nowrojee have argued that regional enforcement actions may be validly undertaken without the prior authorization of the Council provided that the enforcement action "is consistent with the Principles and Purposes of the United Nations."[37] This argument, attractive as it may appear, is hardly compatible and consistent with the clear letter of the Charter as already stated. As I have shown in the preceding pages, the spirit of the Charter is to severely limit the use or the threat of force by states in their relations with one another. An interpretation of the Charter that fosters unilateral resort to force outside the confines of self-defence defeats the intent of the Charter regime. If the use of force by powerful states must be limited, the privilege of determining whether and when such enforcement actions are consistent with the UN Charter must remain in the hands of a legitimate UN Security Council. The next issue is whether, in spite of the absence of a prior authorization of the enforcement action taken by ECOMOG, the Council was competent to ratify such enforcement action.

The Process and Character of Ratification

> *The United Nations is legislator as well as judge and executive and its judgments are political not juridical.*[38]

In examining the nature of the powers of the Security Council to ratify enforcement actions undertaken by regional bodies without its prior authorization, the attitude of the Council in the Dominican matter is perhaps helpful.[39] In that instance, the Soviet Union summoned the Council in September 1960 "to approve the decision of the OAS, so as to give it legal effect and render it more effective."[40] Another member of the Council, Poland, joined the Soviet Union in arguing that the "Security Council is entitled to annul or revise as well as complete regional measures."[41] It is remarkable that no member of the Council doubted the powers of the Council to annul, revise, or complete enforcement actions undertaken by a regional body.

However, the crucial determinant here was whether the sanctions imposed on the Dominican Republic amounted to enforcement actions as contemplated by Article 53 of the Charter.

The position of the Council is consistent with its paramount role as the ultimate guardian of peace and security in the world. In principle, the primacy of the Council in the maintenance of peace is not necessarily impaired merely because a regional organization jumped into a conflict before the Council did. The Council may ratify or reverse measure taken by regional bodies if they were undertaken without the Council's permission first being sought and obtained, or even where authorization was given by the Council but exceeded by the regional body. Where, then, does this power come from, and what is the juridical nature and character of the Council's resolutions?

Malintoppi has argued that since it is the apex body of a universal organization committed to certain values and aspirations, the Security Council's resolutions represent the manifestation of what its members believe to be their general feeling.[42] Given the unrepresentative character of the UN Security Council and glaring inconsistencies in the resolution of international crises, one cannot be very enthusiastic about Malintoppi's articulation of the issue. Earlier, I have drawn attention to instances of serious international crisis, even the worst case of genocide since the Nazi Holocaust of European Jews, where the Security Council, for reasons not unrelated to the lack of racial affinity of its permanent members vis-à-vis the victims, or to the absence of geopolitical self-interest in the crisis area, refused to act to maintain global peace, security, and norms.

Another difficulty with Malintoppi's conception is that in the absence of that quality of near-universal repetition that evidences a normative prescription or obligation at international law, it is difficult to believe that a resolution adopted by the five unelected, unrepresentative, concurring permanent members plus five other selected members of the Council is a true reflection of general feeling or opinion on an issue. At best, such resolutions are the product of hard and shrewd behind-the-scenes negotiation between the permanent members of the Council, as opposed to a true attestation of global consensus on the question. If the juridical character of a resolution of the Council is to have qualitative meaning, apart from sheer coercive fiat, such resolutions should substantially pass certain normative tests.

Although Schwebel[43] and Arangio-Ruiz[44] have their doubts about the normative content and character of resolutions (especially those of the General Assembly), most scholars agree that the resolutions passed by the Council, depending upon their content and context, have a normative effect.[45] Higgins[46] and the editors of *Oppenheim* (to mention a few) are of the view that the Council's resolutions passed in the discharge of its responsibilities under Chapter 7 of the Charter are binding on all states. An analogy can be made between treaty obligations at international law and Charter obligations; in addition, the Council, as the apex organ of the UN body, is deemed to portray in many instances the practice of states as to what they consider to be obligatory.

Accordingly, apart from its resolutions passed pursuant to Chapter 7 of the Charter, the Security Council's other resolutions may, depending on the circumstances, generate new norms and also serve as a revelation of the subjective element of international law, i.e., *opinio juris*.[47] This may well be a function of the fact that the permanent members of the Council largely represent the configuration of the balance of military and economic might that are veritable tools in the enforcement of law. In other words, given that the veto powers of the five permanent members of the Council were rewards for their might and valour in battle, rather than their representation of global consensus and regional balance, the bindingness of the Council's resolutions is not an evidence of its internal morality but rather a testament to the efficacy of force in securing obedience and compliance at international law.

On the other hand, the United Nations, in a manner of speaking, acts as a peculiar form of legislative body for the globe. This it does through the process of adoption of resolutions. According to Sir Robert Jenning and Arthur Watts, "resolutions adopted unanimously, being a matter of consensual agreement, are sometimes regarded as equivalent to treaties concluded in simplified form."[48] With specific reference to resolutions passed pursuant to Chapters 7 and 8 of the Charter, which is the raison d'être of the United Nations, there is hardly any doubt that they are more than recommendations. Membership in the UN or any other body entails an obligation to comply with the rules of the organization. Article 25 of the Charter makes clear the normative nature of decisions on international peace taken by the Council as members are obliged to comply with the measures adopted. Where an obligation created by treaties of a regional body conflicts with the Charter obligations of a member of the United Nations, there is no doubt that the Charter provisions will prevail.[49] Similarly, it cannot be questioned that the Council has the legal authority to remove threats to international peace. If it decides to achieve this by authorizing a state or a regional body to use force on its behalf, such use of force is for all practical purposes an exercise of the will of the Council on behalf of the United Nations.

What is required is a clear indication by the Council of the "extent and nature" of the armed force to be used by the agent state or regional organizations.[50] Of course, any such use of force, whether by the Council directly or by any of its appointees, must be geared towards the validation of the principles and purposes of the United Nations. Thus, if states exercising this function on behalf of the Council wish to use less or more force or expand the ambit of the initial mandate, they must first seek and obtain a mandate or change thereof from the Council. This is usually done at the Council by the adoption of relevant resolutions. Reference may be made to the cases of Southern Rhodesia[51] and Yugoslavia. However, it must be noted that recent trends suggest that powerful states make liberal use of ambiguous authorizations that ultimately threaten global order.

Although it is a troubling phenomenon, there is in theory no legal reason at international law why an enforcement action undertaken by a regional organization without prior authorization of the Council may not be subsequently ratified by the Council if circumstances warrant. In the overall context of the Liberian tragedy, although the Council abdicated its primary responsibility to ECOWAS, it follows from the reasoning above that its resolutions on the crisis have a juridical quality. As earlier noted, there are real dangers of abuse, and the possibility that powerful states will cynically exploit this legalistic loophole is not a matter of idle speculation but of regrettable reality. If the spirit of the Charter, which leans towards limited use of force in international relations, is to have meaning, the increasing practice whereby the Security Council ratifies unilateral enforcement actions must be discouraged or severely limited. Global order as presently constituted cannot long survive such forays by the so-called coalitions of the willing.

It is useful to examine the process used by the Council to ratify the ECOWAS enforcement action in Liberia. This process started in 1992. In effect, while the Liberian civil war had blossomed into a full humanitarian and regional crisis within six months of its explosion, the world feigned ignorance of the unfolding tragedy. Attempts by the Liberian Permanent Representative to the United Nations to place the crisis before that body failed.[52] In addition, France, trying to "protect its business interests in the war torn country,"[53] was not very enthusiastic about bringing the crisis to the agenda of the Council.

These structural and procedural problems with the Council need to be addressed. Instead of having only states as members of the Security Council, regional organizations should have seats too, especially when matters of security involving their regions are under consideration. If this arrangement had been in place, the machinations of France (a permanent member of the council) to frustrate UN intervention would have been nipped in the bud. This arrangement would also ensure that other conflicts totally ignored by the Council but no less deadly and destructive would at least be placed on the Council's agenda. More importantly, it seems that the time has come to strip the five permanent members of the Council of their permanent membership and veto powers. It is becoming increasingly clear that the veto-wielding members of the Council neither represent the status of power in modern times nor embody the configuration of global values and all peoples of the world. A democratic Council that is also fully representative of all the peoples of the world would be the first step towards a genuinely democratic and less cynical world polity.

Besides the Rwandan genocide, the neglect of other African crises by the Council in contrast to its keen interest in European conflicts or the oppression of Africans of Caucasian descent, as in Zimbabwe, is perhaps another reminder that racial sympathies sometimes play a role in the degree of intervention on the part of the permanent members of the Council in African conflicts. Contrast global outrage over Mugabe's mistreatment of white Zimbabweans with abject world indifference to the sufferings of millions of people of Southern Sudan, Côte d'Ivoire, Congo, East Timor, and so on. In the words of a church leader in war-ravaged Sudan, "I have told my people: 'let us die silently now ... the world has forgotten us.'"[54] The "political domination and brutal oppression dictated by Khartoum"[55] over the indigenous peoples of Southern Sudan has largely gone unnoticed despite its chronic character. Again, Sudan epitomizes the inequities created by the imposition of artificial boundaries drawn in accordance with colonial preferences rather than historical interests.[56] Its neglect by the Council is one of many instances casting serious doubts on the presumption that members of the Council sometimes have a global rather than a parochial agenda in the maintenance of world peace. Interestingly, since the discovery of crude oil in Southern Sudan, the United States has shown a marked interest in resolving that conflict so that exploitation of the crude oil reserves there will not be hindered by the protracted war.

Unless an honest and serious effort is made to bring a crisis to the attention of the Council and that body fails to act accordingly, it will be difficult to contemplate any regional initiative ostensibly designed to address the situation, even if the Council thereafter purports to ratify such unilateral actions. The mere fact of *ex post facto* ratification should not excuse the cynicism of the permanent members of the Council. The Charter process regulating the use of force ought to be exhausted before any such multilateral actions can be taken by states, including regional bodies. With particular reference to Liberia, Resolution 788 of 1992[57] is the starting point in the ratification of the ECOWAS action by the Security Council. That resolution:

- determined that the situation in Liberia was a threat to "international peace, particularly in West Africa as a whole"
- welcomed and commended ECOWAS actions in Liberia
- condemned all attacks on ECOMOG troops and recognized the ECOWAS action in Liberia as a peacekeeping exercise
- imposed a complete arms embargo on Liberia except for arms destined for ECOWAS in Liberia

- requested all member states to respect the measures established by ECOWAS to bring about a peaceful solution to the conflict in Liberia
- decided that the Council will remain seized of the matter.

Similarly, Resolution 813 of 1993 reaffirmed the abovementioned aspects of Resolution 788. In addition, it demanded that all parties cooperate with the Secretary-General of the United Nations and with ECOWAS to ensure the full and prompt implementation of the Yamoussoukro Accord, and:

- declared its readiness to consider any appropriate measures in support of ECOWAS if any party was unwilling to cooperate in implementation of the Yamoussoukro Accords, in particular the encampment and disarmament provisions
- requested the Secretary-General, in consultation with ECOWAS, to consider the possibility of convening a meeting of the President of the Interim Government of National Unity and the warring factions, after detailed groundwork, to restate their commitment to the implementation of the Yamoussoukro Accord within an agreed timetable.

This unprecedented cooperation between a regional body and the United Nations in peace enforcement and peacekeeping was further cemented by the provisions of Resolution 856 of 1993.[58] This resolution, the third in the series, welcomed the decision of the Secretary-General of the UN to send a technical team to Liberia to gather and evaluate information relevant to the proposed establishment of a United Nations Observer Mission in Liberia (UNOMIL).[59]

An advance team of thirty military observers was dispatched to Liberia to monitor, investigate, and report on ceasefire violations. In addition, the Secretary-General of the United Nations was requested to draw up a framework that would "ensure coordination between the UNOMIL and the peacekeeping forces of ECOWAS and their respective roles and responsibilities." Resolution 856, like the earlier resolutions, "commends ECOWAS for its efforts" to restore peace in Liberia. Resolution 866 of 22 September 1993 went further than the three previous resolutions and is arguably one of the most radical resolutions substantiating the notion that the United Nations apparently "franchised" its primary responsibility for peace enforcement to ECOWAS.[60] The preamble to this resolution "emphasized that the Peace Agreement assigns ECOMOG the *primary responsibility* of supervising the implementation of the military provisions of the Agreement and envisages that the United Nations role shall be to *monitor* and *verify* this process."[61] This aspect of Resolution 866 clearly relegates the UN to the background in monitoring the more aggressive and dominant ECOWAS in the Liberian conflict.

In fact, Resolution 866 itself attests "that this would be *the first peacekeeping mission undertaken with a peacekeeping mission already set up by another organization, in this case ECOWAS*."[62] This admission clearly dispels any notion or illusion that the United Nations was not fully aware of the nature and character of the relationship that it created with ECOWAS in the Liberian conflict. The resolution further noted that this unparalleled arrangement "would contribute significantly to the effective implementation of the Peace Agreement."[63]

To give teeth to this arrangement, a Joint Cease-fire Monitoring Committee (JCMC) composed of three Liberian warring parties, ECOMOG, and the United Nations was established. In addition, UNOMIL as contemplated by Resolution 856 was finally established. UNOMIL was to be composed of military observers as well as medical, engineering, communications, transportation, and electoral components, together with the minimal staff necessary to support it. A critical review of the mandate of UNOMIL leaves the clear impression that ECOMOG, which stood directly in harm's way, was the enforcement arm of the United Nations while UNOMIL purported to be the legitimizing agent of the UN.

This is a curious arrangement, especially in light of the repeated assertions by observers that Third World armies are ill-trained, underequipped, and rascally. This curious transfer of responsibility from the Council to ECOMOG as contained in Resolution 866 may be listed as follows:

- to receive and investigate all alleged incidents of breach of the ceasefire agreement
- to monitor compliance with the embargo on arms supply to the rebels, especially at the Sierra Leone and other borders
- to observe and verify the election process
- to assist in the coordination of humanitarian assistance
- to develop a plan and assess financial requirements for the demobilization of combatants
- to report on any major violations of international humanitarian law to the Secretary-General of the UN
- to train ECOMOG engineers in mine clearance and, in cooperation with ECOMOG, to coordinate the identification of mines and assist in the clearance of mines and unexploded bombs[64]
- without participation in enforcement operations,[65] to coordinate with ECOMOG in the discharge of ECOMOG's separate responsibilities both formally and informally.

It is perhaps pertinent at this stage to comment on the composition of UNOMIL and its role in the entire regime. UNOMIL consisted of several contributions of personnel and materials from several member states of the

UN. At its height, it consisted of at least 400 military observers drawn from such states as Austria, Bangladesh, Belgium, Brazil, China, Congo, the Czech Republic, Egypt, Guinea-Bissau, Hungary, India, Jordan, Kenya, Malaysia, Nepal, Netherlands, Pakistan, Poland, the Russian Federation, the Slovak Republic, Sweden, and Uruguay.[66] Its military command was held sequentially by Major General Sihandar Shami of Pakistan, Colonel David Magonone of Kenya, Major General Mahmoud Falka of Egypt, and Major General Ismael Opande of Kenya. Clearly, UNOMIL was dominated by soldiers drawn from the so-called Third World, while ECOMOG was completely a West Africa armed force.

On the other hand, voluntary contributions for UNOMIL's budget came from many countries, especially Denmark, France, Japan, the Netherlands, Norway, the United Kingdom, Canada, and the United States. The list of donors tilts heavily to the West. In addition, the General Assembly adopted a general resolution assessing the contributions to be made towards the financing of UNOMIL.[67] It is also pertinent to note that the expenses of UNOMIL were clearly declared by the General Assembly to be "expenses of the Organization to be borne by Member states in accordance with Article 17, paragraph 2 of the Charter of the United Nations."[68]

In effect, it is difficult to dodge the inference that the ECOMOG/UNOMIL action in Liberia was, technically speaking, a United Nations operation with all its legal implications. In addition to establishing UNOMIL, Resolution 866 of 1993 encouraged all member states of the OAU to send additional troops to ECOMOG, and also established a trust fund to offset some of the costs of the ECOWAS action of Liberia. The assessed contributions were augmented by voluntary contributions from several states. Perhaps the tentative interpretation could be made that while black Africans were to engage in the more dangerous work of confronting and subduing the rebels, with the high casualties inherent in such operations, other members of the Third World dominated the buffering and legitimating UNOMIL. Finally, the West was content to contribute some money from the safety of Europe and North America. In contrast, no such qualms or fears of suffering casualties were exhibited in the Kosovo intervention by NATO or by the US in the Gulf War. It is difficult to escape the inference that while Europeans could die in Kosovo for fellow Europeans and Americans could die for oil in Kuwait, no European or American would die for black Africans in a conflict which presented no economic or political advantage to the great powers of the day.

Yet the allied and combined activities of ECOMOG/UNOMIL formed an aspect of the subsequent resolution of the Council in 1994. In Resolution 911 of 1994, the Council "welcomed the close cooperation between UNOMIL and ECOMOG" and stressed "the importance of continued full cooperation and coordination between them in the implementation of their respective tasks."[69] Further, it implored all parties to the conflict to cooperate with ECOMOG in its efforts to resolve the crisis. It should be remembered that the resolution once again affirmed the determination of the Council to remain actively involved in the matter.

At its 3,442nd meeting, held on 21 October 1994, the Security Council reviewed the events in Liberia and for the first time acknowledged, through Resolution 950 of 1994, that the Liberian crisis was a "threat to international peace."[70] Resolution 950 also condemned "the widespread killings of civilians and other violations of international humanitarian law by the factions in Liberia, and the detention and the maltreatment of UNOMIL observers, ECOMOG soldiers and other international personnel."[71] Hence, the Council demanded that all factions in the dispute respect the status of ECOMOG and UNOMIL personnel. Resolution 950 reminded all persons of the Council's decision to remain actively involved in the matter. With the situation in Liberia further deteriorating and some of the neighbouring states pouring arms into that country, the Council passed a resolution noting "with concern that there has been a continuing inflow of arms into Liberia in violation of the existing arms embargo"[72] and urging ECOWAS to convene a meeting for the purposes of tightening the application of the embargo.

Further attesting to the desire of the Council to have ECOMOG directly resolve the crisis in Liberia, when the patience of Nigeria and Ghana (the two leading contributors to ECOMOG) wore thin and a pullout of ECOMOG from Liberia was seriously contemplated, the Council became alarmed and reiterated the need for the ECOWAS states to maintain their troops in ECOMOG. These concerns were reflected and reiterated in Resolution 985 of 1995. In fact, this resolution was one of the most far-reaching efforts by the Council to curtail the inflow of arms into Liberia, as it constituted the full Council into a committee to monitor such inflow.

Further, the proceeds from the United Nations Trust Fund for Liberia could hardly be utilized effectively to relieve the hardship imposed on Liberians caught up in the conflict. In this season of despair, the Council, through Resolution 1001 of 1995, "reaffirmed the continued necessity for ECOMOG and UNOMIL to cooperate in fulfilling their respective mandates and to this end urge[ed] the ECOMOG to enhance its cooperation with UNOMIL *at all levels* to enable the mission to discharge its mandate."[73] In addition, it urged ECOMOG to take necessary action to provide security for UNOMIL observers and civilian staff. The Abuja Accord,[74] signed on 19 August 1995, is probably the most significant step towards the resolution of the Liberian crisis, as the subsequent disarming of the rebels and the return to "democratic" governance in Liberia are based on it. This agreement supplemented the Cotonou Accord, the Akosombo Accord, and the Accra Agreement. Its importance is equally reflected in the decisions of the Security Council as embodied in Resolution 1014 of 1995.[75]

This resolution not only continues the numerous statements of support by the Council for the ECOWAS initiative but made a case for additional resources in terms of troops, equipment, and logistics for ECOMOG in Liberia to oversee the implementation of the various aspects of the agreement, in particular the disarmament and demobilization process. Because of the importance of some of its features and to better appreciate the subsequent discussion on this aspect of the Liberian crisis, some of the resolution's very pertinent aspects are summarized below. They include the:

- adoption of measures to enhance the relationship between UNOMIL and ECOWAS
- provision of financial, logistical, and other assistance in support of ECOMOG to enable it to carry out its mandate
- encouragement of UN member states, in particular African countries, to consider providing troops to the expanded ECOMOG
- demand that all factions in the conflict respect the status of ECOMOG and UNOMIL
- encouragement of the OAU to continue its post-conflict peace-building collaboration with ECOWAS in promoting the cause of peace in Liberia.

After the adoption of Resolution 1014, ECOMOG began deploying its troops throughout the areas hitherto occupied by the rebels. However, this process suffered another setback as one of the rebels led by General Roosevelt Johnson attacked ECOMOG in Tubmanburg on 28 December 1995 and killed several of the troops.[76]

Following the Tubmanburg incident, the United Nations, acting in concert with the OAU, dispatched mediators to the affected areas to negotiate a return to relative normalcy. This event and similar violations of the ceasefire agreements and breach of fundamental norms of war necessitated the strengthening of ECOMOG. Some African states, such as Tanzania, sent troops to ECOMOG, which was duly "appreciated" by the council in Resolution 1020 of 1995.[77] This resolution adjusted the mandate of UNOMIL in the following manner:

- to exercise its good offices to support the efforts of ECOWAS and the Liberian National Transitional Government (LNTG) to implement the peace agreements and to cooperate with them for this purpose
- to investigate allegations of ceasefire violations
- to monitor compliance with the other military provisions of the peace agreements, including disengagement of forces, disarmament, and observance of the arms embargo, and to verify their impartial application

- to assist in the maintenance of assembly sites agreed upon by ECOMOG, the LNTG, and the factions in the implementation of a program for demobilization of combatants
- to observe and verify the election in consultation with the OAU and the ECOWAS.

In addition, Resolution 1020 of 1995 urged all UN member states to continue their material and logistic support for ECOMOG and reiterated that the presence of UNOMIL was wholly predicated upon the security provided by ECOMOG. In other words, UNOMIL would not be in Liberia but for ECOMOG, which had substantially created the conducive environment for its stay. In this context, Resolution 1020, like previous resolutions, stressed the need for close contacts and enhanced coordination between UNOMIL and ECOMOG in their operational activities at all levels.

To further reinforce the impression that the ECOMOG/UNOMIL activities in Liberia were directly under the control and guiding auspices of the Council, Resolution 1020 affirmed the decision of the Council to remain directly involved in the matter. These activities by the Council did not necessarily bring about an immediate end to the crisis. There were repeated attacks on ECOMOG and unarmed civilians by the rebels, and so the Council considered and adopted Resolution 1041 of 1996.[78] Paragraphs 4 and 5 of this resolution not only condemned the attacks but also commiserated with the victims. It addition, it reiterated the status of ECOMOG and UNOMIL as peacekeepers and demanded that such status be accorded its traditional respect.

The peace process in Liberia suffered serious setbacks again as the warring factions escalated the violence. The escalating violence caused ECOWAS to resolve not to recognize any government in Liberia that emerged by sheer force of arms.[79] On the other hand, the West African states of Nigeria and Ghana, who were the backbone of ECOMOG, were compelled to threaten their immediate withdrawal from the peacekeeping exercise. At the debates of the Security Council in May 1996, these developments forced the Council to adopt Resolution 1059 of 1996 condemning the ceasefire violations and "encouraging the ECOWAS to consider ways and means to strengthen ECOMOG and persuade the faction leaders to resume the peace process."[80]

The Council also expressed its support for the ECOWAS stance not to recognize any illegitimate but forcefully effective government in Liberia.[81] Another significant aspect of Resolution 1059 is that it reiterates the ultimate dependence of UNOMIL on ECOMOG. Thus, according to paragraph 8 of its preamble, the Council stressed that "the presence of UNOMIL in Liberia is predicated on the presence of ECOMOG and its commitment to ensure the safety of UNOMIL military observers."[82] This is further evidence that the UN franchised the exercise of coercive powers in restraining the rebels to ECOMOG, and that UNOMIL relied on ECOMOG's firepower.

As the peace process gained momentum, the Council adopted another resolution affirming once again the need for closer cooperation and coordination between UNOMIL and ECOMOG.[83] The process of disarming the warring factions had begun in earnest, however, as evidenced by Security Council Resolution 1100 of 1997.[84] The last of the Council's resolutions on the Liberian crisis is Resolution 1116 of 1997. This resolution not only extended the mandate of UNOMIL to its terminal date of 27 July 1997 but also expressed the gratitude of the Council to all the members of the international community that had supported ECOMOG in its action in Liberia.[85]

It is abundantly evident that the resolutions of the Council on the Liberian crisis had the clear legal effect of ratifying the ECOMOG initiative as lawful,[86] but the jurisprudential ramifications of this extraordinary chain of events have to be explored by scholars, particularly the impact on the future of global peace and security. It was not only the Council that took an active part in approving the ECOWAS action in Liberia. At its eighty-fifth plenary meeting, the UN General Assembly, by an unanimous resolution, affirmed its "appreciation to the international community for its support of the peace plan for Liberia of the ECOWAS ... and hopes that the continuing efforts made at the sub-regional and international levels aimed at a peaceful resolution of the Liberian [conflict] will, within the shortest possible time, lead to national reconciliation, reconstruction and development."[87]

Further, at the eighty-ninth plenary meeting of the General Assembly held on 16 December 1992, another unanimous resolution was adopted expressing universal "appreciation for the continuing mediatory efforts of the ECOWAS to find a peaceful solution to the Liberian crisis."[88] This second global acclamation was immediately followed by another unanimous resolution adopted at the ninety-secnd plenary meeting, held on 18 December 1992.[89] This resolution restated global validation of the ECOWAS action in Liberia and called upon the international community to quickly contribute humanitarian relief materials to the embattled country. The spate of universal approval and commendation of the ECOWAS action in Liberia is also apparent in another unanimous resolution adopted by the General Assembly at its eighty-fifth plenary meeting held on 20 December 1993.[90] Here the General Assembly expressed its appreciation of the ECOWAS efforts to resolve the crisis. The approbation of this regional effort in conflict management and resolution was completed by another General Assembly resolution adopted at the ninety-fourth plenary meeting held on 23 December 1994.[91]

Despite the near-universal acclamation of the ECOWAS action in Liberia, some disturbing issues are raised by it. The first is the question of why it was so conveniently popular within the United Nations Security Council. The second is the impact of this precedent on the Charter regime regarding the use of force by regional bodies or some powerful states backed by their allies. This may best be evaluated in the context of the NATO bombing of Yugoslavia, and perhaps the US threat to use force in Iraq outside the confines of the UN mechanism. Third, how can the lapses in the ECOWAS action in Liberia be usefully evaluated so as to enhance a coordinated framework for regional/universal cooperation for the maintenance of international security under the United Nations framework?

With respect to the first question, the ECOWAS action in Liberia was not the first regional initiative advertised as an attempt to secure regional security and peace. Previous cases exist at international law where multilateral actions supposedly premised on concerns for regional security have been undertaken but have been condemned by the international community. In some of those cases, the fear of hegemonism masking as regional concern for peace was quite real.[92] Although unilateral actions are forbidden by the Charter,[93] regional organizations have under certain circumstances employed themselves in the maintenance of peace. The cases of the OAU in Chad and the OAS in Haiti readily come to mind. A short comparison may be useful here.

In 1981 members of the OAU sent a peacekeeping force to separate the warring factions led by Goukhoni Weddeye and Hissene Habre in Chad.[94] This measure was greeted with acclaim across Africa and touted as the beginning of African solutions to African problems. Chad is the fifth largest country in Africa and, until the recent discovery of oil there, was regarded as one of the poorest states in the world, with 90 percent of its territory generally referred to as useless. Since its independence from France in 1960, its governance has been marked by incompetence, foreign meddling (mainly by France and Libya), ethnic rivalry, and corruption.[95] These factors gave rise to internal rebellions, which, like the Liberian case, blossomed with the end of the Cold War. These rebellions have been generally acknowledged to be largely sponsored by Ghaddafi of Libya, with the ostensible aim of having the upper hand in the two countries' perennial dispute over the uranium-rich Aouzou strip bordering both countries.

The OAU decision to intervene has been justified on the grounds of African states' suspicion of foreign intervention in African crises, especially since the Congolese crisis of the 1960s, which is generally perceived to have sabotaged the government of Patrice Lumumba. Similarly, the plan by the embattled President Weddeye of Chad to bring Chad into a political union with Libya had disturbed security concerns in that region, warranting the speed with which the decision to intervene was made. With the promise of logistical support from France and the United States, the OAU intervened to stop the conflict and pre-empt Ghaddafi's plan of a "greater Islamic State."[96] Accordingly, troops from Nigeria, Senegal, and

Zaire were dispatched to Chad under the auspices of the OAU. The agreement for such dispatch was signed in Nairobi, Kenya, on 28 November 1981.[97] Soon after the arrival of the OAU peacekeepers, the beleaguered government of Weddeye, which had invited the OAU's intervention, was overturned by forces loyal to Hissene Habre.[98] The intervention by the OAU faltered and collapsed.

Although the OAU intervention in Chad, hampered by a lack of resources and an absence of sincerity on the part of President Weddeye and the opposing political force of Hissene Habre, was a failure, its legality has not been questioned. Like the Liberian case, however, its domination by Nigeria[99] and lack of credibility arising from the perceived biases of the interveners[100] raises similar questions regarding the limitations of peacekeeping operations by regional bodies. It is arguable that if Nigeria had been ready and willing to spend as much as it did in Liberia and succeeded in its overall objective, the OAU peacekeeping effort in Chad would have succeeded and would have been favourably perceived. In addition to Weddeye's undoubted right to invite the OAU, which he did (although, like President Doe of Liberia, he was beleaguered and was finally ousted within four months of inviting the OAU), the extant issue is whether the test of legality under the circumstances depends on the ultimate military success of the enforcement action by a regional organization. Does the end justify the means of intervention? This question dovetails into the second issue – the precedent-setting impact of the Security Council's ratification of the ECOWAS action on the Charter regime. Before examining this issue, a quick reference to the Haiti case may be helpful.

In the Haiti case, Jean-Bertrand Aristide, who won an internationally supervised election to become the president of Haiti, was overthrown in a military coup on 30 September 1991.[101] The Organization of American States (OAS) reacted quickly with a package of diplomatic and economic sanctions against the junta led by General Raul Cedras. In addition, the OAS resolved not to recognize the illegitimate junta. Upon the invitation of the deposed President Aristide,[102] it established a civilian mission to pave the way for his return to power, and the necessary mechanism was put in place. On 17 May 1992, the OAS ad hoc Meeting of Consultation of Foreign Ministers passed a resolution urging member states to adopt whatever measures were necessary to restore democracy in Haiti.[103]

Thereafter, the UN Secretary-General began working in consultation with the OAS on the restoration of democracy in Haiti. The argument by the Security Council that the Haitian crisis was an internal problem of Haiti in which it could not lawfully intervene soon yielded to a determination by the Council under Chapter 7 of the Charter that the crisis was a threat to international peace.[104] Accordingly, the Council authorized members of the OAS "to use all necessary means to facilitate the departure from Haiti of the military leadership and the restoration of the legitimate authorities of the government of Haiti,"[105] and the OAS Multinational Force or what the Pentagon called Operation Restore Democracy entered Haiti to pave the way for the United Nations Mission in Haiti (UNMIH), which organized the return of Aristide and maintained peace in the interim.

Unlike the OAU in Chad, where there was no UN collaboration with a regional organization in the enforcement of peace, the ECOWAS/UNOMIL cooperation in Liberia and the OAS/UNMIH collaboration in Haiti raises some troubling issues and lessons. The first point is that the legitimacy of the latter two cases depends largely on the recognition of the requirement that the Security Council must assume control, directly or indirectly, in the enforcement action. Second, for such regional enforcement actions to be legitimate, they must be premised upon a recognized institutional, procedural, and substantive framework. Although this condition is ostensibly designed to screen out hegemonic tendencies from a regional or multilateral decision to intervene in a crisis, there is a real and present danger that powerful states in the region or elsewhere with vested interests in the troubled states may hijack or at least unduly dominate the policy and operations of the interventionist force.

Third, the crisis forming the subject of the intervention must be one that clearly rises to the level of a threat to international peace. The determination of this is a prerogative of the Council and cannot be delegated. However, regional organizations, because of their proximity to the crisis, may have a margin of appreciation of the danger originally unavailable to the Council, which they should bring to the attention of the Council. This is not the same as their making the determination that a particular state of affairs constitutes a threat to international peace. It is not every crisis in a state, real or imaginary, that affords a gateway to Article 53 or that, *ipso facto,* constitutes an exception to Article 2(7) of the Charter. Again, given recent trends regarding the use of force outside the machineries or multilateral framework of the UN, this point can hardly be overemphasized.

On the second issue of the precedent-setting impact of the Security Council ratification of the ECOWAS action on the Charter regime of Chapters 7 and 8, an eloquent example of the potential for abuse is seen in the controversy over the NATO bombing of Yugoslavia in April and May 1999. The human casualties in that unilateral action have been estimated at 2,000 deaths and there were thousands of refugees.[106] Compared with the Rwandan genocide, the Sierra Leonean conflict, and the Zairean debacle, the Kosovo crisis pales into a manageable size, yet there were radically different reactions to the two sets of tragedies.[107] The result is that the motives behind the responses to this set of tragedies invite scrutiny, and also show the need for constraining the impulse by states to unilaterally resort to force in international relations.

Although editorial opinions and news reports seem to support the right of forceful humanitarian intervention, the existence of that right in the post-Charter era has been very difficult to establish and, indeed, is very controversial. While this issue is outside the scope of this book, it can be noted that the prevalent view is that the right of humanitarian intervention, if it existed, did not survive the Charter.[108] Moreover, the conception of humanity deserving of salvation from tragedies is often tainted with racial undertones or considerations or cynical geopolitical and economic actions. The pertinent question here is whether the ratification of the ECOWAS action in Liberia by the Security Council did not set a dangerous precedent so that powerful states can engage in illicit enforcement actions with the real or even vague hope that the Council will ratify such acts. It would seem that we are entering an age when these fears are justified.

A related issue, especially with respect to the bombing of Yugoslavia and the touchstone of military success as a factor in determining the legality of such interventions, is the validity of the peace agreement between Yugoslavia and NATO concerning cessation of the bombing and the resolution of the Kosovo crisis. Article 52 of the 1969 Vienna Convention on the Law of Treaties voids any treaty concluded upon the use or threat of use of force contrary to principles of international law as embodied in the Charter. The question then is, if the use of force by NATO in Yugoslavia was contrary to principles of international law as embodied in the Charter, of what normative force is the peace agreement between NATO and Yugoslavia and similar agreements purportedly endorsed and ratified by the Council? Can we build collective security on acts of dubious legality? This is not the central issue in this book, but only shows the quagmire into which the Security Council's rash of ratifications of unauthorized regional enforcement actions has thrown international law.

Although an appreciation of Article 53 of the Charter in good faith leaves room for the possibility of *ex post facto* authorization by the Council of regional enforcement actions,[109] the probability of abuse, as already indicated, is high. In further reference to the Kosovo crisis, it is remarkable that when France called for a UN Security Council resolution to authorize the deployment of NATO peacekeepers, the US State Department flatly refused, insisting that "NATO should be able to act independently of the United Nations."[110] Apparently, the US knew that its unilateral actions in Yugoslavia would in the fullness of time be "ratified" by the Council. It is possible that the US drew inspiration from the Liberian precedent. This instance is not isolated, as shown by the continual bombing of Iraq by the US and Britain.[111] In the Iraq case, the US and its allies, by a tortured redefinition of the content and meaning of Resolution 678 of 1990,[112] which authorized the initial allied repulsion of Iraqi aggression against Kuwait, have bypassed the Security Council and continually engaged in unilateral enforcement actions against Iraq.

Returning to the Kosovo crisis, it is instructive to note that former President Clinton had declared that "unless human tragedy is caused by natural disaster, there is no such thing as a purely significant humanitarian enterprise."[113] Thus, although the determination by the Council that the situation in Yugoslavia constituted a threat to international peace was made by Resolution 1199 of 1998, Yugoslavia was requested to take urgent steps to arrest the deteriorating humanitarian condition.[114] To remove any doubt, the Council expressly reserved for itself the prerogative of deciding whether Yugoslavia had remedied the situation, and, if not, to "consider further action and additional measures to maintain or restore peace and stability in the region."[115]

Despite this and President Clinton's earlier disavowal of altruism in interventions ostensibly geared towards averting humanitarian tragedies, NATO proceeded to engage in enforcement actions against Yugoslavia without prior reference to or approval by the Security Council. This high-handed defiance and isolation of the Council by NATO may mark the beginning of a competitive relationship between both bodies, which can hardly be masked by the subsequent "ratification" of the NATO conduct by the Council. The overall impact of this is a gradual and steady destruction of the framework of the Charter on the regime regulating international use of force. As Cassese rightly warns, "one cannot confine oneself to hoping that this dramatic departure from the UN standards will remain an exception. Once a group of powerful states has realized that it can freely escape the strictures of the UN Charter and resort to force without any censure, except for that of public opinion, a Pandora's box may be opened."[116]

Sadly enough, it seems that the box is already opened: the Security Council was made to legitimize the NATO actions in Yugoslavia when it adopted a resolution echoing NATO's earlier objectives.

5
Reconfiguring Collective Security in Africa

The deficits in legitimate domestic governance and the absence of an established political order commanding general consent have been identified as the ultimate cause of most civil wars.[1] In postcolonial Africa, attempts to resolve the issue of legitimacy of governance have unfortunately been crudely reduced to elections supervised by retired politicians and human rights organizations from the industrialized world. In the process, little emphasis has been placed on redressing the destabilizing consequences of the colonial mutilation of Africa, the erosion of African precolonial history, external meddling in Africa, and the failure of leadership among African peoples and nationalities.

In resolving the issue of legitimacy of governance, it should be noted that there is no universal theory of legitimacy. Rather, as with democracy, there is a theorem and within this theorem lies the irreducible criterion of popular legitimism. As Okafor has rightly observed, the doctrine of legitimism is subject to historical and cultural changes: "Legitimism which originally meant dynastic or monarchical legitimism, has now divorced itself of its rather unfortunate ancestry and has come to be centred on the concept of popular legitimism."[2] Within the fundamental template of popular assent to the machinery of governance, the processes of achieving popular legitimism may be as varied as the history, culture, aspirations, and values of any given society. For African states, this must necessarily involve a deconstruction and reconstruction of the structure and concept of African statehood, a pan-Africanist reorientation, economic self-determination for African peoples, and a redefinition of leadership in the continent.

Reconceiving African Statehood and Governance

In the preceding chapters, I have examined the origins of the rebellion in Liberia and its impact on neighbouring states and how those states responded to the crisis. It is desirable to draw some lessons from the underlying causes of that conflict, its inherently expansive nature, the method of purported resolution, and ancillary issues. The first lesson is that the African political class will have to accept the fact that the Berlin Conference–created postcolonial states as presently constituted are an unworkable and dangerous colonial heritage. There is a compelling need for bold and imaginative thinking on the issue of African nation-statism. African states must therefore re-examine the cartographical makeup of postcolonial Africa. In doing so, serious consideration should be given towards two workable options. The first is a creative application of the doctrine of self-determination for African peoples within those colonial contraptions. The second and ideal option would be to examine the feasibility of having a pan-African state constituted on the basis of federation of African peoples and nations. These measures are founded on a critical reappraisal of the parameters of legitimate governance in postcolonial Africa. This task and inquiry has already been dealt with decisively in the recent and authoritative works of Makau Wa Mutua and Obiora Okafor.[3] Further analysis of the issues already dealt with by Mutua and Okafor need not detain us here.

For purposes of clarity, however, it should be reiterated that in addition to an unviable state structure, chronic bad governance, predatory economic structures, disgruntled and fractured elitism, and chronic abuse of human rights, particularly economic and social rights, have often embittered Africans and driven them to violence. Hence, the vulnerability of the African state to violent resistance to the entrenched order. The telling lesson here is that a resolution of African crises and serial state failure must go far beyond the simplistic prescriptions of periodic "democratic elections" often demanded of African states by external forces and institutions with little understanding or appreciation of African history and anomie. Although they apparently mean well, the powerful states of Europe and North America must rethink their fixation with periodic elections as the panacea for African state failure and violent crises. As evidence already in the public domain shows, most of those elections are hollow rituals. In the absence of a radical restructuring of African statehood and the emergence of forms and structures of government designed by Africans with a profound sense of African precolonial history and at properly convened conferences of African nationalities and peoples, the uncritical adoption of Western concepts of democracy will continue to be what it is: mere window dressing. The fact of the matter is that African states as presently constituted are fundamentally incapable of genuine geopolitical stability. Copying Western democracies by the uncritical adoption of multiparty politicking as a quick fix is a route riddled with terror and unnecessary bloodshed.

There is hardly any "election" in Africa that is not besmirched with allegations of rigging or electoral malpractice. More worrisome is the practice by which bloodthirsty rebels and notorious perpetrators of war crimes in Africa's numerous conflicts are appeased with the prospect of "legitimate" rule through sham elections overseen by "foreign observers" and "human rights activists." Yet some of these contraptions have been hailed as models of democracy. While these bogus elections and democracies in Africa may satisfy Western power elites, human rights activists, and other well-meaning but misguided "saviours" of Africa, critical African thinkers who are painfully aware of African culture and history must reject them and chart new ways for the continent. The cycle of impunity has to be broken. The notion that Africa is a clean slate on which all sorts of foreign ideals can be inscribed without reference to African history is as ridiculous as it is tragic.

Often, allegations of electoral malpractice constitute the launching pad for internecine violence and consequent violent state breakdown. In the Congo/Katangese war, one of the main issues was the power of the president to dismiss the prime minister. The Nigeria/Biafra war was substantially about the type of federal structure in Nigeria that would give expression to its cultural and ethnic diversity. In Liberia the 1989-96 war was about a dysfunctional state, a disgruntled elite, a botched election, and the inordinate ambitions of a despot with superpower support. In Somalia the corrupt and debauched regime of Siad Barre pushed the Horn of Africa into a bizarre conflict. In Zaire, Mobutu Sese Seko's expiration has left in its wake a civil war,[4] which is eliciting an uncertain response from the Southern African Development Community.[5]

With this spate of internal conflicts, the concept of legitimacy of governance[6] has deservedly assumed greater significance. In addition to an inherently unsustainable legacy of inorganically formed, hastily contrived colonial states, illegitimacy of governance may be manifested in injustice in the distribution of state resources, denial of effective participation in governance, and absence of transparency and accountability in the political process. These factors prevent the penetration of popular desires into the instruments and character of governance.

Another task is to re-examine the role of social, economic, and cultural rights in the African polity. The International Covenant on Civil and Political Rights posits certain normative values as essential constitutive elements of a legitimate government. While its preamble recognizes the inherent dignity of the human person and the foundation of global peace on human freedom and justice, Article 2 enjoins all state parties to the covenant to respect diversity of political opinions.[7] Indeed, Article 2 further enjoins the parties to fashion constitutional and legislative processes for the effective enjoyment of political and civil rights in the domestic polity. Save for public emergencies, during which certain civil and political rights may be temporarily abridged under the narrow conditions stipulated in its Article 4, Article 5 of the covenant forbids any limitations on the enjoyment of civil and political rights by individuals and groups of individuals in state parties to the covenant. The norms of the covenant expressly and implicitly recognize that civil and political rights can best be enjoyed under representative governments, transparent and accountable to members of the state in an orderly and peaceful manner. The General Assembly of the United Nations has equally underscored the elements of good governance, including the holding of free and fair elections at periodic intervals,[8] respect for human rights in all its ramifications,[9] the movement towards strong anti-corruption measures, and the pursuit of sound social policies by the government. In effect, the concept of legitimacy of governance is "philosophical, legal and political,"[10] and its central position within the international normative regime is well established.

These are noble ideals but it would be naive to suppose that constitutional prescriptions and economic ideologies forged in the cultural furnace of European and North American experiences will automatically flourish in Africa without necessary adaptation. Similarly, it would be simplistic to assert that the conflicts in Africa that threaten international peace are necessarily a function of the continent's heterogeneity. Rather, the tinderbox is ignited by the inherently flawed cartography of African colonial states and a reductionist pursuit of policies that run against the grain of international norms on the social and economic rights of peoples and similar norms, particularly the African Charter of Rights of Peoples, designed to promote full and unfettered enjoyment of human rights, particularly social and economic rights.[11]

In Africa, with a panoply of ethnic groups split across several states,[12] the need for a scrupulous respect for these norms of international law can hardly be overstated. Similarly, fiscal federalism or economic self-determination, which are irreducible norms in the International Covenant on Economic, Social and Cultural Rights, must be scrupulously enforced. A situation where people of a particular ethnic group are made to believe, with good reason, that resources from their part of the country are unfairly used to develop other parts of the country at their expense does not bode well for civil stability. In contemporary Nigeria, this is one cause that perceptive scholars fear is capable of violently destabilizing that country. If Nigeria collapses, the events in Rwanda, Sierra Leone, and Liberia combined may not match the destruction and potential savagery that such a tragedy would unleash on the continent. It is equally remarkable that the economic exploitation of crude oil in Southern Sudan by the Khartoum regime at the expense of the Southern Sudanese peoples fuels the civil war in that country. Similarly, undue economic advantages acquired and maintained on the basis of discredited concepts such as colonialism and apartheid in South Africa or racism in colonial Zimbabwe must be lawfully, systematically, and equitably dismantled. It would be foolish to expect or hope that merely holding periodic multiparty elections in African states without lawfully redressing those inequities would create a stable polity.

As the Liberian case has shown, when a certain group of people bonded by a common heritage or ethnicity corners the wealth of the state for themselves, that cannot endure too long or create a sense of belonging among those on the other end. According to Gambari, "one of the swiftest ways to the destruction of a state is to give preference to one particular tribe over another, or to show favour to one group of people rather than another."[13] Similarly, the empowerment of the people by mass education needs to be encouraged to enhance transparency and faith in governance. Those whom illiteracy has rendered impervious to external stimuli or contending ideas can hardly appreciate democracy and its virtues. Democracy and respect for human rights thrive in literate societies. The high illiteracy rate in Liberia enabled oppression and domination. These are some of the issues that domestic governments and human rights activists would do well to confront.

The short point in the abovementioned is that civil conflict in Africa is essentially a problem of colonial heritage exacerbated by domestic ill-governance, which is often fostered by powerful external patrons and unfavourable economic situations. It is not a coincidence that African states, usually characterized by incongruous borders, lack of democratic accountability, impotent judicial systems, and gross and systemic denial of economic and social rights have achieved notoriety in state failure.[14] I am not suggesting here that only autochthonous modes of governance reflecting the culture and aspirations of African peoples would instantaneously conjure political stability and economic development.[15] Rather, legitimate state boundaries and culturally responsive modes of governance afford, in the long run, the best avenue for the prevention and management of grievances that lead to violent internal conflicts.

Those Africans who argue that the colonial state must remain the way it has been since 1885 are seriously mistaken. Similarly, it would be worthwhile for African thinkers and policy makers to revisit, recreate, and revalidate traditional methods of legitimate governance that African peoples can relate to.[16] It is noteworthy that, of late, several African countries at various international forums have declared and reaffirmed the direct relevance of good governance to continental peace, economic progress, stability, and collective security.[17] This is evident in the June 1990 Organization of African Unity (OAU) Declaration on the Political and Socio-Economic Situation in Africa, recognizing the direct interdependence of collective security on good governance in the continent.

At the African Leadership Forum held in Kampala in May 1991, a conference on Security, Stability, Development, and Cooperation in Africa modelled on the Conference on Security and Cooperation in Europe offered a holistic framework for good governance and collective security. The conference clearly identified democratization, popular participation, and accountability as the key to security and stability in the continent. At the thirty-fifth summit of the OAU (now renamed the African Union) in Algiers, held on 10-14 July 1999, the heads of state of African countries, while acknowledging the points above, adopted a unanimous resolution to isolate any government in the region that comes to power by force of arms. In addition, the body resolved to suspend the membership of any country under military rule. While one cannot really be sanguine about the seriousness of the OAU's resolve in this regard, the rise of the consciousness of the inherent dangers of illegitimate governance among African states is a welcome development.[18]

Without a doubt, these sentiments and developments are steps in the right direction, but more serious work needs to be done. The most important process towards a postcolonial stability in Africa would demand a radical rethinking of the doctrine of *uti possidetis juris* and inviolability of the colonial borders. The second step would require a recentring of traditional African values of governance and communal rights, particularly the economic, social, and cultural rights of African peoples.[19] The economic situation in Africa, which has been notoriously worsened by an exploitative global economic regime, unworkable Structural Adjustment Programmes (SARs), domestic graft and corruption, and appropriation and theft of the state purse by rulers, is an explosive mix. Legitimate governance can hardly be sustained on empty wallets and stomachs. According to a United Nations report, African countries lost $50 billion between 1986 and 1992 as a result of falling commodity prices. It is interesting to note that the rebellion in Liberia was also fuelled by the economic downturn in that country.

With the fall in revenue and the loss of foreign economic aid, which had previously flowed by virtue of Liberia's geopolitical relevance during the Cold War, the incompetence and illegitimacy of the Doe regime became more pronounced. The fall of the Berlin Wall has both symbolically and practically permitted a massive movement of financial and human capital to Central and Eastern Europe by Western European and North American governments and corporations. In fact, the movement of scarce African highly skilled labour (the brain drain) to Europe and America may not be unconnected with the bad governance and consequent strife in African countries. It is not accidental that African countries suffering from civil strife are those where economic institutions have all but collapsed. The obvious loser is the African continent and its peoples. African scholars, thinkers, scientists, and leading intellectuals who proffer solutions from the "safety" of European and North American institutions and talk-fests would seriously have to reconsider their priorities and the effectiveness of their location in salvaging a deeply troubled continent.

The international community can avoid and reduce cases of internal civil strife in other ways, including revisiting the normative regime on the law on recognition of governments and non-intervention.[20] African states have tended to ignore the negative normative impact of according recognition to cutthroat warlords in control of the capital cities of their countries. It is quite revealing that in the Liberian crisis, ECOWAS and the UN Security Council passed resolutions declaring that they would not recognize any government in Liberia that emerged from the smoking barrel of the gun. If the Doe government, which came to power by literally slitting the belly of President Tolbert, had been denied international recognition, the normative impact might have been enormous.

The point is that the international community would do well to collectively refuse to sanctify raw might as right. Of course, there is practical wisdom in not ignoring an effective government, but such governments need not be publicly recognized or consorted with as though coming to power on the blood of victims of human rights abuses were of no significance. Such public recognition expressly and implicitly confers undeserved international legitimacy on the rogue government. The virtues of a collective and unified avoidance and shunning of such governments can hardly be overstated. To paraphrase Professor Thomas Franck, there is power in legitimacy among nations. It is interesting to recall that when the Doe government emerged, some states refused to recognize it but others chose to do business with it. There is a high normative value in the interrelationship of governments. States would do well to actively explore the provisions of Article 41 of the International Covenant on Civil and Political Rights providing for the making of complaints to the Human Rights Committee (established by Article 28 of the Covenant) regarding infractions of the obligations created in the Covenant. It is remarkable that no state, not even members of ECOWAS, saw fit to lodge a formal complaint at the Human Rights Committee against the excesses of Samuel Doe.

African multilateral organizations should clearly articulate and publicize the criteria for legitimate statehood and good governance in their area, and errant governments should not be welcome in their fold. This approach worked perfectly well in Lesotho in 1994. In that country, the King, for no ostensible reason, sacked the prime minister and appointed a new one. This arbitrary and illegal conduct threw the country into turmoil. The Southern African Development Community (SADC) immediately issued an ultimatum denying legitimacy to the usurper and threatening sanctions against the whimsical King, whereupon the King immediately restored the prime minister to office. Similar attempts have failed elsewhere for lack of serious resolve.[21] Scholars such as Okafor and Franck and Munansangu[22] agree that such measures on delegitimation will have normative, jurisprudential, political, or socio-economic effect on both the rogue government and on the international order. If international law is to be more than congealed politics, such measures will aid, modify, and humanize the political processes by which international law is made and validated. Jurisprudentially, it may result in the nullification and invalidation of the official processes of the rogue government in the eyes of the international community.[23] It may also result in loss of sovereign, diplomatic, or jurisdictional immunities. Politically, such governments may not participate in and derive the benefits of mutual international intercourse. Economically, they may be punished with sanctions and their assets frozen or seized like those of the Cedras regime in Haiti. In the normative sense, such measures would enhance the character of international law in its compliance-pull and strengthen its capacity to attract habitual obedience.[24] These lessons are immanent in the Liberian crisis[25] and show up the inadequacies in contemporary assumptions and practices of international law.

In addition to rethinking and reconstructing the African states in terms of cartography and norms of governance, the role of regional organizations in the maintenance of global peace and security at the Security Council must be redefined and clarified. Regional agencies have a role to play within the framework of the UN Charter towards managing and resolving conflict, but must do so within the confines of international law. The relationship between regional bodies and the Security Council may be enhanced, coordinated, and strengthened for fruitful collaboration for the maintenance of global peace. However, it can hardly be gainsaid that avoidance measures are better than measures geared towards mitigation of actual damage from civil conflicts.

The systemic incoherence in the world order regarding the application or enforcement of international norms is cause for anxiety. For example, while the Security Council made the determinations that the situations in Iraq and Liberia, respectively, constituted threats to international peace, it responded differently to both crises. For Iraq, it amassed the greatest armada and arsenal known to humanity to expel that country's forces from Kuwait. On Liberia, the Council pontificated on peace and "approved"[26] of ECOWAS initiatives. The Council's refusal or unwillingness to effectively intervene in Sudan, Congo, and Sierra Leone gives room for regional assertiveness and potential hegemony. The apparent inconsistency inherent when "the butchers of Tiananmen and the Butcher of Ham are embraced so that the United Nations can repel the Butcher of Baghdad"[27] undermines the international order of security and normativity. In the Rwandan genocide, the Council pretended that nothing happened, yet nearly a million Rwandans were massacred within 100 days. Without doubt, meta-legal considerations such as geopolitical relevance and racial affinity between victim states and members of the Security Council have often influenced the Council's articulation and execution of its responsibility.

This unfortunate dialectical interaction between normativity and narrow interests is a betrayal of the high ideals with which the United Nations was established. It is tragic that institutions often defeat the ideals for which they first came into being. In the prescient words of Edward Carr, "the ideal once embodied in an institution, ceases to be an ideal and becomes the expression of a selfish interest, which must be destroyed in the name of a new ideal. This constant interaction of irreconcilable forces is the stuff of politics. Every political situation contains mutually incompatible elements of utopia and reality, of morality and power."[28] Although this prognosis is no cause for despair, international lawyers should use the unfortunate circumstances of the Liberian crisis as veritable materials for examining ways of enhancing the contemporary regime of collective security, most probably beginning with reform of the Security Council.[29]

Regional Bodies and Collective Security

The proper role of regional organizations in the maintenance of global security is often a difficult issue to resolve. Diverse scholarship on the desirable relationship between regional organizations and the United Nations[30] in the maintenance of international peace and security have identified the salient battle for supremacy[31] between these two regimes. In spite of the clear primary role of the Security Council in the maintenance of global peace, centripetal forces of regionalism tend to give the impression that both regimes are at par, or at worst are in a gladiatorial stance. This state of affairs partly explains the self-afflicted paralysis of the Council.

It can hardly be denied that the Council takes action mainly when the interests of its permanent members are involved. Witness its action in Haiti and in Iraq, where the interests of a superpower were involved. Compare that with its inaction in the Chechnya and Tibetan crises, where the interests of other permanent members are involved. If those are juxtaposed with its complete indifference to the chronic conflict in Southern Sudan[32] and empty exhortations on Burundi, Ethiopia, Sierra Leone, Zaire, Guinea-Bissau, and several other places, the unfortunate realpolitik of the Council becomes obvious. In those cases where it does not clearly abdicate its role to maintain peace, the Council becomes a platform for ineffective "conciliatory, hortatory or condemnatory"[33] rhetoric and platitudes on peace.

This situation apparently fuels the emergence of regional or ad hoc actions to secure global peace independent of the Council. This trend is dangerous. The situation is hardly helped by the Charter of the United Nations in its provisions on the proper role of regional organizations in the maintenance of international peace. The Charter is not an exemplar of precision and clarity in legal drafting, as it does not delimit with relative certainty the boundaries and terms of association between regional organizations and the Council. Thus, the task of delimiting and defining this important relationship appears to be a function of uncoordinated and nebulous state practice. Towards striking a balance between the Council and regional initiatives, a few suggestions derived from the ECOWAS action in Liberia are worthy of consideration.

As an aside, the provisions of Article 43 of the Charter, which provides for a unified military force capable of securing peace in troubled states, has unfortunately not been realized. The UN has regrettably abandoned any serious examination of this option. If the UN had a unified military force of its own, it is arguable that the self-serving criteria that determine when and how great powers intervene in hot spots would have been significantly reduced. In the face of UN inertia on this front, instead of the standing army contemplated by the Charter, the United Nations Secretariat would do well to actualize its currently proposed arrangement whereby units of the armed forces of some states will be specially designated a United Nations force ready to be deployed at short notice.[34] While this arrangement is being examined, it is perhaps more fruitful to examine how the existing regional bodies may be harmonized and their abilities and potentials harnessed for securing global peace within the existing framework of the Charter.

On this issue, Tom Farer has pertinently suggested that the existing relationship between the United Nations and the various regional bodies be urgently redefined for clarity.[35] The scope of the respective areas of autonomy as well as of competence and expertise of regional organizations should be clearly established. A situation like Liberia's, where ECOWAS, an organization designed for regional economic integration, grapples with the problems of peacekeeping and military enforcement of peace, leaves much to be desired. ECOWAS lacked the experience, infrastructure, logistics, and personnel for the task, and this obviously affected its performance.

Although the Charter does not define the relationship between the United Nations and regional organizations, it would be prudent to categorize and delimit the latter depending on their constitutive treaties, focus, and specialized competence. At the moment, no one can say with appreciable certainty which regional organizations in any part of the globe could function under Chapter 8 of the UN Charter. Regional bodies dealing with educational, scientific, economic, environmental, or other diverse concerns should be clearly recognized as such, and their areas of special competence and expertise delimited. This is probably the better way to bring about closer cooperation between both regimes. Peace enforcement should not be an all-comers affair. The much-expected regime of close cooperation between the UN and regional organizations should be on a clearly established basis of recognition of competence.

Further, regional bodies should be encouraged to exchange information with the Council. This can be achieved by inviting them to attend meetings of the Council where matters of security affecting their respective regions are at issue. The Council and regional organizations should have the power to introduce matters to the respective agendas of each organ where necessary. Where such efforts to compel the active involvement of the Council fail, the regional body may ask for the Council's authorization to intervene in the conflict. If this arrangement had been in place, the reactionary efforts by Zaire and Ethiopia at the Council that prevented a timely response to the Liberian crisis would probably have failed. Similarly, the inherent danger of abuse in *ex post facto* ratifications would be obviated.

A symbiotic relationship between regional organizations and the Council should be fostered.[36] The present fluid and distant relationship on security is undesirable. Former UN Secretary-General Boutros Boutros-Ghali, in apparent rationalization of this fluid state of affairs, hailed it as affording some "useful flexibility conducive to a rich variety of complementary roles."[37] Arguing further, he posited that "just as no two regions or situations are the same, so the *design of cooperative work* and its division of labour must adapt to the realities of each case with flexibility and creativity."[38] While these optimistic words for the contemporary relationship between the United Nations and the regional bodies have some element of truth, unfortunately there is no design of cooperative work, the existence of which the Secretary-General assumed. This is hardly an ideal situation.

It is pertinent to recall that Boutros-Ghali took an unprecedented step in 1994. On 1 August, he held a meeting with the heads of all regional organizations committed to the maintenance of regional security, such as the Commonwealth of Independent States (CIS), the European Union (EU), League of Arab States, NATO, the OAU, ECOWAS, and so on.[39] At the meeting, it was reiterated that the United Nations has the primary responsibility, but the need for some decentralization of that mandate under the Charter was acknowledged. What then shall be the nature of this much-heralded era of decentralization of authority?

From a sober examination of the relationship between ECOWAS and the Security Council in the management of the Liberian crisis, it can hardly be denied that some element of clear devolution and decentralization of authority is necessary. The contemporary practice by which regional bodies such as NATO, ECOWAS, and the SADC or such other so-called coalitions of the willing literally determine by themselves the existence or otherwise of threats to international peace, and bypass the Security Council by formulating and enforcing responses thereto, is not only illegal but extremely dangerous. Indeed, it strikes at the very essence of the existence of the Council.[40]

The question of primary jurisdiction in the maintenance of peace, globally or regionally, can hardly be resolved in favour of regional bodies.[41] Where the Council is unable to act, it may then clearly and within narrow limits authorize a regional body recognized as existing for the purposes of Chapter 8 of the Charter to deal with the matter. In such a situation, the Council must retain political and legal control over the intervention. Such a delegation of authority should be on very clear terms, leaving no room for a perpetual extension by a regional body or a group of powerful states. For instance, the mandate to a regional body to intervene may be limited in time and renewable by the Council every three months.

The redefinition of the relationship between regional organizations and the Council should be articulated before crises emerge, and where violent conflicts arise that threaten international peace, the role of the two regimes should be clearly defined. A few lessons derived from the ECOWAS action in Liberia may be helpful. Because of the proximity of regional organizations to the conflict,[42] it is not difficult to foresee a situation where, blinded by the dusts of the conflict, such organizations bring their own agendas and perspectives to the conflict and thus may compound an already grave and complex situation. In the Liberian case, it was no secret that the francophone states and their anglophone counterparts brought their mutual suspicions and prejudices to bear upon their perception of the problem.

However, the maintenance of international peace and security by the Council does not necessarily mean that it must be involved in every aspect of crisis detection and peace enforcement. It may delegate some of its functions to regional bodies and yet maintain direct control of the extent of the use of force and formulate general policies behind such actions. It has been suggested that in addition to non-permanent members of different continents sitting as members of the Council, regional organizations with security interests should be relied upon for information regarding the state of security in their respective regions. This acknowledges that regional organizations are best situated to appreciate the emergence of threats to international peace at their earliest stages, yet it hardly addresses the problem of the regional bodies' absence of standing at the Council. This is one way of bringing objectivity to the way the Council determines that a threat to international peace exists.

How will the information relevant for making such a determination be effectively used if the regional bodies have no competence to place such issues on the Council's agenda? It is probable that information gathered by regional bodies may end up as a bulky and dust-ridden file in an obscure office at the United Nations. If the information is passed on to the continental representatives at the Council, chances are it may never see the light of day. Again, Liberia is a case in point.[43]

There is therefore a need for a review of the procedural rules to enable regional bodies to place emerging crises on the Council's agenda. This calls for a clearer definition of the scope of authority of regional bodies and how they can best be utilized while remaining under the direction of the Council. There is no denying the reality that a concerted global approach to conflict prevention, management, and resolution is far preferable to regional initiatives.

The question of funding of operations has profound implications. What happened in Liberia is again instructive. It has been estimated that as at 1994, the estimated sum of $12 billion was expended in the ECOWAS action. Of this, only thirty percent was contributed by the United Nations Trust Fund. Almost 70 percent was borne by Nigeria. Several of the West African troops in Liberia were paid their salaries directly by their respective governments. Several West African states could hardly afford the cost of keeping their troops in Liberia. This raised at least two dangers.

First, as the salaries were in some cases unpaid for months, some of the peacekeepers began to engage in activities incompatible with their peacekeeping status. Substantial and serious cases of looting, expropriation, and theft of Liberian assets by the ECOMOG peacekeeping troops have been widely reported,[44] as was extortion of the traumatized Liberians. Second, regional enforcement actions have shown that they are more or less unilateral in character even when cloaked in the toga of the regional machinery. This is more pronounced in the aspect of funding and when the peacekeepers are paid from the respective accounts of their different countries. Loyalty is split, and contributing countries who can afford to pay their soldiers are more likely or potentially able to hijack the supposed regional and collective effort.

The ECOWAS action in Liberia was largely dominated and inspired by the military government in Nigeria. Of the US$12 billion spent by ECOWAS in the crisis, Nigeria accounted for an estimated $8 billion, hence the impression and allegation that the ECOWAS action in Liberia was in fact a Nigerian quest for hegemonic control of West Africa. Similar allegations have been made in the ECOWAS intervention in the Sierra Leonean crisis.[45] The NATO intervention in Kosovo has been perceived as a US attempt to impose its will and vision in the Balkans. The current SADC intervention in the Zairean crisis has been inspired by Zimbabwe, whose prime minister, Robert Mugabe, is suspected to harbour ideas about Zimbabwean leadership of southern Africa.[46] To reduce and possibly avoid this debilitating suspicion when regional enforcement actions are in place, the funds for the maintenance of peacekeeping troops should be placed in one pool regardless of the contribution of any state, and managed by the civilian administrative body of the relevant regional organization and/or in consultation with the UN.

In addition, a professional civilian staff to monitor and document the excesses of the military aspect of enforcement actions should be institutionalized and made answerable to the office of the Secretary-General of the United Nations. The office of the Secretary-General should be made to work in liaison with the regional organization and should also serve as a clearinghouse for regional bodies already at work in trouble spots. Unlike the UN Special Representative or High Commissioner, which are usually appointed after the conflict has been resolved, this kind of agency would serve as an information-gathering and collation centre during the enforcement of peace by a regional organization, to ensure that human rights abuses by peacekeepers and warring factions are not left undocumented and ultimately unpunished.[47]

In the Liberian case, the ECOMOG/UNOMIL peacekeepers were alleged to have abused women and young girls, siring over 25,000 children in the process.[48] In Sierra Leone, allegations of sex-for-food dogged British aid workers there. A UN Special Representative who merely visits refugees from the conflict and flies back to New York or Geneva to deliver a special report is absolutely useless in the documentation and collation of incidents of human rights abuses perpetrated in the field of conflict. On the sexual abuse of Liberian women and girls, the Nigerian-dominated contingent, with over 5,000 troops in ECOMOG, accounts for 50 percent of the children born to the peacekeepers; the remaining 50 percent is divided among Ghanaian, Guinean, Gambian, and Sierra Leonean fathers. Most of the girls were between thirteen and sixteen years of age, and reportedly had affairs with ECOMOG soldiers in return for food and protection during the war.

In the absence of an effective civilian machinery to supervise the conduct of ECOMOG troops, over 85 percent of the young girls sexually abused by the peacekeepers have yet to locate the soldiers or establish contacts between them and the "ECOMOG children." Sadly, a combination of a paucity of reliable documentation of the atrocities by the warring factions and the peacekeepers and an absence of political will has made it impossible for criminal charges to be pressed against the perpetrators of those crimes.[49] As already indicated, similar allegations of sexual abuse have been made against European and African aid workers in the refugee camps of Sierra Leone.[50]

Furthermore, the norms on intervention should be codified. Just as the United Nations International Law Commission has researched and codified several applicable norms, the time has come for a body of experts to evaluate the cases of multilateral enforcement actions and come up with principles that may be adopted by the UN General Assembly in the form of a declaration. In this context, a few suggestions may be worth trying.

First, no regional enforcement action may be countenanced without the express authorization of the Council first sought and obtained. *Ex post facto* ratifications of unilateral regional enforcement actions leave ample room for abuse and arbitrariness and do great damage to the normative order on use of force.

Second, no regional organization purporting to enforce international peace may enter a field of conflict without an effective ceasefire in place. The attack on ECOMOG troops by the National Patriotic Front of Liberia (NPFL) rebels was largely due to the absence of an effective ceasefire before ECOMOG purported to enforce one.[51] This factor also contributed to the protracted nature of the conflict and actual intervention, and literally made ECOMOG a party to the conflict.

Third, there must be clear lines demarcating the combatants themselves and the interventionist forces. A situation in which the rebels, the vestiges of government troops, and the ECOMOG peacekeepers had little or no clear lines of demarcation contributed to the high casualty rate and the chaotic nature of the conflict and its resolution by the interventionist forces. Similarly, the absence of a clearly demarcated line of conflict and intervention obscured the apportionment of responsibility for human rights abuses perpetrated during the conflict. Where the lines of separation are not clear, it is very easy for such crimes to go undetected or, if detected, to remain unpunished.

Fourth, the interventionist force must be clearly neutral. This may best be achieved by a prior express authorization of the Council and scrupulous compliance with the regional organization's constitutional mechanism. The ad hoc manner in which ECOWAS approved and ratified its decision to intervene in Liberia cast serious doubts on its neutrality, and this in turn impacted negatively on its perception by the warring factions.

Fifth, the mandate of the regional enforcers of peace must be subject to the overriding authority of the Security Council.

Finally, to ensure collective security, the international community must first secure social distributive justice. Within the African context, with a multitude of ethnic groups split across different frontiers of that continent's fifty-three countries, the practice of a holistic concept of collective security and distributive social justice secured by legitimate state boundaries and good governance is the antidote to the civil conflicts ravaging the continent. Collective security and social justice, in the words of Nigerian novelist Chinua Achebe, are "two sides of the same coin."[52]

Conclusion

The legality of the ECOWAS intervention in Liberia from the standpoint of collective security in a dynamic world has been established in this book. However, the Liberian state in its structure, polity, and organization raises questions regarding the nature of statehood in Africa, and regarding the mode of governance and raison d'être of African states. With the first question comes an urgent need to re-examine the utility of the *uti possidetis juris* stance on colonial African boundaries. The second requires a redefinition of the parameters of governance in Africa. I have sought to show that without a fundamental restructuring of the African state, the contemporary fixation on "democratic" elections supervised by external observers is an empty ritual. These pretensions have a marginal role in the search for stability in postcolonial Africa. Further, the causes of the Liberian conflict raise interesting issues concerning the impact of global events and phenomena on the stability and security of most African states. The intervention itself marked the first active collaboration in peacekeeping between a regional organization and the United Nations. This development presents an interesting but potentially dangerous precedent. Some concluding observations are now pertinent.

First, although the fundamental cause of African political instability remains the colonial legacy in Africa, particularly the Berlin Conference boundaries and the disruption of that continent's political evolution, a part of the blame lies with the failure of domestic leadership and the inequities of the international economic regime. An ethnic enclave is not necessarily a paragon of political stability and economic justice if the political leadership is devoid of courage, integrity, wisdom, and a sense of history. Second, the regime on recognition of governments needs urgent reappraisal.

Regarding interventions by regional bodies or powerful states acting in concert with their allies, several issues are raised. The first is whether a regional organization can use force to maintain peace within its area of relevance. Given the paralysis of the UN Security Council and the increasing marginalization of Africa in global relevance, it may be impractical to insist that Africans should fold their arms and watch their fellow Africans perish. With notorious UN indifference or halfhearted responses to armed conflicts in Sudan, Zaire, Angola, Chad, Ethiopia, Eritrea, Guinea-Bissau, Sierra Leone, Uganda, Somalia, Burundi, and other flashpoints in Africa, the temptation for relatively powerful neighbouring states to seize the initiative and intervene cannot be ignored. This is particularly troubling when the chords of ethnic affiliations have survived the European division of Africa at the 1884-85 Berlin Conference. One need only recall the Watutsi (Tutsi) crisis in Central/East Africa, which found expression in the Rwandan genocide, the Zairean war, and several other crises in that part of the continent.

However, the dangers of abuse inherent in the ECOWAS precedent may be worse than the Security Council's indifference and cynicism. The question is how to improve the relationship between the Council and regional organizations in maintaining and enforcing peace. In this context, one cannot fail to question the responsibility of members of the Council, especially the permanent members. Is their primary responsibility to global concerns held hostage by their selfish national interests? If the permanent members of the Council look out for their respective national interests at the expense of their responsibility to the globe, the attitude is ominous. Further, the world is at risk in an era when regional organizations assume primary responsibility for the maintenance of global peace on their own terms, without substantive reference to the Council.

Such unilateralist attitudes veiled in enthusiastic campaigns to eliminate evils across the globe are becoming rampant, and the Security Council is increasingly assuming the pathetic role of a legitimizer and ratifier of its usurped legal responsibility. There is no indication that this trend will not continue, and its impact on UN Charter law will be enormously negative. The legal order in a violent world appears to be at the cusp of drastic upheavals in which unilateral enforcement actions orchestrated by "coalitions of the willing" are gradually replacing collective responses to violations of international law. It is a dangerous prospect and foreshadows a return to the primitive age of rule by might. If the concept and practice of collective security are to have meaning at international law, it must be not only through a collective effort led by a legitimate, representative, and responsible Security Council but also through a perception of security in its holistic character, undefiled by parochial and cynical tendencies of powerful states.

The words of Polish contemporary poet Wislawa Szymborska provide a fitting close to this book:[1]

Oh, the leaky boundaries of man-made states!
How many clouds float past them with impunity;
How much desert sand shifts from one land to another;
How many mountain pebbles tumble into foreign soil
In provocative hops!

Notes

Chapter 1: The Myth of African Statehood

1 Charles C. Boone, *Liberia as I Know It* (Richmond, CT: Negro Universities Press, 1970) at page 51. See also Roger Clark, "Stephen Spielberg's *Amistad* and Other Things I Have Thought about in the Past Forty Years: International (Criminal) Law, Conflict of Laws, Insurance and Slavery" (1999) 30 Rutgers L.J. 371.

2 But see Marc Weller, *Regional Peacekeeping and International Enforcement: The Liberian Crisis* (Cambridge: Grotius Publications, 1994) at 18-19. He argues that the colonization of Liberia was a genuinely humanitarian act.

3 Abayomi Cassel, *Liberia: History of the First African Republic* (New York: Fountainhead Publishers, 1970). The greatest forced human migration in recorded history, the continental slave trade lasted over 400 years. See also Lerone Bennet Jr., *Before the Mayflower: A History of Black America,* 6th ed. (New York: Penguin Books, 1993) at 29; Clark, *supra* note 1 at 23-44.

4 The exact number of black people lost in the slave trade is uncertain. However, precolonial Africa was densely populated. According to Cheikh Anta Diop, the dean of precolonial African history, "it has been estimated that the slave trade swallowed up one hundred to three hundred million individuals, dead or shipped to America": Cheik Anta Diop, *Precolonial Black Africa: A Comparative Study of the Political and Social Systems of Europe and Black Africa, from Antiquity to the Formation of Modern States* (New York: Lawrence Hill Book, 1987) at 142.

5 Boone, *supra* note 1 at 1-2. Some African chiefs and traders also partook in the slave trade.

6 Edward Knappman, ed., *Great American Trials* (Detroit: Gale Research Press, 1994) at 91-94. See also Cassel, *supra* note 3 at 11.

7 E. Dunn and S. Holsoe, *Historical Dictionary of Liberia* (London: Scarecrow Press, 1985) at 5. Save for Cuba and Brazil, the institution of slavery was at this time beginning to lose economic force.

8 Charles Wilson, *Liberia* (New York: William Sloan Associates, 1947) at 8; Cassel, *supra* note 3 at 13-20.

9 Cassel, *ibid.*

10 Boone, *supra* note 1 at 27. See also Gus Liebenow, *Liberia: The Evolution of Privilege* (Ithaca, NY: Cornell University Press, 1969) at 9.

11 Cassel, *supra* note 3 at 26-28.

12 For a fuller account of the origins of Liberia, see Amos Beyan, *The American Colonization Society and the Creation of the Liberian State: A Historical Perspective, 1822-1900* (Lanham, MD: University Press of America, 1991).

13 Liebenow, *supra* note 10 at 5.

14 Boone, *supra* note 1 at 82.

15 Liebenow, *supra* note 10 at 15.

16 Merran Fraenkel, *Tribe and Class in Monrovia* (London: Oxford University Press, 1964) at 14. To the consternation of the natives, the Americo-Liberians wore three-piece suits in tropical

heat, had large houses, and kept their Christian faith and Anglo-Saxon names, of which they hardly knew the meanings. It was only in the early 1970s that the Liberian leaders deigned to wear any clothes indicative of their African pedigree. For over 150 years, the official attire in Liberia was a suit. See also Harry Johnston, *Liberia* (London: Hutchinson, 1906) at 219.

17 R. Earle Anderson, *Liberia: America's African Friend* (Chapel Hill: University of North Carolina Press, 1952) at 8.

18 Fraenkel, *supra* note 16 at 8-9.

19 As quoted in Liebenow, *supra* note 10 at xviii-xix.

20 C.O.C. Amate, *Inside the OAU: Pan-Africanism in Practice* (New York: St. Martin's Press, 1986) at 35.

21 Anderson, *supra* note 17 at 35.

22 Edith Holden, *Blyden of Liberia* (New York: Vintage Press, 1966).

23 Martin Lowenkopf, *Politics in Liberia: The Conservative Road to Development* (Stanford, CA: Hoover Institution Press, 1976) at 3.

24 Gabriel Omoden, "Brief History of Liberia" in Margaret Vogts, ed., *Liberian Crisis and ECOMOG: A Bold Attempt at Peacekeeping* (Lagos: Gabumo Publishing, 1992) at 23.

25 *Ibid.* at 36.

26 R.C.F. Maugham, *The Republic of Liberia* (New York: Negro Universities Press, 1969) at 57.

27 This political party founded in 1860 dominated the entirety of Liberia for 125 years. Although Liberia has never been officially a one-party state, during the period of the dominance of the TWP, it was one to all intents and purposes.

28 Irvin Kaplan *et al.*, "The Society and Its Environment" in Nelson Harold, ed., *Liberia: A Country Study* (Washington, DC: American University Press, 1985) at 104.

29 The pervasive nature of the Masonic Lodge in Liberia was equally reflected in the fact that membership in the Lodge was not treated with secrecy; instead it was a badge of honour used to open doors in Liberia. Almost every Liberian of substance belonged to the Masonic Lodge.

30 Liebenow, *supra* note 10 at xx. It is arguable that Tubman stood between Scylla and Charybdis. The natives outnumbered the Americo-Liberians by over 100 to 1. True democracy would in effect uproot the existing order. On the other hand, sustaining the status quo in its entirety would lead to a bloodbath that could wipe out the elite. To worsen matters, Kwame Nkrumah of Ghana and Sekou Toure of Guinea, with their pan-African message, were at this time stoking the fire of political freedom for African natives.

31 Nicholas Kristoff, "What Is Democracy Anyway?" *New York Times* (5 March 2002). Editorial/ Op-ed.

32 *Keesing's Contemporary Archives,* annual volumes (London: Longman Publications, 1989-98) at 30405.

33 Ahmadu Sesay, "The Historical Background to the Liberian Crisis" in Vogts, *supra* note 24 at 35; Ahmadu Sesay, "Collective Security or Collective Disaster? Regional Peace-Keeping in West Africa" (1995) 26 Security Dialogue 2 at 205.

34 Quote attributed to Crocker by Mark Huband, *The Liberian Civil War* (London: Frank Cass Publishers, 1998) at 27.

35 Quote attributed to Schultz by Huband, *ibid.*

36 David Steven, *Third World Coups d'état and International Security* (Baltimore: Johns Hopkins University Press, 1987) at 7. In a rather belated admission of collusion, Herman Cohen, then the US Assistant Secretary of State for African Affairs, in his testimony before the Congress observed that "it [the coup] represented the takeover of Liberia by the majority of the people. You must remember that for over 100 years, a minority of Liberians controlled that country and essentially excluded the majority of the population ... They did nothing to bring up the indigenous people ... It was an internal colonial system ... Doe was living in terrible squalor, which essentially represented the conditions of the indigenous people." See Weller, *supra* note 2 at 50. Yet the United States accorded the minority government legitimacy and never once used its good offices to raise the issue.

37 R. Welch, "The OAU and International Recognition: Lessons from Uganda" in Yassin El-Ayouty, ed., *The OAU after Ten Years* (New York: Praeger, 1975) at 103-17.

38 Born in 1921, Jean-Bedel Bokassa was president of the Central African Republic from 1966 to 1979. He declared himself president-for-life in 1972 and crowned himself "emperor" of the so-called Central African Empire. This megalomaniac was erratic and peculiarly violent. He was overthrown by French troops in 1979, who reinstated David Dacko as president. Exiled to France and Côte d'Ivoire, Bokassa was arrested and tried for torture, murder, and cannibalism. He was convicted and sentenced to death, but the death penalty was commuted to life in prison. Bokassa died ignominiously in 1996.

39 Edward Quashigah, "Legitimacy of Governments and Resolution of Intra-National Conflicts in Africa" (1995) 7 A.J.I.C.L. 284.

40 See note 38.

41 "Belgium Apologizes for Lumumba Killing" *BBC News* (6 February 2002), online: BBC News <http://news.bbc.co.uk/he/English/world/Africa>, accessed 2 May 2002.

42 "Mideast Turmoil Sends Oil Firms to W. Africa" *Chicago Sun Times* (23 September 2002) A10.

43 For a succinct analysis of this tendency, see Obiora Okafor, "The Global Process of Legitimation and the Legitimacy of Global Governance" (1998) 10 A.J.I.C.L. 20.

44 Kristoff, *supra* note 31.

45 For an excellent analysis of this issue, see Okafor, *supra* note 43.

46 Binaifer Nowrojee, "Joining Forces: United Nations and Regional Peacekeeping: Lessons from Liberia" (1995) 18 Harv. Hum. Rts. J. 50 at 134.

47 *Keesing's Contemporary Archives,* vol. 28 (London: Longman Publications, 1982) at 31281.

48 *Keesing's Contemporary Archives,* vol. 30 (London: Longman Publications, 1984) at 32715.

49 Raymond Copson, *Conflict among the African States* (Ph.D. Dissertation, Johns Hopkins University, 1971) at 53. The indifference of the Soviet Union to the Liberian tragedy is not unrelated to the cold relations between these two countries throughout the rule of Doe. Ghana/Doe relations were hardly free of recriminations over Doe's constant allegations that Ghana wanted him out of the Liberian presidency.

50 The committee submitted a draft constitution on 11 April 1983, which Liberians approved by a popular referendum in July 1994.

51 *Keesing's Contemporary Archives,* vol. 31 (London: Longman Publications, 1985) at 33322.

52 *Keesing's Contemporary Archives,* vol. 32 (London: Longman Publications, 1986) at 34146.

53 Virtually all coup attempts against Doe were alleged by him to have extra-Liberian backing. It is also interesting that the Quiwonkpa coup of 1985, which was arguably the most serious attempt to unseat Doe, was launched from the Liberian border town of Nimba and with West African nationals. Similarly, the Taylor rebellion, which started in 1989, was launched from this same border town and with West African nationals as part of the rebel army. There may therefore be some element of truth in Doe's persistent assertion that neighbouring states were subverting his regime.

54 World demand for Liberia's major products of iron ore, rubber, and timber was falling rapidly. It deserves mention that global inequities in trade often destabilize Third World governments.

55 *Keesing's Contemporary Archives,* vol. 33 (London: Longman Publications, 1987) at 34978.

56 The Nimba County is a classic example of the consequences of the partition of Africa by Europe at the Berlin Conference of 1884-85. Here, the borders of three West African countries -- Liberia, Guinea, and Côte d'Ivoire – intersect. Most of the coups against Doe were allegedly launched from this region. Further, the Berlin Conference boundaries are notoriously fractious and controversial. See Dennis Austin, "The Uncertain Frontiers: Ghana and Togo" (1963) 1 J. Modern Afr. Stud. 1.

57 *Keesing's Contemporary Archives,* vol. 34 (London: Longman Publications, 1988) at 35884.

58 *Keesing's Contemporary Archives,* vol. 35 (London: Longman Publications, 1989) at 36610. The government moved in over 1,000 soldiers to quell the insurrection. In the process, atrocities of ethnic character were committed by the troops. This set the stage for the massive exile of the Dan/Gio, who supported the subsequent rebellion by Charles Taylor.

59 *Amnesty International Annual Report* (London: Amnesty International Publications, 1989) at 62-63; *Amnesty International Annual Report* (London: Amnesty International Publications, 1990) at 151.

60 *Keesing's Contemporary Archives,* vol. 36 (London: Longman Publications, 1990) at 37132.

61 Anthony Ofodile, "The Legality of ECOWAS Intervention in Liberia" (1994-95) 32 Colum. J. Transnat'l L. 381 at 384.

62 Kofi Oteng Kufour, "The Legality of the Intervention in the Liberian Civil War by the ECOWAS" (1993) 5 A.J.I.C.L. at 527.

63 Charles Ghankay Taylor was born in 1948 in Arthington, near Liberia's capital of Monrovia. He is half Americo-Liberian; his mother was from the Gola nation. Taylor's rise to power is traceable to his activities at Bentley College, Waltham, Massachusetts, where he graduated with a degree in economics in 1977. There is evidence to show that as one of the most articulate and vocal chairpersons of the Union of Liberian Associations in the United States, he harangued Liberian President William Tolbert when the latter visited the United States in 1979. Taylor organized and led a raucous demonstration outside the Liberian mission in New York City to protest Tolbert's policies. The noisy affair enabled him to meet with President Tolbert; subsequently, Taylor was invited to Liberia, where he stayed until the April 1980 coup by army sergeant Samuel Doe.

Charles Taylor's political experience, personal charisma, and background in economics made him a strong candidate for the position of director of the General Services Agency (GSA) of Liberia. The GSA was the purchasing agency of the Liberian government. In 1983 Taylor was accused of defrauding the agency to the tune of over US$1 million. When a warrant for his arrest was issued, Taylor fled to the United States in October 1983.

A warrant for Taylor's extradition to Liberia was issued in 1984 and he was arrested by US federal agents in Massachusetts. Taylor spent sixteen months in the Plymouth House of Corrections. In September 1985, he and four other inmates escaped from the jail. The three other inmates were recaptured but Taylor escaped to Libya, where he was sheltered by Muammar Ghaddafi. As already noted, on Christmas Eve 1989, Taylor resurfaced in Liberia as leader of the rebel National Patriotic Front (NPFL). This band of mercenaries and refugees soon became the breeding ground for the most brutal rebel movement to afflict West Africa.

64 Augustine Konneh, *Religion, Commerce and the Integration of the Mandingo in Liberia* (New York: University Press of America, 1996) at 132.

65 *Amnesty International Annual Report* (London: Amnesty International Publications, 1991) at 142 [hereinafter *Amnesty International 1991*]

66 Sources from the Office of the UN High Commissioner for Refugees claimed that 500,000 people had fled from the conflict to neighbouring countries – some 300,000 to Guinea, 120,000 to Côte d'Ivoire, and 80,000 to Sierra Leone. A further 1 million were believed to have been internally displaced. Monrovia's population jumped from 400,000 to over 1 million.

67 Lindsay Barret, "Liberia: The Nimba Equation" *West Africa* (17-23 February 1993) 1-7.

68 Christopher Clapham, *Africa and the International System: The Politics of State Survival* (Cambridge: Cambridge University Press, 1996) at 20.

69 Stephen Wright and Emeka Okolo, "Nigeria: Aspirations of a Regional Power" in Stephen Wright, ed., *African Foreign Policies* (Boulder, CO: Westview Press, 1999) at 107-29.

70 Robert Jackson and Carl Rosberg, *Personal Rule in Africa: Prince, Autocrat, Prophet, Tyrant* (Berkeley: University of California Press, 1982); Jona Rono, "Kenyan Foreign Policy" in Wright, *ibid.*

71 The Security Council considered the situation in Liberia for the first time on 22 January 1991, a little over a year after the conflict broke out: *Yearbook of the United Nations,* 1991 (New York: Martinus Nijhoff, 1992) at 132.

72 Interim Government of National Unity of Liberia, Final Communiqué of the National Conference of All Liberian Political Parties, Patriotic Fronts, Interest Groups and Concerned Citizens, Banjul, Gambia, 29 August 1990. Reproduced in Weller, *supra* note 2 at 89-93.

73 Weller, *supra* note 2 at 100.

74 ECOWAS Authority of Heads of States and Governments, Decision A/DEC.1/11/90 Relating to the Approval of the Decisions of the Community Standing Mediation Committee Taken during Its First Session from 6-7 August 1990, Bamako, Republic of Mali, 28 November 1990. Reproduced in Weller, *supra* note 2 at 111-20.

75 *Africa South of the Sahara,* 27th ed. (London: Europa Publications, 1998) at 598; *Yearbook of the United Nations,* 1992 (New York: Martinus Nijhoff Publishers, 1993) at 191.
76 The ULIMO split along ethnic lines, with ULIMO-K led by Alhaji Koromah supporting and defending Liberian Mandingoes. It was alleged to have strong backing from other Mandingoes in Guinea. The ULIMO-J was a predominantly Krahn army and was alleged to be operating from Sierra Leone.
77 *Amnesty International Report* (London: Amnesty International Publications, 1993) at 191-92.
78 See Letter from the Chargé d'Affaires of the Permanent Mission of Côte d'Ivoire to the United Nations Addressed to the President of the Security Council, 15 January 1991. Reproduced in Weller, *supra* note 2 at 127.
79 *Ibid.*
80 *Amnesty International Annual Report* (London: Amnesty International Publications, 1994) at 196.
81 *Keesing's Contemporary Archives,* vol. 40 (London: Longman Publications, 1994) at 39898.
82 *Amnesty International Annual Report* (London: Amnesty International Publications, 1995) at 195.
83 Thomas Woewiyu led a revolt against Charles Taylor and claimed that Taylor had been removed as the leader of the NPFL. Taylor sought refuge in Côte d'Ivoire but returned to Liberia after the revolt had succeeded only in creating a splinter group called the CRC-NPFL. There were now seven rebel groups.
84 "Statement on Developments in the Peace Process" *Panafrican News Agency* (27 July 1995), online: Panafrican News Agency <http://www.africanews.org>, accessed 8 November 1998.
85 *Keesing's Contemporary Archives,* vol. 41 (London: Longman Publications, 1995) at 40669.
86 *Amnesty International Annual Report* (London: Amnesty International Publications, 1996) at 210.
87 *Amnesty International Annual Report* (London: Amnesty International Publications, 1997) at 218-20.
88 *Amnesty International Annual Report* (London: Amnesty International Publications, 1998) at 235.
89 Huband, *supra* note 34 at 52-53.
90 Makau Wa Mutua, "Why Redraw the Map of Africa: A Moral and Legal Inquiry" (1995) 16 Mich. J. Int'l L. 1113.
91 Nwafor Azinna, *United Nations Use of Armed Forces in Internal War: Conditions for the Maintenance of International Stability* (Ph.D. Dissertation, University of Michigan, 1969) at 16.
92 George Kelly and Linda Miller, *Internal Wars and International Systems: Perspectives in Method* (New York: AMC Press, 1969) at 1. For a recent and informative analysis of the "curse" of statehood in Africa, see Basil Davidson, *The Black Man's Burden: Africa and the Curse of the Nation-State* (New York: Times Books, 1996).
93 Mutua, *supra* note 90. See also Crawford Young, "The Heritage of Colonialism" in John Harbeson and Donald Rothchild, eds., *Africa in World Politics* (Boulder: CO: Westview Press, 1991) 19.
94 Ali Mazrui, "The Africans: A Triple Heritage" (documentary) (Annenberg, CPB, 1986).
95 "Partitioning of Africa at the Berlin Conference, General Act of the Conference at Berlin, 26 February 1885" (1884-85) 76 British and Foreign States Report 4.
96 Fraenkel, *supra* note 16 at 27.
97 The scramble for Africa started in 1830 when the French invaded Algeria. The British quickly took over Egypt and the Suez Canal. Not to be outdone, King Leopold of Belgium seized huge tracts of land in Central Africa, and Germany followed suit in South-West Africa. In order to have an orderly process of pillaging Africa, European powers (with the sole exception of Switzerland), China, and the United States met in Berlin and signed the treaty, the General Act of the Conference of Berlin, on 26 February 1885, giving legal effect to claims of different powers and recognizing their territories in Africa. This devastating venture was subsequently justified by the argument that Africans were racially inferior and therefore

constituted wards of the "superior" white race – the so-called burden of the white man. Remarkably, this racist justification of colonialism was at odds with previous European scholarship, which had accepted the historicity of the African basis of European civilization, tracing the origins of Greek philosophy to ancient civilizations of Africa, and monotheism to ancient Egypt. See Mutua, *supra* note 90.

98 The foundations of European civilization are derived from classical Greek civilization, which in turn derived its religion, mathematics, philosophy, and much else from ancient African civilizations. For an analytic deconstruction of the racist construction of human civilization, see Martin Bernal, *Black Athena: The Afro-Asiatic Roots of Classical Civilization* (Camden, NJ: Rutgers University Press, 1987); Basil Davidson, *The African Past* (New York: Grosset and Dunlap, 1967).

99 Ethnologue, online: <http://www.ethnologue.com/show_country.asp?name=Liberia>, accessed 20 February 2003. This phenomenon gives rise to irredentism and accusations of subversion. Kwame Nkrumah of Ghana was given to issuing threats to the effect that Ghana would invade Togo so as to unite the Ewes in both countries. Togo accused Ghana of complicity in the assassination of Togolese President Sylvanius Olympio.

100 Mutua, *supra* note 90 at 1135.

101 J.C. Anene, *The International Boundaries of Nigeria 1885-1960* (London: Longman Publications, 1970), as cited in Mutua, *ibid.* at 1114.

102 Mutua, *ibid.* at 1135.

103 *Case Concerning the Land and Maritime Boundary between Cameroon and Nigeria* (*Cameroon* v. *Nigeria,* Equatorial Guinea intervening), 10 October 2002, [2002] I.C.J. Rep. General List No. 94. The Efik nation of Nigeria has threatened secession from Nigeria if the judgment of the Court ceding the peninsula to Cameroon is accepted by the government of Nigeria. See "Bakassi Threatens to Declare Own Republic" *Thisday* (29 October 2002) 1.

104 Liebenow, *supra* note 10 at 31-32.

105 *Ibid.* at 36. See also Davidson, *supra* note 92 at 203.

106 James Minahan, *Nations without States: A Historical Dictionary of Contemporary National Movements* (London: Greenwood Press, 1996) at 99.

107 Robert Jackson, *Quasi-States: Sovereignty, International Relations and the Third World* (Cambridge: Cambridge University Press, 1990) at 22.

108 *Charter of the OAU,* 25 May 1963, 479 U.N.T.S. 39. See Articles 3(3) and 3(5). Earlier attempts by some prescient African leaders such as Julius Nyerere to rethink the colonial borders and create a pan-African federation were killed at conception. See Davidson, *supra* note 92 at 184.

109 Christopher Clapham, "The Foreign Policies of Ethiopia and Eritrea" in Wright, *supra* note 69 at 84. Similar campaigns labelled as "separatist," "secessionist," and "irredentist" in Sudan, Nigeria/Biafra, Congo/Katanga, Ghana/Ewe/Togo, and Somalia/Kenya have not been successful.

110 Asiwaju Anthony, "Borders and Borderlands as Linchpins for Regional Integration in Africa: Lessons of the European Experience" in Clive Schofield, ed., *World Boundaries,* vol. 1 (London: Routledge, 1994) at 41-57.

111 For a fuller consideration of such arguments, see Mutua, *supra* note 90. There is abundant evidence to show that the frontiers of African states command little or no respect among African peoples. See Davidson, *supra* note 92 at 187-204. See also Shedrack Agbakwa, "Reclaiming Humanity: Economic, Social, and Cultural Rights as the Cornerstone of African Human Rights" (2002) 5 Yale Human Rts. & Dev. L.J. 177.

112 Michael Brown, ed., *The International Dimensions of Internal Conflicts* (Cambridge, MA: MIT Press, 1996) at ix.

113 Rhoda Howard, "Civil Conflict in Sub-Saharan Africa: Internally Generated Causes" (1995) 51 Int'l J. 27.

114 John McGhie, "Kenya: White Terror" *BBC News* (9 November 2002), online: BBC News <http://news.bbc.co.uk/1/programmes>, accessed 9 November 2002. See also Davidson, *supra* note 92 at 25.

115 As quoted in Mutua, *supra* note 90 at 1144.
116 Pat Utomi, "On the Cost of Government" *The Guardian* (15 October 2002) 5; Bright Ewulu, "Government Officials Consume 80% of Nigeria's Revenue" *Daily Trust* (7 November 2002) 1.
117 Richard Sandbrook, *The Politics of African Economic Recovery* (Cambridge: Cambridge University Press, 1993) at 93.
118 Stephen Stedman, "Conflict and Conciliation in Sub-Saharan Africa" in Brown, *supra* note 112 at 21.
119 Donald Rothchild, "Ethnic Bargaining and State Breakdown in Africa" (1995) 1 Nationalism and Ethnic Politics 21 at 54-72.
120 *Amnesty International Annual Report* (London: Amnesty International Publications, 1992) at 173.
121 James Crawford, *The Creation of States in International Law* (Oxford: Clarendon Press, 1979) at 230.
122 E.K. Quashigah, "Protection of Human Rights in the Changing International Scene: Prospects in Sub-Saharan Africa" (1994) 6 A.J.I.C.L. 84 at 93.
123 Clapham, *supra* note 68 at 20.
124 Thomas Callaghy, "Africa and the World Economy: Caught between the Rock and Hard Place" in Harbeson and Rothchild, *supra* note 93 at 56.
125 Another pathetic case is that of Equatorial Guinea under the regime of Marcias Nguema. According to an observer for the International Commission of Jurists, "the funds of the state had become totally confused with those of Marcias Nguema ... Marcias as Head of State, took the national treasury to his palace at Nzeny-Ayeng ... he administered the funds of the state from his house": quoted in Richard Kiwanuka, "The Meaning of 'People' in the African Charter of Human Rights" (1988) 82 A.J.I.L. 98.
126 "Bernard Kouchner: The Man Behind MSF" *BBC News* (15 October 1999), online: BBC News <http://news.bbc.co.uk/1/hi/world/europe/40632.stm>, accessed 26 February 2003.
127 Houghouet-Boigny of Côte d'Ivoire, who never did any private work or business but served his country instead, admitted having some billions stashed away in foreign banks.
128 It is a notorious fact that many African rulers maintained personal rule for over 20 years. Houghouet-Boigny of Côte d'Ivoire ruled for 28 years, Kenyatta of Zambia died in office after 18 years, Moi of Kenya ruled for 24 years, Mugabe of Zimbabwe has spent 22 years in office, and Eyadema of Togo has clocked 34 years in office.
129 Quashigah, *supra* note 122 at 96.
130 US House of Representatives, Subcommittee on Africa of the Committee on Foreign Affairs, 101st Congress, 2nd Session, Hearing on US Policy and the Crisis in Liberia, 19 June 1990. Reproduced in Weller, *supra* note 2 at 43.
131 *Ibid.*
132 Richard Falk, "A New Paradigm for International Legal Studies: Prospects and Proposals" in Richard Falk and Friedrich Kratochwill, eds., *International Law: A Contemporary Perspective* (Boulder, CO, and London: Westview Press, 1985) at 651-702.
133 Makau Wa Mutua, "The Ideology of Human Rights" (1996) 36 Va. J. Int'l L. 589; Kristoff, *supra* note 31.
134 At the 1990 Franco-African Summit at La Boulle, France, in June 1990, the late French President Mitterand, ostensibly speaking for the Western world, articulated the policy that future aid to African states would be tied to "good governance."
135 Rono, *supra* note 70 at 106-9.
136 Shephard, Anna, "The Economics of Democracy" *African Report* March-April 1992) 18 at 29.
137 Ike Nwachukwu, ed., *Nigeria and the ECOWAS since 1985: Towards a Dynamic Regional Integration* (Enugu, Nigeria: Fourth Dimension Publishers, 1995) at 105.
138 I am careful, however, not to explain every crisis on this basis.
139 Empirical surveys indicate that given its number of countries, the West African subregion has the highest number of coups d'état in the world, and is also the most politically unstable region in the world.

140 Richard Falk, "The Grotian Moment: Unfulfilled Promise, Harmless Fantasy, Missed Opportunity?" (1997) 13 Int'l Insights 3.
141 Nwachukwu, *supra* note 137 at 13.
142 Paul Szasz, "The Rise of Nationalism and the Breakup of States: The Fragmentation of Yugoslavia" (1994) 50 A.S.I.L. Proc. 33. Of all the African states, few, such as Somalia, Botswana, and Lesotho, approximate a nation, with common history of nomadic expansion, common language and culture, and common religion. Souadia Toural, *Somali Nationalism* (Cambridge, MA: Harvard University Press, 1963) 24.
143 *Amnesty International 1991, supra* note 65 at 145.
144 Stephen Ellis, "Liberia 1989-1994: A Study of Ethnic and Spiritual Violence" (1995) 94 African Affairs 168.
145 Kwesi Aning, "The International Dimensions of Internal Conflict: The Case of Liberia and West Africa" (Accra, Ghana: CDR Working Papers, 97.4, June 1997).
146 *Ibid.* The US State Department further confirmed Burkinabe/Libyan support for the rebels of the NPFL.
147 *Ibid.* Ghana has always had the reputation in African politics of being virulently opposed to conservative tyranny. In the Congo crisis, Ghana's Kwame Nkrumah, in denouncing Congolese leader Moise Tsombe for inviting Belgium to intervene in the crisis, had written: "You have assembled in your support the foremost advocates of imperialism and colonialism in Africa and the most determined opponents of African freedom. How can you, an African, do this?" See Ali Mazrui, *Toward a Pax Africana* (Chicago: University of Chicago Press, 1967) at 38.
148 Aning, *supra* note 145 at 7. Doe accused Ghana of sponsoring the Quiwonkpa coup attempt of November 1985.
149 *Ibid.*
150 Byron M. Tarr, "The ECOMOG Initiative in Liberia: A Liberian Perspective" (1993) 21-22 J. Opinion 74.
151 Weller, *supra* note 2 at 151. See also Osisioma Nwolise, "The Internationalization of the Liberian Crisis and Its Effects on West Africa" in Vogts, *supra* note 24 at 58.
152 Candy Shiner, "Peacekeepers Caught Up in Renewed War in Liberia" *Christian Science Monitor* (12 October 1991) 1.
153 Huband, *supra* note 34 at 212.
154 W. Ofuatey-Kodjoe, "Regional Organizations and the Resolution of Internal Conflicts: The ECOWAS Intervention in Liberia" (Autumn 1994) Int'l Peacekeeping 261-302.
155 Yeebo Zaya, *Ghana: The Struggle for Popular Power – Rawlings: Saviour or Demagogue?* (London: New Beacon Books, 1991) at 56.
156 Huband, *supra* note 34 at 212.
157 Weller, *supra* note 2 at 52. In protest, the US recalled its ambassador to Burkina Faso.
158 The late Ivorian president was also father-in-law to President Compaore of Burkina Faso. Similarly, because of the ideological and personal relationship between Kwame Nkrumah of Ghana and Sekou Toure of Guinea, the latter occasionally threatened to invade Ghana so as to reinstall the former after he had been overthrown. In 1963 Sawaba ethnic dissidents had aided their kith and kin in Togo to launch an assassination attempt on President Hamani Diori of Niger. It is common knowledge that the radical government of Nkrumah of Ghana harboured dissidents and socialist-minded rebels in Africa who were fleeing their respective states. On this, see Immanuel Wallerstein, *Africa: The Politics of Unity* (New York: Random House, 1965) at 101-8.
159 Stuart Croft and Adrian Treacher, "Aspects of Intervention in the South" in Andrew Dorman and Thomas Otte, eds., *Military Intervention: From Gunboat Diplomacy to Humanitarian Intervention* (London: Dartmouth Publishing, 1995) 130 at 147.
160 Jibrin Ibrahim, "Towards a Nigerian Perspective on the French Problematic in Africa" in Haruna Jacob and Massoud Omar, eds., *France and Nigeria: Issues in Comparative Studies* (Ibadan: Credu Niger Press, 1992) 55 at 67. The sympathies of France for Biafra during the civil war in Nigeria (1967-70) were generally construed by the Nigerian government as an attempt to balkanize Nigeria and reduce its influence in West Africa. See Femi Otubanjo

and Seye Davies, "Nigeria and France: The Struggle for Regional Hegemony" in B. Akinyemi and F. Otubanjo, eds., *Nigeria since Independence* (Ife, Nigeria: University of Ife Press, 1994) at 73-86.

161 "Sierra Leone Peace Deal Agreed" *BBC News,* online: BBC News <http://news.bbc.co.UK>, accessed 7 July 1999. See also Commonwealth News Release, 99/08, "Commonwealth Secretary-General Calls for Urgent International Action to Save Sierra Leone" (2 February 1999).

162 Commonwealth News Release, *ibid.*

163 *International Assistance to Sierra Leone,* GA Res. 48/196, UN GAOR, Supp. No. 49, UN Doc. A/ 48/49 (1993) at 171.

164 *Ibid.* In addition to other resolutions of the General Assembly, Resolution 49 of 1994 appealed to the world community to help the states around Liberia contend with the refugee crisis. See GA Res. 49/26, UN GAOR, Supp. No. 49, UN Doc. A/49/49 (1994).

165 Mark Doyle, "Sierra Leone: Worse Than Kosovo?" *BBC News* (3 July 1999), online: BBC News <http://news.bbc.co.uk>, accessed 18 November 2002.

166 "Liberia's War Is Said to Spill into Ivory Coast" *New York Times* (5 September 1993) A3 at A21.

167 Resolution 1343 of 7 March 2001, UN Doc. S/Res/1343 (2001); See also General Assembly Resolution 55 of 5 December 2001.

168 William Reno, "Reinvention of an African State" (1995) 16 Third World Quarterly 16 at 110.

169 Stedman, *supra* note 118 at 170.

170 *Yearbook of the United Nations* (New York: Martinus Nijhoff, 1995) 396.

171 UN Doc. S/Res/788 (1992). On the formation of the ULIMO and LDF in Sierra Leone, see Peter Da Costa, "Diversionary Tactics?" *West Africa* (29 April-5 May 1991) 645 at 650.

172 Stedman, *supra* note 118 at 246.

173 UN Doc. S/Res/985 (1995).

174 Brown, *supra* note 112.

175 Julia Preston, "250,000 Rwandans Flee to Tanzania in One Day" *Boston Globe* (30 April 1990) at A12.

Chapter 2: Collective Security and the Liberian Conflict

1 Jaye Ellis, "The Regime as a Locus of Legitimacy in International Law" (1997) 13 Int'l Insights 65 at 116.

2 M.V. Naidu, *Collective Security and the United Nations: A Definition of the UN Security System* (New York: St. Martin's Press, 1974) at 4.

3 Otto Pick and Julian Critchley, *Collective Security* (London: Macmillan, 1974) at 15; Joel Larus, *From Collective Security to Preventive Diplomacy* (New York: John Wiley, 1965).

4 Grant Dexter, *Canada and the Building of Peace* (Toronto: Canadian Institute of International Affairs, 1944) at 141.

5 Naidu, *supra* note 2 at 5.

6 Pick and Critchley, *supra* note 3 at 27. In spite of Soviet enthusiasm in 1934 to revive the concept of collective security and thus contain Hitlerite expansionism and aggression, the League woefully failed and Stalin, in despair, "continued to promote his country's national interest by his own means": *ibid.* Save for providing a forum for minimal multilateral contacts, the League was a failure as an instrument of collective security.

7 R.A. Akindele, *The Organization and Promotion of World Peace: A Study of Universal-Regional Relationships* (Toronto: University of Toronto Press, 1976) at 3.

8 Among the Igbos of Nigeria, this philosophy is summarized in the pithy saying that no one can finish a meal prepared by the entire community and that no matter the size of the pot and the dexterity of the skill, no single person can engorge the entire community with food for too long.

9 Hans Kelsen, *Collective Security at International Law* (Washington, DC: US Government Printing Office, 1957) at 3.

10 H.L.A. Hart, *The Concept of Law* (Oxford: Clarendon Press, 1961) at 89.

11 Kelsen, *supra* note 9.

12 Henry Kissinger, *A World Restored* (Boston: Houghton Mifflin, 1957) at 11.
13 Inis Claude, *Swords into Ploughshares,* 3rd ed. (New York: Random House, 1964) at 32.
14 The ancient Greek city-states that combined against aggression from Sparta and Athens almost always broke up their alliance as soon as the common enemy was routed.
15 Those "marriages of convenience" collapsed as soon as the common enemy was defeated. Similar tendencies were apparent in medieval Europe.
16 B.S. Chimni, *International Law and World Order* (New Delhi: Sage Publications, 1993).
17 James Golden *et al.*, eds., *NATO at Forty: Change, Continuity and Prospects* (London: Westview Press, 1989) at 22.
18 Christopher Jones, *Soviet Influence in Eastern Europe: Political Autonomy and the Warsaw Pact* (New York: Praeger, 1981) at 6-8. Both regional security arrangements, like the ECOWAS PMAD, embody the concept that aggression against one member is aggression against all other members.
19 Paul Butuex, *The Politics of Nuclear Consultation in NATO since 1965-80* (London: Cambridge University Press, 1983) at 34.
20 John K. Gailbraith and Stanislav Menshikov, *Capitalism, Communism and Coexistence* (Boston: Houghton Publishing, 1988) at 2; Alastair Buchan, *Change without War* (London: Chatto and Windus, 1974) at 22.
21 Regional arrangements appear to be the compromise. Defenders of this watered-down substitute contend that it is a partial realization of the grander vision of the pure concept of collective security – a peculiar state of being "slightly pregnant." This limited vision of collective security and its defence by Lester Pearson arguably cost him the job of United Nations Secretary-General, a job that he was otherwise eminently qualified for. See Krishna Menon, *India and World Politics: Krishna Menon's View of the World* (Toronto: Oxford University Press, 1968) at 107.
22 Quincy Wright, *International Law and the United Nations* (New York: Publishing House, 1960) at 15. For his part, Claude bemoans the situation and asserts that the "mountainous resolve" by states at the close of the Second World War to establish a universal collective security shrank to a "mousy commitment." See Inis Claude, "The United Nations and the Use of Force" (1961) 532 International Conciliation 325-28.
23 Naidu, *supra* note 2 at 3. But see Wolfgang Friedman, "The United States Policy and the Crisis of International Law" 59 A.J.I.L. 857. He makes the argument that since 1956, there was a prevailing regime of "limited use of force" and that states took particular interest in justifying their actions before the United Nations. In his view, these two factors show that the doctrine of collective security system is alive and well.
24 It seems that the Charter of the United Nations itself contemplated the present position, as Chapter 8 provides for the exercise of certain functions that, in an effective international collective security system, would have been an absolute prerogative of the United Nations itself.
25 *Legality of the Threat or Use of Nuclear Weapons,* Advisory Opinion of 8 July 1996, [1996] I.C.J. Rep. 226.
26 Gene Lyons and Michael Mastanduno, "State Sovereignty and International Intervention" in Gene Lyons and Michael Mastanduno, eds., *Beyond Westphalia? State Sovereignty and International Intervention* (Baltimore: Johns Hopkins University Press, 1995) 240 at 250.
27 Thomas Weiss and Jarat Chopra, "Sovereignty under Siege" in Lyons and Mastanduno, *ibid.* at 87.
28 H. Grotius, *De Jure Belli ac Pacis* (1646) (New York: Carnegie Translation, 1925) at 112.
29 Frederick Kratochwill, "Sovereignty as Dominium" in Lyons and Mastanduno, *supra* note 26 at 23-30.
30 The Peace of Westphalia was among the series of international agreements reaffirming the inviolability and sovereignty of the emerging fraternity of Christianized European states.
31 For a telling and analytical deconstruction of this Eurocentric perception of the modern state in the milieu of human rights, see Makau Wa Mutua, "Savages, Victims, and Saviours: The Metaphor of Human Rights" (2001) 42 Harv. Int'l L.J. 201.
32 Obiora Okafor, "Is There a Legitimacy Deficit in International Legal Scholarship and Practice?" (1997) 13 Int'l Insights 91.

33 *Mitchell and Others* v. *D.P.P.,* [1986] (C.L.R) Constitutional & Administrative L.R. at 155. On the impact of this trend on municipal law, see Roderick MacDonald, "Metaphors of Multiplicity: Civil Society, Regimes, and Legal Pluralism" (1998) 15 Ariz. J. Int'l L. 75.
34 Karsten Nowrot and Emily Schabacker, "The Use of Force to Restore Democracy: International Implications of the ECOWAS Intervention in Sierra Leone" (1998) 14 Am. U. Intl. L. Rev. 321-412.
35 Jost Dulbreck, "Globalization of Law, Politics, and Markets: Implication for Local Law: A European Perspective" (1993) 1 Ind. J. Global Legal Stud. 9 at 36.
36 *International Covenant on Civil and Political Rights,* 1966, 999 U.N.T.S. 171 (1966). See also David Luban, "Just War and Human Rights" (1980) 9 Philosophy and Public Affairs J. 160 at 166-81.
37 On the nature of new customary international law, see the *North Sea Continental Cases* (Federal Republic of Germany/Denmark; Federal Republic of Germany/Netherlands), [1969] I.C.J. Rep. 3.
38 Mark Zacker, "The Decaying Pillars of the Westphalian Temple" in James Rosenau, ed., *Governance without Government* (New York: Cambridge University Press, 1992) 40 at 58.
39 Robert Jackson, "International Community beyond the Cold War" in Lyons and Mastanduno, *supra* note 26 at 59.
40 For a general discussion of these concerns, see Mutua, *supra* note 31.
41 E.K. Quashigah, "Protection of Human Rights in the Changing International Scene: Prospects in Sub-Saharan Africa" (1994) 6 A.J.I.C.L. 84 at 93.
42 *Charter of the United Nations,* 26 June 1945, 892 U.N.T.S. 1 (1973) [hereinafter *UN Charter*].
43 Rosalyn Higgins, *The Development of International Law through the Political Organs of the United Nations* (Cambridge: Cambridge University Press, 1963) at 2.
44 Thomas Franck, "The Emerging Right to Democratic Governance" (1992) 86 A.J.I.L. 46 at 81.
45 *UN Charter, supra* note 42.
46 Lori F. Damrosch, ed., *Enforcing Restraint: Collective Intervention in Internal Conflicts* (New York: Council on Foreign Relations Press, 1993) at 502.
47 E.Y. Benneh, "Review of the Law on Non-Intervention" (1995) 7 A.J.I.C.L. 139 at 155.
48 Stephen Schnably, "The Santiago Commitment as a Call to Democracy: Evaluating the OAS Role in Haiti, Peru and Guatemala" (1994) 25 U. Miami Inter-Am. L. Rev. 393.
49 I.L.M 1305 (1990).
50 *Case Concerning the Continental Shelf (Libyan Arab Jamahiriya/Malta),* 3 June 1985, [1985] I.C.J. Rep. 13.
51 As reproduced in Damrosch, *supra* note 46 at 193.
52 Commission on Human and Peoples Rights, *Eighth Annual Activity Report, 1994-1995,* Thirty-First Ordinary Session, 26-28 June 1995, Addis Ababa, Ethiopia.
53 *Declaration of the OAU Ad-Hoc Committee on Southern Africa on the Question of South Africa,* Harare, Zimbabwe, 21 August 1989. See Gino Naldi, ed., *Documents of the OAU* (London: Mansel Publishing, 1992) at 79. This declaration was unanimously endorsed by the Movement of Non-Aligned States at its summit meeting in Belgrade and formed the basis for the Declaration on Apartheid and Its Destructive Consequence in Southern Africa adopted by the UN General Assembly on 14 December 1989.
54 Domingo Acevedo, "The Haitian Crisis and the OAS Response: A Test of Effectiveness in Protecting Democracy" in Damrosch, *supra* note 46 at 119.
55 Max Kampelman, "Foreword" in Damrosch, *supra* note 46 at vii-ix.
56 The Standing Mediation Committee was set up by the Authority of Heads of States and Governments, and was made up of Gambia, Ghana, Mali, Nigeria, and Togo. See *Extract from the Final Communiqué of the ECOWAS Authority of Heads of States and Governments Meeting,* Banjul, Gambia, 30 May 1990; reproduced in Marc Weller, *Regional Peacekeeping and International Enforcement: The Liberian Crisis* (Cambridge: Grotius Publications, 1994).
57 *Report of the Secretary-General on the Question of Liberia,* UN Doc. S/25402, 12 March 1993, para. 12.
58 *Supra* note 56.

59 Comfort Ero, "ECOWAS and the Sub-regional Peacekeeping in Liberia," online: <http://www.jha.ac.articles/a005.htm>, accessed 25 February 2003.
60 Douglas Rimmer, *The Economies of West Africa* (New York: St. Martin's Press, 1985) at 2. At its formation, ECOWAS had fifteen members: Benin, Burkina Faso, Côte d'Ivoire, Gambia, Ghana, Guinea, Guinea Bissau, Liberia, Mali, Mauritania, Niger, Nigeria, Senegal, Sierra Leone, and Togo. Cape Verde, the sixteenth member, joined in 1977.
61 *Treaty of the Economic Community of West African States (ECOWAS),* 28 May 1975, 14 I.L.M. 1200.
62 Preamble and Article 12 of the ECOWAS treaty, *ibid.*
63 Stephen Wright, "The Changing Context of African Foreign Policies" in Stephen Wright, ed., *African Foreign Policies* (Boulder, CO: Westview Press, 1999) [hereinafter *African Foreign Policies*] 1 at 16.
64 Julius Okolo, "The Development and Structure of ECOWAS" in Julius Okolo, ed., *West African Regional Cooperation and Development* (Oxford: Westview Press, 1990) [hereinafter *West African Regional Cooperation*] 15 at 20.
65 Ralph Onwuka, *Development and Integration in West Africa: The Case of the Economic Community of West Africa (ECOWAS)* (Ife, Nigeria: University of Ife Press, 1982) at 53.
66 Olatunde Ojo, "Nigeria and the Formation of ECOWAS" (1988) 34 Int'l Org. 45.
67 Okolo, *supra* note 64 at 25.
68 John Heilbrunn, "The Flea on Nigeria's Back: The Foreign Policy of Benin" in *African Foreign Policies, supra* note 63 at 43.
69 Daniel Bach "Franco-phone Regional Organizations and ECOWAS" in Okolo, *supra* note 64 at 54.
70 Articles 5(2) and 5(3).
71 Article 6 of the ECOWAS Treaty.
72 Articles 8 and 9.
73 Reproduced in Weller, *supra* note 56.
74 Phil Williams, *North Atlantic Treaty Organization* (London: Transaction Publishers, 1994) at 4.
75 Neil Fodor, *The Warsaw Treaty Organization: A Political and Organizational Analysis* (London: Macmillan, 1990) at 16.
76 Reproduced in Weller, *supra* note 56 at 19-22.
77 Article 4.
78 See Chapters 7-8 of the United Nations Charter, of which later.
79 Kelsen, *supra* note 9 at 43.
80 Naidu, *supra* note 2 at 63.
81 David Brown, "The Role of Regional Organizations in Stopping Civil Wars" (1996-97) 41 A.F.L. Rev. 235 at 260.
82 The United Nations itself recognizes and addresses the ECOWAS as a regional body. See SC Res. 813, UN SCOR, 48th Sess., 3187th Mtg., UN Doc. S/Res/813 (1993) 1.
83 Hilaire McCoubrey and Nigel White, *International Organizations and Civil Wars* (Aldershot, UK: Dartmouth Press, 1995) at 31.
84 Robert Jackson, "The Grotian Moment in World Jurisprudence" (1997) 13 Int'l Insights 35-56.
85 Kofi Oteng Kufour, "The Legality of the Intervention in the Liberian Civil War by the ECOWAS" (1993) 5 A.J.I.C.L. 528.
86 Ibrahim Babangida, "The Imperative Features of Nigeria's Foreign Policy and the Crisis in Liberia" in Ike Nwachukwu, ed., *Nigeria and the ECOWAS since 1985: Towards a Dynamic Regional Integration* (Enugu, Nigeria: Fourth Dimension Publishers, 1995) at 105.
87 *Ibid.* It is interesting to observe that similar arguments but of a humanitarian nature were made by NATO in its bombing of Yugoslavia. See Bruno Simma, "NATO, the UN and the Use of Force: Legal Aspects" (1998) 10 E.J.I.L. 1.
88 UN Doc. S/PV.2974 (22 January 1991).
89 Babangida, *supra* note 86 at 106.
90 *Ibid.* at 109.

91 Louis Henkin, *How Nations Behave: Law and Foreign Policy,* 2nd ed. (New York: Columbia University Press, 1979) at 155.

92 Subhas Khare, *Use of Force under the United Nations Charter* (New Delhi: Metropolitan Book Co., 1985) at 132.

93 H. Lauterpacht, *The Function of Law in the International Community* (Oxford: Clarendon Press, 1933) at 286.

94 For example, *Declaration on the Inadmissibility of Intervention into the Domestic Affairs of States and the Protection of Their Independence and Sovereignty*, GA Res. 2131, UN GAOR, 20th Sess., Supp. No. 14, UN Doc. A/6014 (1965) 11; *Declaration on Principles of International Law Concerning Friendly Relations and Co-operation among States in Accordance with the Charter of the United Nations*, GA Res. 2625, UN GAOR, 25th Sess., Supp. No. 28, UN Doc. A/8028 (1970) 121; *Definition of Aggression,* GA Res. 3314, UN GAOR, 29th Sess., Supp. No. 31, UN Doc. A/9631 (1974) 142; *Charter of the OAU,* 25 May 1963, 479 U.N.T.S. 39.

95 *Case Concerning Military and Paramilitary Activities in and against Nicaragua (Merits)* (*Nicaragua* v. *United States*), [1986] I.C.J. Rep. 14.

96 *Corfu Channel Case (Merits),* [1949] I.C.J. Rep. 4.

97 Kufour, *supra* note 85. See also Anthony Ofodile, "The Legality of ECOWAS Intervention in Liberia" (1994-95) 32 Colum. J. Transnat'l L. 381.

98 A. Roxburgh, "The Sanction of International Law" (1920) 14 A.J.I.L. 26.

99 This intervention was condemned by the General Assembly in a resolution. See United Nations General Assembly, The Situation in Geneva, GA Res. 38/7, UN GAOR, 43rd Plenary Meeting, 2 November 1983, (1983), reprinted in William Gilmore, *The Grenada Intervention: Analysis and Documentation* (London: Mansell Publishing, 1984) at 107-8. The purported invitation to intervene was largely dismissed, as the authority to make the invitation was in grave doubt.

100 This intervention was condemned in a Security Council draft resolution that failed because of a Soviet veto. See UN SCOR, 23d Year, 1442d Mtg., (1968) at 34. Note also that the purported invitation to intervene in this case and in the case of Hungary were dismissed, as they were patently manufactured and/or coerced.

101 GA Res. 3314 (29) UN GAOR, 6th Comm., UN Doc. A/9890, Annex, (1974).

102 Ann Thomas and A.J. Thomas, *Non-Intervention* (Dallas: Southern Methodist University Press, 1956) at 3.

103 Richard Little, *Intervention: External Involvement in Civil Wars* (London: M. Robertson, 1975) at 2.

104 Ernest Oppenheim, *International Law* [H. Lauterpacht, ed.], vol. 9 (London: Longman Publications, 1992) at 432 [hereinafter *Oppenheim's International Law*].

105 Richard Connaughton, *Military Intervention in the 1990s* (New York: Routledge, 1992) at ix.

106 Ellery Stowell, *Intervention in International Law* (Washington, DC: John Byrne, 1921) at 47.

107 Thomas and Thomas, *supra* note 102 at 14.

108 F.X. De Lima, *Intervention in International Law* (The Hague: Pax Nederland, 1971) at 126.

109 Lauterpacht, *supra* note 93 at 286.

110 *Ibid.* at 141.

111 Hannis Taylor, *A Treatise on Public International Law* (Chicago: Callaghan, 1901) at 140. The Holy Alliance was a group of royals from the crowns of Austria, Prussia, and Russia. Emperor Francis I of Austria, King Frederick William III of Prussia, and Tsar Alexander I of Russia signed a treaty on 26 September 1815 by which they united in a "Holy Alliance."

112 Stowell, *supra* note 106 at 387.

113 D. Bowett, *Self Defence in International Law* (Manchester, UK: Manchester University Press, 1968) at 53.

114 Stowell, *supra* note 106.

115 *Ibid.* This distinction appeared to lay the test upon which the legality of interventions would be judged for centuries. Castlereagh dismissed the Holy Alliance as "sublime mysticism and nonsense," and Metternich of Austria later ridiculed it as "a loud sounding nothing." See Baron De Savigny, *Metternich and His Times* (London: Longman Publications, 1962).

116 Robert Jennings and Arthur Watts, eds., *Oppenheim's International Law,* 9th ed. (London: Longman Publications, 1992) at 447.

117 P.H. Winfield, "The History of Intervention in International Law" (1922-23) 3 B.Y.I.L. 138.
118 *Ibid.*
119 *Ibid.* at 137.
120 OAS, Inter-American Juridical Committee, *Differences between Intervention and Collective Action,* OR OEA/Ser.1/VI.2 (1996).
121 James Oliver Murdoch, "Collective Security Distinguished from Intervention" (1962) 56 A.J.I.L. 500.
122 See Jennings and Watts, *supra* note 116; Oppenheim's *International Law, supra* note 104.
123 F. Kirgis, *International Organizations in Their Legal Setting: Documents, Comments, and Questions* (St. Paul, MN: West Publishing, 1993) at 2.
124 Ian Brownlie, *International Law and the Use of Force* (Oxford: Clarendon Press, 1963) at 145.
125 Bowett, *supra* note 113 at 52. Similar requests of Indonesia by Australia were also rejected.
126 Roger Shiner, *Norm and Nature: The Movements of Legal Thought* (Oxford: Oxford University Press, 1992) at 187.
127 Anthony Clark, "The United Nations, Regional Organizations and Military Operations: The Past and the Present" (1995) 7 Duke J. Int'l & Comp. L. 3-33.
128 William Durch, *Evolution of UN Peacekeeping: Case Studies and Comparative Analysis* (New York: St. Martin's Press, 1993).
129 E. Luard, ed., *The International Regulation of Civil Wars* (New York: New York University Press, 1972) at 8; John Norton Moore, "Toward an Applied Theory for the Regulation of Intervention" in John Norton Moore, ed., *Law and Civil War in the Modern World* (Baltimore: Johns Hopkins University Press, 1974) at 3.

Chapter 3: The Liberian Conflict and International Law on Foreign Intervention in Domestic Conflicts

1 Anthony Ofodile, "The Legality of ECOWAS Intervention in Liberia" (1994-95) 32 Colum. J. Transnat'l L. 381.
2 This intervention was condemned in a Security Council draft resolution that failed because of the Soviet veto. See E.J. Czerwinski and Jaroslaw Peilkalkiewicz, eds., *The Soviet Invasion of Czechoslovakia* (New York: Praeger, 1973). Note also that the purported invitation to intervene in this case and in the case of Hungary were dismissed, as they were patently manufactured and/or coerced.
3 Heather Wilson, *International Law and the Use of Force by National Liberation Movements* (Oxford: Clarendon Press, 1988) at 7.
4 Kofi Oteng Kufour, "The Legality of the Intervention in the Liberian Civil War by the ECOWAS" (1993) 5 A.J.I.C.L. at 527. This is an interesting argument. The two countries (Burkina Faso and Côte d'Ivoire) that initially opposed the intervention were acknowledged to have financed and equipped the rebels.
5 H.G. Schermers, *International Institutional Law* (Alphen aan den Rijn, Netherlands: Sijthoff and Noordoff, 1980) at 391.
6 The states in question were Burkina Faso and Côte d'Ivoire. Although the activities of these two states may not have met the austere requirements posed by the *Nicaragua Case,* of which more later, these two countries, for diverse reasons, supported the NPFL.
7 Note that Burkina Faso and Côte d'Ivoire changed their minds and supported the intervention when they allegedly discovered "NPFL sponsored attempts to destabilize" their own countries. See Ofodile, *supra* note 1.
8 Louise Doswald-Beck, "The Legal Validity of Military Intervention by the Invitation of the Government" (1985) 56 B.Y.I.L. 189.
9 *Definition of Aggression,* GA Res. 3314, UN GAOR, 29th Sess., Supp. No. 31, UN Doc. A/9631 (1974) 142.
10 *Ibid.* In 1964, Britain intervened in Tanzania, Uganda, and Kenya to help incumbent governments quell internal mutinies. France has intervened more than a dozen times in African states to help beleaguered governments regain control in the face of attempted military coups d'état.
11 David Wippman, "Military Intervention, Regional Organizations and Host-State Consent" (1996) 7 Duke J. Int'l & Comp. L. 209-39.

12 Rein Mullerson, "Intervention by Invitation" in L. Damrosch and D. Scheffer, eds., *Law and Force in the New International Order* (Boulder, CO: Westview Press, 1991) 128 at 129.
13 "Eighth Report on State Responsibility" (1979) 2 Y.B.I.L. Comm'n 36.
14 Tom Farer, "Panama: Beyond the Charter Paradigm" (1990) 84 A.J.I.L. 503. But see Anthony D'Amato, "The Invasion of Panama Was a Lawful Response to Tyranny" (1990) 84 A.J.I.L. 516.
15 Quincy Wright, "United States Intervention in Lebanon" (1959) 53 A.J.I.L. 120.
16 On Hungary, see UN SCOR, 14th Sess., 746th Mtg., UN Doc. S/PV (1956) at 4. On Czechoslovakia, see UN SCOR, 26th Sess., UN Doc. S/PV.1441 (1968). On Afghanistan, see *The Situation in Afghanistan,* General Assembly Resolution 35/37 of 20 November 1980.
17 David Wippman, "Change and Continuity in Legal Justification for Military Interventions in Internal Conflicts" (1996) 27 Colum. H.R.L. Rev. 435-85.
18 Tom Farer, "A Paradigm of Legitimate Intervention" in L.F. Damrosch, ed., *Enforcing Restraint: Collective Intervention in Internal Conflicts* (New York: Council on Foreign Relations Press, 1993).
19 *Case Concerning Military and Paramilitary Activities in and against Nicaragua (Merits)* (*Nicaragua* v. *United States*), [1986] I.C.J. Rep. 14 at 126 [hereinafter *Nicaragua Case*].
20 Note that although the US intervention in Panama ousted a dictatorial regime, it was widely condemned as "a flagrant violation of international law." See GA Res. 44/240, UN GAOR, 44th Sess., Supp. No. 49, 88th Plen. Mtg., 29 December 1989 (1989) 52. See also Louis Henkin, "The Invasion of Panama under International Law: A Gross Violation" (1991) 29 Colum. J. Transnat'l L. 293.
21 Article 38 of the Statute of the International Court of Justice. See also *The Paquete Habana Case* 175 U.S. 677 (1900).
22 Louis Henkin, "Use of Force: Law and US Policy" in Louis Henkin, ed., *Right v. Might: International Law and the Use of Force* (New York: Council on Foreign Relations Press, 1991) 61 at 67.
23 Wippman, *supra* note 11.
24 Reproduced in (1966) Y.B.I.L.C. 240 at 247-49.
25 Article 53, *Vienna Convention on the Law of Treaties,* signed at Vienna, 23 May 1969, 500 U.N.T.S. 95 (1969).
26 *Western Sahara,* Advisory Opinion, [1975] I.C.J. Rep. 12.
27 Wippman, *supra* note 11. The Chadian situation is a case in point. The inviting government collapsed soon after the invitation was made to the OAU.
28 John Perkins, "The Right of Counter-Intervention" (1986) 17 Ga. J. Int'l & Comp. L. 171.
29 Eli Lauterpacht, "The Contemporary Practice of the UK: Survey and Comment V" (1957) 3 I.C.L.Q. 92 at 99-102. See also Eli Lauterpacht, "Independence and Intervention" (1964) B.P.I.L. 3 at 22-23.
30 William Hall, *A Treatise on International Law,* 8th ed. (Oxford: Clarendon Press, 1924) at 347.
31 Rosalyn Higgins, "International Law and Civil Conflict" in E. Luard, ed., *The International Regulation of Civil Wars* (New York: New York University Press, 1972).
32 *Western Sahara, supra* note 26.
33 Article 1 of UN Human Rights Covenants (1966), 993 (1976) U.N.T.S. 3; Article 1(4) of Geneva Protocol 1 1977 Additional to the Geneva Conventions of 1949, 75 U.N.T.S. 85 (1950).
34 Geneva Protocol (1977) 16 I.L.M. 1442.
35 Marc Weller, *Regional Peacekeeping and International Enforcement: The Liberian Crisis* (Cambridge: Grotius Publications, 1994).
36 Article 11 of the 1948 Convention on the Prevention and Punishment of the Crime of Genocide, which entered into force in 1951, defines genocide as the intentional destruction, in whole or in part, of national, racial, ethnic, or religious groups. See J.G. Starke, *An Introduction to International Law,* 9th ed. (London: Butterworths, 1984) at 60-61.
37 HR 345, 101st Cong., 2d sess. (7 March 1990).
38 Weller, *supra* note 35.
39 *Ibid.*

40 *Ibid.* at 53.
41 *Ibid.* On the legal consequences of de facto and *de jure* recognition of governments, see *Haile Selassie* v. *Cable and Wireless Ltd.* (1938) L.R. ch. 839 (No. 2).
42 David Wippman, "Enforcing the Peace: ECOWAS and the Liberian Crisis" in Damrosch, *supra* note 18 at 210.
43 *Ibid.*
44 Letter of President Samuel Kanyon Doe to the Chairman and Members of the Ministerial Meeting of the ECOWAS Standing Mediation Committee (14 July 1990). Reproduced in Weller, *supra* note 35.
45 Weller, *ibid.* From the moment the idea was mooted, Charles Taylor opposed it, arguing that it amounted to a breach of Liberian sovereignty and the right of the Liberian peoples to self-determination. He threatened that his forces would kill any interventionist forces. The NPFL rebels made good their threat as they engaged in private acts of reprisals against citizens of ECOWAS countries that supported the intervention.
46 UN GAOR, 45th Sess., 27th Mtg., UN Doc. A/45/PV.27 (1990) 61. The African members of the Security Council (Ethiopia and Zaire), for their self-serving reasons, frustrated the attempts to place the crisis on the agenda of the Security Council.
47 ECOWAS Standing Mediation Committee, Decision A/DEC.1/8/90, on the ceasefire and establishment of an ECOWAS Monitoring Group for Liberia, Banjul, Gambia, 7 August 1990. Reproduced in Weller, *supra* note 35 at 69. In spite of the opposition of the NPFL to the ECOMOG intervention, President Lansana Conté of Guinea, speaking for ECOWAS, insisted that "we do not need the permission of any party involved in the conflict to implement the decisions reached in Banjul. So with or without the agreement of any of the parties, ECOWAS troops will be in Liberia." See Weller, *ibid.* at 66. Yormie Johnson of the INPFL welcomed the intervention, saying that he was "ready to die to make the Monrovia port conducive for ECOWAS landing." Initially, President Doe, holed up inside the presidential villa, was dilatory as his envisaged plan to use the intervention as a shield and recover his position failed. Contrary to Doe's expectation, ECOWAS decided to set up an interim government independent of him and the rebels. However, he noted his "happiness with the ECOWAS intervention ... but hoped that it [ECOMOG] would not take sides." See Weller, *ibid.* at 88.
48 Mark Weisburd, *Use of Force: The Practice of States since World War II* (University Park, PA: Pennsylvania State University Press, 1997) at 2.
49 Malcolm Shaw, "The International Status of National Liberation Movements" in Frederick Snyder and Surakiart Sathirathai, eds., *Third World Attitudes toward International Law* (Dordrecht, Netherlands: Martinus Nijhoff, 1986) 145 at 150.
50 Edward Kwakwa, *The International Law of Armed Conflicts: Personal and Material Field of Application* (Dordrecht, Netherlands: Martinus Nijhoff, 1992).
51 Christine Gray, "Host-State Consent and UN Peacekeeping in Yugoslavia" (1996) 7 Duke J. Int'l & Comp. L. 241. Similar consensus was reached in the cases of Namibia, Cambodia, and Mozambique, but these wars were of a totally different character from the Liberian war. See also Milan Sahovic, "Non-Aligned Countries and the Current Regulation on the Use of Force" in Antonio Cassese, ed., *The Current Legal Regulation of the Use of Force* (Dordrecht, Netherlands: Martinus Nijhoff, 1986) 470 at 479. But see Damrosch, *supra* note 18 at 10.
52 Weller, *supra* note 35 at 49. See also Jeffrey Goldberg, "A War without Purpose in a Country without Identity" *New York Times Magazine* (22 January 1995) 37.
53 Megan McKenna, "The Reintegration of Child Soldiers in Liberia," online: UNICEF <http://www.unicefusa.org/issues98/nov98/Liberia_jump>, accessed 28 February 2003.
54 Human Rights Watch Interview, <http://www.hrw.org>, accessed 14 March 1999. See also Yael Danieli *et al.*, eds., *International Response to Traumatic Stress* (New York: Bayword Publishing, 1998).
55 *Ibid.*
56 Damrosch, *supra* note 18.
57 George Nolte, "Restoring Peace by Regional Action: International Law Aspects of the Liberian Conflict," cited in Wippman, *supra* note 11 at 225.

58 Michael Reisman, "Humanitarian Intervention and Fledgling Democracies" (1995) 18 Fordham Int'l L.J. 794. It is interesting that the United States did not condemn the recent botched coup d'état against democratically elected President Hugo Chavez of Venezuela.

59 SC Res. 1132, UN SCOR, 51st Sess., 3822d Mtg., UN Doc. S/Res/1132 (1997) para. 1. Note that ECOMOG intervention was not directly authorized by the Security Council: SC Res. 1156, UN SCOR, 52d Sess., 3861st Mtg., UN Doc. S/Res/1156 (1998).

60 Malvina Halberstam, "The Copenhagen Document: Intervention in Support of Democracy" (1993) 34 Harv. Int'l L.J. 163.

61 OAS Doc. CP/SA/896/92 (1 April 1992) and CP/Doc.2248/92 (1 April 1992), as cited in Domingo Acevedo, "The Haitian Crisis and the OAS Response: A Test of Effectiveness in Protecting Democracy" in Damrosch, *supra* note 18. The military coups d'état in Burundi and Sierra Leone, which had satisfied the test of effectiveness, were frustrated by international isolation and delegitimation.

62 UN SCOR, 49th Sess., 3413th Mtg., UN Doc. S/Res/940 (1994) at 1. Note also that this was the first time that the Security Council was authorizing the use of force for the restoration of "democracy."

63 [1962] I.C.J. Rep. 151.

64 *Supplement to An Agenda for Peace: Position Paper of the Secretary-General on the Occasion of the Fiftieth Anniversary of the United Nations,* UN SCOR, 50th Sess., UN Doc. S/1995/1 (1995) paras. 34-35 (emphasis added).

65 Mats Berdal, "The Security Council, Peacekeeping and Internal Conflicts after the Cold War" (1996) 7 Duke J. Int'l & Comp. L. 71. He notes at 75 that "as of late 1994, there had been 130 fatalities in the UN forces in Yugoslavia ... and as of early 1996, there had been 410 fatalities in UN peacekeeping operations in the former Yugoslavia."

66 Richard Connaughton, "Time to Clear the Doctrine Dilemma" (1994) 21 Jane's Defence Weekly 19.

67 Margaret Vogts, "The Problems and Challenges of Peace-Making: From Peace-Keeping to Peace Enforcement" in Margaret Vogts, ed., *Liberian Crisis and ECOMOG: A Bold Attempt at Peacekeeping* (Lagos: Gabumo Publishing, 1992).

68 Nico Schrijver, "Introducing Second Generation Peacekeeping: The Case of Namibia" (1997) 6 A.J.I.C.L. 1. See also Sylvester Ekundayo, "ECOMOG – A Model for African Peacekeeping" *AfricaNews* (16 October 1998) 2 at 12. According to him, "it should be emphasized that the concept, nature and scope and practice of peacekeeping are changing rapidly with the emergence of new types of conflict situations in the continent. Both the United Nations and the ECOWAS have recognized this, and have had to adapt traditional peacekeeping to meet specific intra-state conflicts such as verification of cease-fire agreements, security/protection for refugees and humanitarian relief workers, demobilization and disarmament of combatants, and observation of democratic political processes in the form of elections and referenda."

69 Jinmi Adisa, "The Politics of Regional Military Cooperation: The Case of ECOMOG" in Vogts, *supra* note 67 at 217.

70 Walter Shawn, "Protecting the Avatar of International Peace and Security" (1995) 7 Duke J. Int'l & Comp. L. 93 at 102.

71 In Cambodia, the UN peacekeepers exercised sovereign authority within the state, and in Somalia they adopted enforcement measures to stop the anarchy, starvation, and bloodletting. See Kufour, *supra* note 4; Ofodile, *supra* note 1.

72 R.A. Akindele, *The Organization and Promotion of World Peace: A Study of Universal-Regional Relationships* (Toronto: University of Toronto Press, 1976) at 3.

73 H. Lauterpacht, "The Grotian Tradition" (1946) 23 B.Y.I.L. at 30-38.

74 Josef Kunz, "Individual and Collective Self Defence in Article 51 of the Charter of the United Nations" (1947) 41 A.J.I.L. 872-79.

75 D.W. Bowett, *Self Defence in International Law* (Manchester, UK: Manchester University Press, 1968) at 6.

76 Hans Kelsen, "Collective Security and Collective Self Defence under the Charter" (1948) 42 A.J.I.L. 875.

77 Max Sorensen, *A Manual of Public International Law* (London: Macmillan, 1968) at 765.

78 Laura Dickinson, "The Analogy between Natural Persons and International Law in the Law of Nations" 26 Yale L.J. 265; Myres McDougal and Florentino Feliciano, *International Law of War* (New Haven, CT: Yale University Press, 1994).
79 *R.* v. *Bottrell* (1981), 60 C.C.C. (2d) 211; *R.* v. *Deegan* (1979), 49 C.C.C. (2d) 417; Section 34(1), *Criminal Code,* R.S.C. 1985, c. C-34, s. 1.
80 C.G. Fenwick, *The Principles of International Law* (New Haven, CT: Yale University Press, 1962) at 125.
81 Yoram Dinstein, "International Law as a Primitive Legal System" (1986-87) 19 NYU J. Int'l Law 1 at 12.
82 Myres McDougal and Florentino Feliciano, *Law and Minimum World Public Order: The Legal Regulation of International Coercion* (New Haven, CT: Yale University Press, 1961) at 246-60.
83 Ian Brownlie, "The Use of Force in Self Defense" (1961) 37 B.Y.I.L. 183.
84 Oscar Schacter, "Self Defence and the Rule of Law" (1989) 83 A.J.I.L. 259.
85 M. Shaw, *International Law* (London: Grotius Publications, 1991) at 698.
86 G. Schwarzenberger, *A Manual of International Law,* 6th ed. (South Hackensack, NJ: Professional Books, 1976) at 153.
87 Henry Wheaton, *Elements of International Law* (Washington, DC: Carnegie Endowment for International Peace, 1936).
88 (1975) 14 I.L.M. 1117.
89 F.X. De Lima, *Intervention in International Law: With a Reference to the Organization of American States* (The Hague: Pax Nederland, 1971) at 94.
90 A. Pearce-Higgins, "The Monroe Doctrine" (1924) 5 B.Y.I.L. 114.
91 R.I.I.A. Documents, Cmd. 3109 (1928) at 25.
92 Hans Wehberg, *The Outlawry of War* (Washington, DC: Carnegie Endowment for International Peace, 1931) at 86.
93 Bowett, *supra* note 75 at 213.
94 *Nicaragua Case, supra* note 19 at 220. See particularly Judge Jennings.
95 Dinstein, *supra* note 81. See also F.B Schick, "The North Atlantic Treaty and the Problem of Peace" (1950) 62 Juridical Rev. 26.
96 McDougal and Feliciano, *supra* note 82 at 248.
97 But see Hans Kelsen, "Is the North Atlantic Treaty in Conformity with the Charter of the United Nations?" (1951) 19 U. Kan. City L. Rev. 1-15.
98 J.W. Verzijl, *International Law in Historical Perspective* (Leyden, Netherlands: A.W. Sijhoff, 1968) at 225.
99 Von Glahn, *Law among Nations* (Boston: Allyn and Bacon, 1996) at 563.
100 McDougal and Feliciano, *supra* note 82 at 238-41.
101 Robert Jennings and Arthur Watts, eds., *Oppenheim's International Law,* 9th ed. (Boston: Addison-Wesley Longman, 1996) at 214-21. See also A. Karlsrud, "The Seizure of the Danish Fleet, 1807" (1938) 32 A.J.I.L. 280.
102 E. Miller, "Self Defense, International Law, and the Six Day War" 20 Isr. L.R. 49.
103 Lauterpacht, *supra* note 73 at 180.
104 "Judgment" in *The Trial of German War Criminals: Proceedings of the International Military Tribunal Sitting in Nuremberg, Germany* (London: HMSO, 1946) at 208.
105 Subhas Khare, *Use of Force under the United Nations Charter* (New Delhi: Metropolitan Book Co., 1985) at 74.
106 Oscar Schacter, "The Right of States to Use Armed Force" (1984) 82 Mich. L. Rev. 1620.
107 Yoram Dinstein, *War, Aggression and Self Defence* (Cambridge: Grotius Publications, 1994) at 251. Dinstein notes that between 1920 and 1939 there was little treaty support for the doctrine of anticipatory collective self-defence in Europe, especially with reference to the Convention for the Definition of Aggression of 1933, the Pact of Balkan Entity of 1934, and the Sadabad Pact of 1939.
108 R.Y. Jennings, "The *Caroline* and the *McCleod Cases*" (1938) 32 A.J.I.L. at 117.
109 *Ibid.* See also Wheaton, *supra* note 87 at 441.
110 McDougal and Feliciano, *supra* note 78 at 588. In a rather extreme case, the US Army in 1916 struck deep into Mexican territory to permanently incapacitate some bandits who

had engaged in cross-border raids from Mexico to US territory. See G.A. Finch, "Mexico and the United States" (1917) 17 A.J.I.L. at 399-406.

111 C.M.H. Waldock, "The Regulation of the Use of Force by Individual States" in *General Course on Public International Law,* 81 Hague Recueil des Cours de l'Académie de droit international, no. 2 (1952) 455.

112 Kelsen, *supra* note 76 at 641.

113 Phillip Jessup, *A Modern Law of Nations* (New York: Macmillan, 1948) at 166.

114 Henkin, *supra* note 22.

115 *Ibid.* at 141.

116 Dinstein, *supra* note 107 at 18.

117 McDougal and Feliciano, *supra* note 82 at 233.

118 *Nicaragua Case, supra* note 19 at 103.

119 But see the contrary opinion of Judge Jennings at page 543, *ibid.*

120 (1947) U.N.T.S. 21, at 93.

121 P. Pirrone, "The Use of Force in the Framework of the OAS" in Cassese, *supra* note 51 at 123.

122 Kunz, *supra* note 74 at 877. See also Waldock, *supra* note 111 at 445; H. Armstrong, "Regional Pacts: Strong Ports or Storm Cellars?" (1948) 27 Foreign Affairs 337.

123 It should be noted that there is no general right to intervene on the basis of disapproval of another state's economic, political, social, or foreign policy. In the Court's view, "for such a general right to come into existence would involve a fundamental modification of the customary law of non-intervention": *Nicaragua Case, supra* note 19.

124 Josef Kunz, "The Bogota Charter of the Organization of American States" (1948) 42 A.J.I.L. 508.

125 Dinstein, *supra* note 107 at 24. See also Schick, *supra* note 95.

126 But see Kelsen, *supra* note 97.

127 *Ibid.*

128 W.C. Greig, "Self Defence and the Security Council: What Does Article 51 Require?" (1991) 40 I.C.L.Q. 366.

129 Barry A. Feinstein, "The Legality of the Use of Armed Force by Israel in Lebanon – June 1982" (1985) 20 Isr. L.R. 362. It is interesting to note that the Israeli incursion deep into Lebanese territory in June 1982, which purported to effectively cripple the prospects of future attacks by militant Palestinians operating from Lebanon, has been justified by Israel on this principle.

130 But see Bruno Simma *et al.*, eds., *The Charter of the United Nations: A Commentary* (Oxford: Oxford University Press, 1994) at 662-78. They contend that there is no acceptable definition of "armed attack."

131 Mark Huband, *The Liberian Civil War* (London: Frank Cass Publishers, 1998) at 65.

132 *Corfu Channel Case (Merits),* (*United Kingdom* v. *Albania*), [1949] I.C.J. Rep. 4 at 18.

133 Ofodile, *supra* note 1 at 384. Candy Shiner, "Peacekeepers Caught Up in Renewed War in Liberia" *Christian Science Monitor* (12 October 1991) at 1. See also Kwesi Aning, "The International Dimensions of Internal Conflict: The Case of Liberia and West Africa," online: <http://www.cdr.dk/working_papers/wp-97-4.html>, accessed 28 February 2003; D. Elwood Dunn, "The Civil War in Liberia" in Taisier M. Ali and Robert Matthews, eds., *Civil Wars in Africa: Roots and Resolution* (Montreal and Kingston: McGill-Queen's University Press, 1999) at 89.

134 R. St. MacDonald, "The Nicaragua Case: New Answers to Old Questions" (1986) 34 Can. Y.I.L. 224.

135 Pierluigi Lamberti Zanardi, "Indirect Military Aggression" in Cassese, *supra* note 51 at 111.

136 *Nicaragua Case, supra* note 19 at 630, para. 195.

137 *Ibid.* at 126.

138 Reproduced in Weller, *supra* note 35 at 18.

139 *Ibid.*

140 *Ibid.*

141 *Ibid.*

142 Article 13 of PMAD.

143 Article 18 of PMAD.

144 *Ibid.*

145 *International Assistance to Sierra Leone,* GA Res. 48/196, UN GAOR, 48th Sess., Supp. No. 49, UN Doc. A/48/49 (1993) at 171.

146 *Ibid.,* para. 5.

147 *Ibid.,* para. 6. Note also that in addition to other resolutions of the General Assembly, Resolution 49 of 1994 appealed to the world community to aid the states around Liberia in contending with the refugee crisis. See GA Res. 49/26, UN GAOR, 49th Sess., Supp. No. 49, UN Doc. A/49/49 (1994).

148 Kufour, *supra* note 4 at 534.

149 Article 1 of the PMAD defines "Authority" as "the Authority of Heads of States and Governments as defined in Article 8 of the ECOWAS Treaty." See Weller, *supra* note 35 at 20.

150 *Ibid.*

151 *Ibid.*

152 ECOWAS Authority of Heads of States and Governments, Decision A/DEC.9/5/90, Relating to the Establishment of the Standing Mediation Committee, Banjul, Republic of Gambia, 30 May 1990. Reproduced in Weller, *supra* note 35 at 38-39.

153 *Ibid.*

154 ECOWAS Authority of Heads of States and Governments, Decision A/DEC.1/11/90 Relating to the Approval of the Decisions of the Community Standing Mediation Committee Taken during Its First Session from 6-7 August 1990, Bamako, Republic of Mali, 28 November 1990. Reproduced in Weller, *supra* note 35 at 111-20.

155 Weller, *supra* note 35 at 60.

156 *Ibid.* As already noted, these decisions were subsequently ratified by the full body of the Authority of Heads of States and Governments of ECOWAS.

157 Louis Henkin, *How Nations Behave: Law and Foreign Policy,* 2nd ed. (New York: Columbia University Press, 1979) at xii.

158 Annex, UN Doc. S/21485 (10 September 1990).

159 Annex, UN Doc. S/24811 (16 November 1992).

Chapter 4: The UN Charter and the Ratification of the ECOWAS Action by the Security Council

1 Pittman Potter, "Foreword," in R.A. Akindele, ed., *The Organization and Promotion of World Peace: A Study of Universal-Regional Relationships* (Toronto: University of Toronto Press, 1976), at ii.

2 Boutros Boutros-Ghali, *Report of the UN Secretary-General, United Nations Observer Mission in Liberia,* 26 August 1994, UN Doc. S/1994/1006. Also reproduced in Marc Weller, *Regional Peacekeeping and International Enforcement: The Liberian Crisis* (Cambridge: Grotius Publications, 1994) at 440-446.

3 Louis Henkin, *How Nations Behave: Law and Foreign Policy,* 2nd ed. (New York: Columbia University Press, 1979) at 155.

4 Philip Gourevitch, "The Triumph of Evil" (interview), online: Public Broadcasting System <http://www.pbs.org/wgbh/pages/frontline/shows/evil/interviews/gourevitch.html>, accessed 4 May 2002. For a chilling but critically acclaimed account of the Rwandan genocide, see Philip Gourevitch, *We Wish to Inform You that Tomorrow We Will Be Killed with Our Families* (New York: Farrar, Straus and Giroux, 1998) [hereinafter *We Wish to Inform You*].

5 Peter Rosenblum, "Irrational Exuberance: The Clinton Administration in Africa" (2002) 101 Current History 195 at 201.

6 *Assessment of the Special Representative of the Secretary-General,* UN SG, UN Doc. S/25402 (12 March 1993).

7 Hilaire McCoubrey and Nigel White, *International Organizations and Civil Wars* (Aldershot, UK: Dartmouth Press, 1995).

8 *Charter of the United Nations,* 26 June 1945, 892 U.N.T.S. 1 (1973) [hereinafter *UN Charter*].

9 *Ibid.*

10 *Ibid.*

11 Article 39 (emphasis added).

12 H.A. Amankwah, "International Law, Dispute Settlement and Regional Organizations in the African Setting" in Frederick Snyder and Surakiart Sathirathai, eds., *Third World Attitudes toward International Law: An Introduction* (Dordrecht, Netherlands: Martinus Nijhoff, 1987) at 197-206.
13 Emphasis added.
14 McCoubrey and White, *supra* note 7 at 4.
15 Bruno Simma *et al.*, eds., *The Charter of the United Nations: A Commentary* (Oxford: Oxford University Press, 1994) at 565.
16 Michael Reisman, "Coercion and Self Determination: Construing Article 2(4) of the UN Charter" (1984) 78 A.J.I.L. 642.
17 But see Mark Weisburd, "The Emptiness of the Concept of *Ius Cogens* as Illustrated by the War in Bosnia-Herzegovina" (1995-96) 77 Mich. J. Int'l L. 1.
18 Gourevitch, *supra* note 4.
19 *Ibid.*
20 *Ibid.* On the East Timor tragedy and US indifference, see Charles Krauthammer, "The Limits of Humanitarianism: *Realpolitik* Dictates that the US Take a Backseat in East Timor" *TIME* (Canadian ed.) (27 September 1999) 98.
21 *Reparation Case* (Reparations for Injuries Suffered in the Service of the United Nations), [1949] I.C.J. Rep. 178-79.
22 Jochen Frowein, "Action with Respect to Threats to the Peace, Breaches of the Peace, Acts of Aggression" in Simma *et al., supra* note 15 at 513.
23 Lea Brilmayer, "What's the Matter with Selective Intervention?" (1995) 37 Ariz. L. Rev. 955. The ongoing debate over the alleged difference between "threats to the peace" and "danger to the peace" are not helpful. According to Frowein, "an abstract distinction between the threat to the peace and the mere endangering of peace does not appear possible": Frowein, *supra* note 22 at 623. But see N.D White, *Keeping the Peace: The United Nations and the Maintenance of International Peace and Security,* 2nd ed. (Manchester, UK: Manchester University Press, 1993) at 38-48.
24 Boutros Boutros-Ghali, *Agenda for Peace,* UN Doc. A/47/277-S/24111 (17 June 1992). The "margin of appreciation" is the advantage of proximity possessed by regional organizations in their appreciation of conflicts in their regions.
25 McCoubrey and White, *supra* note 7. See also C.G. Fenwick, "When Is There a Threat to Peace? – Rhodesia" (1967) 61 A.J.I.L. 753-55.
26 H. Freudenschub, "Article 39 of the UN Charter Revisited: Threats to the Peace and the Recent Practice of the UN Security Council" (1993) 46 Aus. J. Pub. & Int'l L. at 1-39.
27 Following the Iraqi invasion of Kuwait in August 1990, the United Nations Security Council adopted Resolution 688 of 5 April 1991 determining that the Iraqi suppression of the Kurds was a threat to international peace.
28 SC Res. 713 (1991). See also Secretary-General's Report, UN Doc. A/46/36 of 2 December 1991.
29 UN Doc. S/Res.788 of 19 November 1992 (1992).
30 J. Wolf, "Regional Arrangements and the UN Charter" (1983) 6 E.P.I.L. 289 at 295.
31 Michael Akehurst, "Enforcement Actions by Regional Agencies with Special Reference to the Organization of American States" (1967) 7 B.Y.I.L. 47.
32 In 1960 there was an unsuccessful attempt by President Trujillo of the Dominican Republic to assassinate President Betancourt of Venezuela. The member states of the OAS, acting under Articles 6 and 8 of the Rio Treaty, agreed to impose sanctions on the Dominican Republic and break diplomatic relations with it. At the Security Council, the Soviet delegate argued that the OAS action amounted to an enforcement action requiring the prior authorization of the Security Council: UN Doc. S/4491 (1960).
33 US Department of State, Bulletin (1962) xlvii at 15.
34 UN Doc. S/PV.992-8 (1962).
35 Christopher Greenwood, "Protection of Peacekeepers: The Legal Regime" (1996) 7 Duke J. Int'l & Comp. L. 185.
36 Georg Ress, "Article 53 of the United Nations Charter" in Simma *et al., supra* note 15.

37 Binaifer Nowrojee, "Joining Forces: United Nations and Regional Peacekeeping: Lessons from Liberia" (1995) 18 Harv. Hum. Rts. J. 50 at 131.
38 Louis Henkin, *supra* note 3 at 168.
39 See UN SCOR, 1960 893d Mtg. (8 September 1960) at 4.
40 UN Doc. S/PV.893, para. 24. The obvious implication, according to Inis Claude, is that the groundwork was being laid by the Soviet Union to disapprove the measures taken by the OAS. See Inis Claude, "The OAS, the UN and the United States" (1964) 565 International Conciliation 36 at 48-49.
41 R. St. MacDonald, "The Developing Relations between Superior and Coordinate Bodies at International Law" (1964) 2 Can. Y.B.I.L. 21.
42 See Malintoppi's arguments in J. Castañeda, *Legal Effects of United Nations Resolutions* (New York: Columbia University Press, 1969) at 170-71.
43 Stephen Schwebel, "The Effect of Resolutions of the UN General Assembly on Customary International Law" (1979) Proc. Am. Soc. Int'l L. 301 at 305.
44 Gaetano Arangio-Ruiz, "The Normative Role of the General Assembly of the United Nations and the Declaration of Principles of Friendly Nations" (1972) 3 Recueil des cours 457.
45 Georges Abi-Saab, "The Development of International Law by the United Nations" in Snyder and Sathirathai, *supra* note 12 at 221.
46 Rosalyn Higgins, "The UN and Law Making" (1970) Proc. Am. Soc. Int'l L. 42.
47 But see Anthony D'Amato, who dismisses the concept of *opinio juris* as "otiose." D'Amato, "Custom and Treaty: A Response to Professor Weisburd" (1988) 21 Vand. J. Transnat'l L. 459.
48 Robert Jennings and Arthur Watts, eds., *Oppenheim's International Law,* 9th ed. (Boston: Addison-Wesley Longman, 1996) at 48.
49 Article 103 of the UN Charter, *supra* note 8.
50 It should be noted, however, that authority should not be delegated without adequate safeguards to prevent national interests from outstripping collective security interests.
51 Myres McDougal and Michael Reisman, "Rhodesia and the United Nations: The Lawfulness of International Concern" (1968) 62 A.J.I.L. 1.
52 Raymond Hopkins, "Anomie, System Reform, and Challenges to the UN System" in Milton Esman and Shibley Telhami, eds., *International Organizations and Ethnic Conflict* (Ithaca, NY: Cornell University Press, 1995) 95.
53 Nowrojee, *supra* note 37 at 142.
54 Julie Flint, "The Unwinnable War" *African Report* (November-December 1993) 46-49.
55 Angela Lloyd, "The Southern Sudan: A Compelling Case for Secession" (1994-95) 32 Colum. J. Transnat'l L. 419.
56 Adila Abusharaf, "The Legal Relationship between Multinational Oil Corporations and the Sudan" (1999) 43 J. Afr. L. 18.
57 UN Doc. S/Res/788 (1992).
58 UN Doc. S/Res/856 (1993).
59 *Ibid.* The creation of UNOMIL was effected pursuant to Resolution 866 of 1993.
60 UN Doc. S/Res/866 (1993).
61 *Ibid.* (emphasis added).
62 *Ibid.* (emphasis added).
63 *Ibid.*
64 *Ibid.*
65 Here the UN acknowledged that the ECOWAS action in Liberia was indeed a peace enforcement action.
66 "UNOMIL Facts and Figures as of 30 June 1997," online: United Nations <http://www.un.org/Depts/DPKO/Missions/UNOMIL_f.htm>, accessed 1 March 2003.
67 *Financing of the United Nations' Observer Mission in Liberia,* GA Res. 49/232, UNGAOR, 49th sess., Supp. No. 49, UN Doc. A/49/49/ (1994) at 281.
68 On the implication of this, see *Certain Expenses of the United Nations Case,* [1962] I.C.J. Rep. 151.
69 UN Doc. S/Res/911 (1994).

70 UN Doc. S/Res/950 (1994).
71 *Ibid.*
72 UN Doc. S/Res/972 (1995).
73 UN Doc. S/Res/1001 (1995) (emphasis added).
74 UN Doc. S/Res/742 (1995).
75 UN Doc. S/Res/1014 (1995).
76 Liberia: UN Report, 01/29/96, <http://www.sas.upenn.edu/African_studies/Urgent_Action/apic_libr196.html>, accessed 3 March 2003.
77 UN Doc. S/Res/1020 (1995).
78 UN Doc. S/Res/1041 (1996).
79 This belated assumption of a higher ground of legitimacy and its probable role as a tool for the reduction or elimination of tyrannical regimes around the world has already been dealt with.
80 UN Doc. S/Res/1059 (1996).
81 *Ibid.*
82 *Ibid.*
83 UN Doc. S/Res/1071 (1996).
84 UN Doc. S/Res/1100 (1997).
85 UN Doc. S/Res/1116 (1997).
86 Thomas Brewer, "Collective Legitimization in International Organizations: Concept and Practice" (1972) 2 J. Int'l L. & Policy 73; Bhupinder Singh Chimni, "Towards a Third World Approach to Non-Intervention: Through the Labyrinth of Western Doctrine" in Snyder and Sathirathai, *supra* note 12 at 73.
87 GA Res. 47/74, UN GAOR, 47th Sess., Supp. No. 49, UN Doc. A/47/49 (1992) 31.
88 *Assistance to Refugees and Displaced Persons in Africa,* GA Res. 47/107, UN GAOR, 47 Sess., Supp. No. 49, UN Doc. A/47/49 (1992) 188.
89 *Assistance for the Rehabilitation of Liberia,* GA Res. 47/154, UN GAOR, 47th Sess., Supp. No. 49, UN Doc. A/47/49 (1992) 114.
90 GA Res. 48/118, UN GAOR, 48th Sess., Supp. No. 49, UN Doc. A/48/49 (1993).
91 *Assistance to Refugees, Returnees and Displaced Persons in Africa,* GA Res. 49/174, UN GAOR, 49th Sess., Supp. No. 49, UN Doc. A/49/49 (1994) 191.
92 Witness the case of Czechoslovakia. Seventeen days after the Warsaw Pact, which bound the members to cooperate on the basis of "the principles of equality, respect for sovereignty and national independence," came into effect, those same members invaded the country on the pretext that there was an internal problem in Czechoslovakia that threatened the subregion. Similar abuses occurred in Hungary. See Richard Falk, ed., *The International Law of Civil War* (Baltimore: Johns Hopkins University Press, 1971) at 419.
93 S.A. Williams and A.L.C. de Mestral, "Justifications for Use of Force," in Hugh Kindred *et al.*, eds., *International Law: Chiefly as Interpreted and Applied in Canada,* 5th ed. (Toronto: Emond Publications, 1993) at 850-51.
94 Ahmadu Sesay, "The Limits of Peace-Keeping by a Regional Organization: The OAU in Chad" (1991) 11 Conflict Quarterly 7-26.
95 Orobola Fasehun and Ahmadu Sesay, *The OAU and Conflict Control* (Ife, Nigeria: Department of International Relations, University of Ife, 1980) [mimeograph] at 12.
96 David Yost, "French Policy in Chad and the Libyan Challenge" *Orbis* (Winter 1983) 965-97.
97 Olusola Ojo and Ahmadu Sesay, "The OAU Peacekeeping Force in Chad: Policy Implementation and Failure" in C.A.B. Olowu and Victor Ayeni, *A Nigerian Reader in the Policy Process* (Ife, Nigeria: University of Ife Press, 1991) 1.
98 C.O.C. Amate, *Inside the OAU: Pan-Africanism in Practice* (New York: St. Martin's Press, 1986) at 187.
99 Nigeria was the main financier in the effort.
100 Certain states contributing troops to the OAU force were accused of bias by some of the warring factions.
101 Domingo Acevedo, "The Haitian Crisis and the OAS Response: A Test of Effectiveness in Protecting Democracy" in Lori Fisler Damrosch, ed., *Enforcing Restraint: Collective Intervention in Internal Conflicts* (New York: Council on Foreign Relations Press, 1993) at 119.

102 *Request from the President of the Republic of Haiti to the Secretary-General of the OAS,* Doc. MRE/doc.3./91 (7 October 1991).
103 *Restoration of Democracy in Haiti,* Resolution MRE/Res. 3/92 (17 May 1992).
104 UN Doc. S/Res/940 (1994).
105 *Ibid.* Note that this was the first time that the Security Council had authorized the use of force for the restoration of democracy.
106 Noam Chomsky, "The Demolition of World Order" *Harper's Magazine* (June 1999) 1517.
107 Antonio Cassese, "*Ex inuria ius oritur:* Are We Moving towards International Legitimation of Forcible Humanitarian Countermeasures in the World Community?" (1999) 10 E.J.I.L. 1-7.
108 Michael Akehurst, "Humanitarian Intervention" in Hedley Bull, ed., *Intervention in World Politics* (New York: Council on Foreign Relations Press, 1984) 285.
109 Simma *et al., supra* note 15 at 3.
110 Chomsky, *supra* note 106 at 16.
111 Jules Lobel and Michael Ratner, "Bypassing the Security Council: Ambiguous Authorizations to Use Force, Cease-Fires and the Iraqi Inspection Regime" (1999) 93 A.J.I.L. 1.
112 Reprinted in 29 I.L.M. 1565 (1990).
113 A TV remark, June 1994. Cited in D. Elwood Dunn, "The Civil War in Liberia" in Taisier M. Ali and Robert Matthews, eds., *Civil Wars in Africa: Roots and Resolution* (Montreal and Kingston: McGill-Queen's University Press, 1999) at 115. See also Rakiya Omaar and Alex de Waal, "The Lessons of Humanitarian Imperialism in Somalia" *War Report* (February-March 1993) at 12.
114 UN Doc. SC/Res/1199 (1998).
115 *Ibid.*
116 Cassese, *supra* note 107.

Chapter 5: Reconfiguring Collective Security in Africa

1 Evan Luard, ed., *The International Regulation of Civil Wars* (New York: New York University Press, 1972).
2 Obiora Okafor, "The Global Process of Legitimation and the Legitimacy of Global Governance" (1998) 10 A.J.I.C.L. 20.
3 Obiora Okafor, *Redefining Legitimate Statehood: International Law and State Fragmentation in Africa* (The Hague: Martinus Nijhoff, 2000); Makau Wa Mutua, "Why Redraw the Map of Africa: A Moral and Legal Inquiry" (1995) 16 Mich. J. Int'l. L. 113.
4 "Ceasefire agreement to halt war in Congo" *CNN News* (10 July 1999), online: CNN <http://www.cnn.com/WORLD/africa/9907/10/congo.summit.01/>, accessed 1 March 2003.
5 The rebellion led by the late Laurent Kabila was expected to lead to an end to the internecine conflicts in Zaire. Events have proven the expectations wrong. Shortly after the emergence of the Kabila regime in Zaire (later renamed Congo), its foreign minister, Bizima Kazare, and a coalition of Banyamulenge (ethnic Tutsis of East Congo) rebelled against the rule of Kabila alleging that he was no better than the late Mobutu and accusing him of corruption, tribalism, and dishonesty of intention in claiming to return the country to democratic rule. The leading figures in the armed rebellion against Kabila include Jean Pierrre Ondekame, a former commander of Kabila's army, which overthrew the regime of Mobutu, and Zahiti Ngoma, an international lawyer formerly with UNESCO. It has been alleged that the rebels who now occupy a significant portion of Congo are backed by the governments of neighbouring Rwanda and Uganda, and because of this, the Congolese government has refused to negotiate with the rebels, described as the "pawns of Rwanda and Uganda." The Southern African Development Community (SADC) reviewed the situation and, noting "the escalating conflict's potential for upsetting the region's precarious balance," decided to intervene. The first measure was to impose an economic blockade against the rebels. In 1999 the SADC intervened militarily. In July 1999 the government of Zaire (Congo) instituted an action at the International Court of Justice against the governments of Uganda, Burundi, and Rwanda for their alleged support of the rebels and aggression against Zaire (Congo).
6 Thomas Franck, "Legitimacy in the International System" (1988) 82 AJ.I.L. 705.

7 *International Covenant on Economic, Social and Cultural Rights,* 16 December 1966, 999 U.N.T.S. 3. See also Stephen Stedman, *Peacemaking in Civil War* (Boulder, CO: Lynne Rienner Publishers, 1991) at 3.
8 UN GAOR, 45th Sess., Supp. No. 49, UN Doc. A/RES/45/150 (1990).
9 Robert Jackson and Doreen Jackson, *Contemporary Government and Politics: Democracy and Authoritarianism* (Scarborough, ON: Prentice Hall, 1993) at 3.
10 E.K. Quashigah, "Legitimacy of Governments and Resolution of Intra-National Conflicts in Africa" (1995) 7 A.J.I.C.L. 284.
11 K.C. Wheare, *Federal Government* (London: Oxford University Press, 1956) at 11.
12 Adila Abusharaf, "The Legal Relationship between Multinational Oil Corporations and the Sudan" (1999) 43 J. Afr. L. 18.
13 Ibrahim Gambari, "Paths to Safe Polity" *The Guardian* (25 May 1999), online: The Guardian <http://www.ngrguardiannews.com/news/htm>, accessed 25 May 1999.
14 Sean Murphy, "The Security Council, Legitimacy and the Concept of Collective Security after the Cold War" (1994-95) 32 Colum. J. Transnat'l L. 201.
15 According to the findings by the London Development Institute, "authoritarian rule is likely to generate higher domestic savings as a basis for higher levels of growth whether by forcing public savings or by promoting inegalitarian policies which indirectly assist growth." See Anna Shephard, "The Economics of Democracy" *African Report* (March-April 1992) 18 at 29. Cited in E.K. Quashigah, "Protection of Human Rights in the Changing International Scene: Prospects in Sub-Saharan Africa" (1994) 6 A.J.I.C.L. 84. Reference may be made to Latin America, Asia, and Ghana.
16 Okey Martin Ejidike, "Human Rights in the Cultural Traditions and Social Practice of the Igbo of South-Eastern Nigeria" (1999) 43 J. Afr. L. 71.
17 "OAU Summit Ends with Democracy Plea" *BBC News* (14 July 1999), online: BBC News <http://www.news2.bbc.co.uk/english/world/africa>, accessed 21 July 1999.
18 Julius Nyerere, "How to Check Coups in Africa" *The Guardian* (25 May 1999), online: The Guardian <http://www.ngrguardiannews.com/news/htm>, accessed 26 May 1999.
19 Shedrack Agbakwa, "Reclaiming Humanity: Economic, Social, and Cultural Rights as the Cornerstone of African Human Rights" (2002) 5 Yale Human Rts. & Dev. L.J. 177.
20 Hersch Lauterpacht, *Recognition in International Law* (Cambridge: Cambridge University Press, 1947) at 68. See also Hans Kelsen, "Recognition in International Law: Some Theoretical Observations" (1941) 35 A.J.I.L. 605.
21 When the Togolese tyrant Gnassingbe Eyadema murdered Sylvanius Olympio, states like Nigeria, Guinea, and Sierra Leone successfully barred Eyadema from attending the inaugural conference of the OAU. However, "when Nkrumah was overthrown in 1966 ... an attempt to deny the usurpers of participatory legitimacy ... failed ... Congo, Guinea, Mali ... refused to take part in the proceedings." See Bolaji Akinyemi, "The Organization of African Unity and the Concept of Non-Interference in Internal Affairs of Member States" in Frederick Snyder and Surakiart Sathirathai, eds., *Third World Attitudes toward International Law: An Introduction* (Dordrecht, Netherlands: Martinus Nijhoff, 1987).
22 T.M. Franck and M.M. Munansangu, *The New International Economic Order: International Law in the Making* (New York: UNITAR, 1982) at 2.
23 *Legal Consequences for States of the Continued Presence of South Africa in Namibia (South West Africa) notwithstanding Security Council Resolution 276,* Advisory Opinion, [1971] I.C.J. Rep. 16.
24 T.M. Franck, *The Power of Legitimacy Among Nations* (New York: Oxford University Press, 1990) at 3.
25 Amos Sawyer, *The Emergence of Autocracy in Liberia: Tragedy and Challenge* (San Francisco: ICS Press, 1992) at 301.
26 *Provisional Verbatim Record, Statement of the President, Mr. Bagbeni Adeito Nzengeya,* UN SCOR, 47th Sess., 2974th Mtg., UN Doc. S/PV:2974 (1991): "The members of the Security Council commend and approve of the efforts made by the ECOWAS Heads of States to promote peace and normalcy in Liberia."
27 Michael Reisman, "Some Lessons from Iraq: International Law and Democratic Politics" (1991) 16 Yale J. Int'l L. 203-15.

28 Reproduced in Okafor, *supra* note 2.
29 There are compelling arguments that the Council has become a "rubber stamp" for US foreign policy. See Okafor, *ibid.*
30 Berhanykun Andemicael, ed., *Regionalism and the United Nations* (New York: Oceania Publications, 1979) at 225.
31 F.C. Okoye, *International Law and the New African States* (London: Sweet and Maxwell, 1972) at 157.
32 Wole Soyinka, *The Open Sore of a Continent: A Personal Narrative of the Nigerian Crisis* (New York: Oxford University Press, 1996) at 25.
33 See generally Antonio Cassese, ed., *The Current Legal Regulation of the Use of Force* (Dordrecht, Netherlands: Martinus Nijhoff, 1986) at 511.
34 "Nigeria, 21 Others Join Global Peacekeeping Outfit" *The Guardian* (3 April 1999), online: The Guardian <http://www.ngrguardiannews.com>, accessed 3 April 1999. Note that the same approach is being pressed by the francophone countries in West Africa for ECOMOG.
35 Tom Farer, "A Paradigm of Legitimate Interventions," in L.F. Damrosch, ed., *Enforcing Restraint: Collective Intervention in Internal Conflicts* (New York: Council on Foreign Relations Press, 1993) at 316.
36 *Ibid.*
37 Boutros Boutros-Ghali, *Agenda for Peace: Preventive Diplomacy, Peacemaking and Peacekeeping* (New York: United Nations, 1984) at 60-65.
38 *Ibid.*
39 Boutros Boutros-Ghali, *Building Peace Development: Report of the Work of the Organization for the 48th to the 49th Session of the General Assembly* (New York: UN Dept. of Information, 1994) at 158.
40 Alan Henrikson, "The UN and Regional Organizations: King Links of a Global Chain?" (1996) 7 Duke J. Int'l & Comp. L. 35.
41 But see Clovis Maksoud, "The Arab World's Quandary" (1991) 8 World Policy Journal 551.
42 Dan Lindley, "Collective Security Organizations and Internal Conflict" in Michael Brown, ed., *The International Dimensions of Internal Conflicts* (Cambridge, MA: MIT Press, 1996) 500 at 556.
43 Michael Wolfers, *Politics in the Organization of African Unity* (London: Methuen, 1967) at 92. See also T.A. Imobighe, "An African High Command: The Search for a Feasible Strategy of International Security" (1980) 79 African Affairs 315.
44 Terrence Lyons, "Liberia's Path from Anarchy to Elections" (1998) 97 Current History 229.
45 Sylvester Ekundayo, "ECOMOG – A Model for African Peacekeeping" *AfricaNews* (16 October 1998) 2 at 12.
46 "Ceasefire agreement to halt war in Congo," *supra* note 5.
47 William Neil, "Human Rights Monitoring versus Political Expediency: The Experience of the OAS/UN Mission in Haiti" (1998) 8 Harv. Hum. Rts. J. 101.
48 Jeff Cooper, "Tracing Missing Fathers" *World News, Inter Press Service* (23 October 1998), online: One World International Foundation <http://www.oneworld.org/ips/oct98/.html>, accessed 22 July 1999.
49 Abraham William, "War Crimes Tribunal for Liberian Warlords" (1996) 11 Perspective 6.
50 But see "Aid Agency 'Lacks Proof' of Abuse" *BBC News* (1 March 2002), online: BBC News <http://news.bbc.co.uk>, accessed 1 March 2002.
51 James Busumtwi-Sam, "Redefining Security after the Cold War" in Taisier Ali and Robert Matthews, eds., *Civil Wars in Africa: Roots and Resolution* (Montreal and Kingston: McGill-Queen's University Press, 1999) 276.
52 Chinua Achebe, *The Trouble with Nigeria* (London: Heinemann, 1983) at 24.

Conclusion

1 Quoted in James Rosenau, *Along the Domestic-Foreign Frontier: Exploring Governance in a Turbulent World* (Cambridge: Cambridge University Press, 1999) at 451.

Bibliography

Treaties and Conventions

Charter of the United Nations, 26 June 1945, 892 U.N.T.S. 1 (1973).

ECOWAS Protocol on Non-Aggression, 22 April 1978.

ECOWAS Protocol Relating to Mutual Assistance on Defence, 29 May 1981.

General Treaty for the Renunciation of War, signed at Paris, 27 August 1928, 1929 Can. T.S. No. 7; 94 L.N.T.S. 57.

Geneva Conventions of 12 August 1949, 75 U.N.T.S. 85 (1950).

International Covenant on Civil and Political Rights, 999 U.N.T.S. 171 (1966); 1976 Can. T.S. No. 47.

Organization of African Unity Charter, 25 May 1963, 479 U.N.T.S. 39.

Treaty of the Economic Community of West African States (ECOWAS), 28 May 1975, 14 I.L.M. 1200.

Vienna Convention on the Law of Treaties, (1969) I.L.M. 679; 1155 U.N.T.S. 33 (1969).

Cases

Case Concerning the Continental Shelf (Libyan Arab Jamahiriya/Malta), 3 June 1985, [1985] I.C.J. Rep. 13.

Case Concerning Military and Paramilitary Activities in and against Nicaragua (Merits) (*Nicaragua* v. *United States*), [1986] I.C.J. Rep. 14.

Certain Expenses of the United Nations Case, Article 17, Paragraph 2, of the Charter, Advisory Opinion of 20 July 1962 [1962] I.C.J. Rep. 151.

The Corfu Channel Case (Merits), (*United Kingdom* v. *Albania*), [1949] I.C.J. Rep. 4.

Haile Selassie v. *Cable and Wireless Ltd.* (No. 2) [1939] Ch. D. 182.

Legal Consequences for States of the Continued Presence of South Africa in Namibia (South West Africa) Notwithstanding Security Council Resolution 276, Advisory Opinion, [1971] I.C.J. Rep. 16.

Legality of the Threat or Use of Nuclear Weapons, Advisory Opinion of 8 July 1996, [1996] I.C.J. Rep. 226.

Mitchell and Others v. *D.P.P.,* [1986] L.R.C. (const.) 35, (1986) A.C. 73.

Reparation for Injuries Suffered in the Sevice of the United Nations, Advisory Opinion of 11 April 1949, [1949] I.C.J. Rep. 174.

R. v. *Bottrell* (1981), 60 C.C.C. (2d) 211.

R. v. *Deegan* (1979), 49 C.C.C. (2d) 417.

Books and Journal Articles

Achebe, Chinua. *The Trouble with Nigeria* (London: Heinemann, 1983).

Abusharaf, Adila. "The Legal Relationship between Multinational Oil Corporations and the Sudan" (1999) 43 J. Afr. L. 18.

Africa South of the Sahara, 27th ed. (London: Europa Publications, 1998).

Agbakwa, Shedrack. "Reclaiming Humanity: Economic, Social, and Cultural Rights as the Cornerstone of African Human Rights" (2002) 5 Yale Human Rights and Development L.J. 177.

Akehurst, Michael. "Enforcement Actions by Regional Agencies with Special Reference to the Organization of American States" (1967) 7 B.Y.I.L. 47.

Akindele, R.A. *The Organization and Promotion of World Peace: A Study of Universal-Regional Relationships* (Toronto: University of Toronto Press, 1976).

Akinyemi, B., and Otubanjo, F., ed. *Nigeria since Independence* (Ife, Nigeria: University of Ife Press, 1994).

Ali, Taisier, and Robert Matthews, eds. *Civil Wars in Africa: Roots and Resolution* (Montreal and Kingston: McGill-Queen's University Press, 1999).

Amate, C.O.C. *Inside the OAU: Pan-Africanism in Practice* (New York: St. Martin's Press, 1986).

Amnesty International Annual Reports, 1990-98 (London: Amnesty International Publications, 1999).

Andemicael, Berhanykun, ed. *Regionalism and the United Nations* (New York: Oceania Publications, 1979).

Anderson, R. Earle. *Liberia: America's African Friend* (Chapel Hill: University of North Carolina Press, 1952).

Anene, J.C. *The International Boundaries of Nigeria 1885-1960: The Framework of an Emergent African Nation* (London: Longman Publications, 1970).

Arangio-Ruiz, Gaetano. "The Normative Role of the General Assembly of the United Nations and the Declaration of Principles of Friendly Nations" (1972) 3 Recueil des cours 457.

Armstrong, H. "Regional Pacts: Strong Ports or Storm Cellars?" (1948) 27 Foreign Affairs 337.

Austin, Dennis. "The Uncertain Frontiers: Ghana and Togo" (1963) June 1:2 Journal of Modern African Studies 1.

Azinna, Nwafor. *United Nations Use of Armed Forces in Internal War: Conditions for the Maintenance of International Stability* (Ph.D. Dissertation, University of Michigan, 1969).

Benneh, E.Y. "Review of the Law on Non-Intervention" (1995) 7 A.J.I.C.L. 139.

Bennet, Lerone Jr. *Before the Mayflower: A History of Black America,* 6th ed. (New York: Penguin Books, 1993).

Berdal, Mats. "The Security Council, Peacekeeping and Internal Conflicts after the Cold War" (1996) 7 Duke J. Int'l & Comp. L. 71.

Bernal, Martin. *Black Athena: The Afro-Asiatic Roots of Classical Civilization* (New Jersey: Rutgers University Press, 1987).

Beyan, Amos. *The American Colonization Society and the Creation of the Liberian State: A Historical Perspective, 1822-1900* (Lanham, MD: University Press of America, 1991).

Boone, C. *Liberia as I Know It* (Richmond, CT: Negro Universities Press, 1970).

Boutros-Ghali, Boutros. *Agenda for Peace: Preventive Diplomacy, Peacemaking and Peacekeeping,* UN Doc. A/47/277-S/24111 (17 June 1992).

–. *Building Peace Development: Report of the Work of the Organization for the 48th to the 49th Session of the General Assembly* (New York: UN Dept. of Information, 1994).

Bowett, D.W. *Self Defence in International Law* (Manchester, UK: Manchester University Press, 1968).

Brewer, Thomas. "Collective Legitimization in International Organizations: Concept and Practice" (1972) 2 J. Int'l L. & Policy 73.

Brilmayer, Lea. "What's the Matter with Selective Intervention?" (1995) 37 Ariz. L. Rev. 955.

Brown, David. "The Role of Regional Organizations in Stopping Civil Wars" (1996-97) 41 A.F.L. Rev. 235.

Brown, Michael, ed. *The International Dimensions of Internal Conflicts* (Cambridge, MA: MIT Press, 1996).

Brownlie, Ian. *International Law and the Use of Force* (Oxford: Clarendon Press, 1963).

Buchan, Alastair. *Change without War* (London: Chatto and Windus, 1974).

Bull, Hedley, ed. *Intervention in World Politics* (New York: Council on Foreign Relations Press, 1984).

Butuex, Paul. *The Politics of Nuclear Consultation in NATO since 1965-80* (London: Cambridge University Press, 1983).

Cassel, Abayomi. *Liberia: History of the First African Republic* (New York: Fountainhead Publishers, 1970).

Cassese, Antonio, ed. *The Current Legal Regulation of the Use of Force* (Dordrecht, Netherlands: Martinus Nijhoff, 1986).

–. "*Ex inuria ius oritur:* Are We Moving towards International Legitimation of Forcible Humanitarian Countermeasures in the World Community?" (1999) 10 E.J.I.L. 1-7.

Castañeda, J. *Legal Effects of United Nations Resolutions* (New York: Columbia University Press, 1969).

Chan, Stephen. "Mirror, Mirror on the Wall ... Are the Democratic States Pacific?" (1948) 28 J. Conflict Resolution 649.

Chimni, B.S. *International Law and World Order* (New Delhi: Sage Publications, 1993).

Clapham, Christopher. *Africa and the International System: The Politics of State Survival* (Cambridge: Cambridge University Press, 1996).

Clark, Anthony. "The United Nations, Regional Organizations and Military Operations: The Past and the Present" (1995) 7 Duke J. Int'l & Comp. L. 3.

Clark, Roger. "Stephen Spielberg's *Amistad* and Other Things I Have Thought about in the Past Forty Years: International (Criminal) Law, Conflict of Laws, Insurance and Slavery" (1999) 30 Rutgers L.J. 371.

Claude, Inis. "The United Nations and the Use of Force" (1961) 532 International Conciliation 325-28.

–. "The OAS, the UN and the United States" (1964) 565 International Conciliation 36.

–. *Swords into Ploughshares,* 3rd ed. (New York: Random House, 1964).

Compton, Richard. "Time to Clear the Doctrine Dilemma" (1995) 21 Jane's Defence Weekly 7.

Connaughton, Richard. *Military Intervention in the 1990s* (New York: Routledge, 1992).

–. "Time to Clear the Doctrine Dilemma" (1994) 21 Jane's Defence Weekly 19.

Copson, Raymond. *Conflict among the African States* (Ph.D. Dissertation, Johns Hopkins University, 1971).

Crawford, James. *The Creation of States in International Law* (Oxford: Clarendon Press, 1979).

Damrosch, L.F., ed. *Enforcing Restraint: Collective Intervention in Internal Conflicts* (New York: Council on Foreign Relations Press, 1993).

Damrosch, L.F., and D. Scheffer, eds. *Law and Force in the New International Order* (Boulder, CO: Westview Press, 1991).

Danieli, Yael, *et al.*, eds. *International Response to Traumatic Stress* (New York: Bayword Publishing, 1998).

Davidson, Basil. *The African Past* (New York: Grosset and Dunlap, 1967).

–. *The Black Man's Burden* (New York: Times Books, 1996).

De Lima, F.X. *Intervention in International Law* (The Hague: Pax Nederland, 1971).

Dexter, Grant. *Canada and the Building of Peace* (Toronto: Canadian Institute of International Affairs, 1944).

Dinstein, Yoram. "International Law as a Primitive Legal System" (1986-87) 19 NYU J. Int'l Law 1.

–. *War, Aggression and Self Defence* (Cambridge: Grotius Publications, 1994).

Diop, Cheik Anta. *Precolonial Black Africa: A Comparative Study of the Political and Social Systems of Europe and Black Africa, from Antiquity to the Formation of Modern States* (Westport, CT: Lawrence Hill Books, 1987).

Dorman, Andrew, and Thomas Otte, eds. *Military Intervention: From Gunboat Diplomacy to Humanitarian Intervention* (London: Dartmouth Publishing, 1995).

Doswald-Beck, Louise. "The Legal Validity of Military Intervention by the Invitation of the Government" (1985) 56 B.Y.I.L. 189.

Doyle, Michael. "Kant, Liberal Legacies and Foreign Affairs" (1983) 12 Philosophy and Public Affairs 205.

Dulbreck, Jost. "Globalization of Law, Politics, and Markets: Implication for Local Law: A European Perspective" (1993) 1 Ind. J. Global Legal Stud. 9.

Dunn, Elwood, and Svend Holsoe. *Historical Dictionary of Liberia* (London: Scarecrow Press, 1985).

Durch, William. *Evolution of UN Peacekeeping: Case Studies and Comparative Analysis* (New York: St. Martin's Press, 1993).

Ejidike, Okey. "Human Rights in the Cultural Traditions and Social Practice of the Igbo of South-Eastern Nigeria" (1999) 43 J. Afr. L. 71.

El-Ayoutry, Yassin, ed. *The OAU after Ten Years* (New York: Praeger, 1975).

Ellis, Jay. "The Regime as a Locus of Legitimacy in International Law" (1997) 13 Int'l Insights 65.

Ellis, Stephen. "Liberia 1989-1994: A Study of Ethnic and Spiritual Violence" (1995) 94 African Affairs 168.

Esman, Milton, and Shibley Telhami, eds. *International Organizations and Ethnic Conflict* (Ithaca, NY: Cornell University Press, 1984).

Ezetah, Reginald. "Are We in a Grotian Moment?" (1997) 13 Int'l Insights 35.

Falk, Richard. "The Grotian Moment: Unfulfilled Promise, Harmless Fantasy, Missed Opportunity" (1997) 13 Int'l Insights 3.

–, ed. *The International Law of Civil War* (Baltimore: Johns Hopkins University Press, 1971).

–, and Friedrich Kratochwill, eds. *International Law: A Contemporary Perspective* (Boulder, CO, and London: Westview Press, 1985).

Farer, Tom. "Panama: Beyond the Charter Paradigm" (1990) 84 A.J.I.L. 503.

Feinstein, Barry A. "The Legality of the Use of Force by Israel in Lebanon – June 1982" (1985) 20 Isr. L.R. 362.

Fenwick, C.G. *The Principles of International Law* (New Haven, CT: Yale University Press, 1962).

–. "When Is There a Threat to Peace? – Rhodesia" (1967) 61 A.J.I.L. 753.

Fodor, Neil. *The Warsaw Treaty Organization: A Political and Organizational Analysis* (London: Macmillan, 1990).

Fraenkel, Merran. *Tribe and Class in Monrovia* (London: Oxford University Press, 1964).

Franck, T.M. "Legitimacy in the International System" (1988) 82 AJ.I.L. 705.

–. "Why a Quest for Legitimacy" (1988) 22 U.C. Davis L. Rev. 53.

–. *The Power of Legitimacy among Nations* (New York: Oxford University Press, 1990).

–. "The Emerging Right to Democratic Governance" (1992) 86 A.J.I.L. 46.

Franck, T.M., and M.M. Munansangu. *The New International Economic Order: International Law in the Making* (New York: UNITAR, 1982).

Freudenschub, H. "Article 39 of the UN Charter Revisited: Threats to the Peace and the Recent Practice of the UN Security Council" (1993) 46 Aus. J. Pub. & Int'l L. 1.

Friedman, Wolfgang. "The United States Policy and the Crisis of International Law" 59 A.J.I.L. 857.

Gailbraith, J.K., and Stanislav Menshikov. *Capitalism, Communism and Coexistence* (Boston: Houghton Publishing, 1988).

Gilmore, William. *The Grenada Intervention: Analysis and Documentation* (London: Mansell Publishing, 1984).

Glahn, Von. *Law among Nations* (Boston, MA: Allyn and Bacon, 1996).

Golden, James, *et al.*, eds. *NATO at Forty: Change, Continuity and Prospects* (London: Westview Press, 1989).

Gonidec, P.F. "The Relationship of International Law and National Law in Africa" (1988) 6 A.J.I.C.L. 12.

Gourevitch, Philip. *We Wish to Inform You that Tomorrow We Will Be Killed with Our Families* (New York: Farrar, Straus and Giroux, 1998).

Gray, Christine. "Host-State Consent and UN Peacekeeping in Yugoslavia" (1996) 7 Duke J. Int'l & Comp. L. 241.

Greenwood, Christopher. "Legal Constraints on UN Military Operations" (1995) 1 IISS Strategic Comments 22.

–. "Protection of Peacekeepers: The Legal Regime" (1996) 7 Duke J. Int'l & Comp. L. 185.

Greig, W.C. "Collective Self Defence: What Does Article 51 Require?" (1991) 40 I.C.L.Q. 366.

Grotius, H. *De Jure Belli ac Pacis* (1646) (New York: Carnegie Translation, 1925).

Halberstam, Malvina. "The Copenhagen Document: Intervention in Support of Democracy" (1993) 34 Harv. Int'l L.J. 163.

Harbeson, John, and Donald Rothchild, eds. *Africa in World Politics* (Boulder, CO: Westview Press, 1991).

Harold, Nelson, ed. *Liberia: A Country Study* (Washington, DC: American University Press, 1985).

Hart, H.L.A. *The Concept of Law* (Oxford: Clarendon Press, 1961).

Henkin, Louis. *How Nations Behave: Law and Foreign Policy,* 2nd ed. (New York: Columbia University Press, 1979).

–. "The Invasion of Panama under International Law: A Gross Violation" (1991) 29 Colum. J. Transnat'l L. 293.

–, ed. *Right v. Might: International Law and the Use of Force* (New York: Council on Foreign Relations Press, 1991).

Henrikson, Alan. "The UN and Regional Organizations: King Links of a Global Chain?" (1996) 7 Duke J. Int'l & Comp. L. 35.

Higgins, Rosalyn. *The Development of International Law through the Political Organs of the United Nations* (Cambridge: Cambridge University Press, 1963).

–. "The UN and Law Making" (1970) Proc. Am. Soc. Int'l L. 42.

Holden, Edith. *Blyden of Liberia* (New York: Vintage Press, 1966).

Howard, Rhoda. "Civil Conflict in Sub-Saharan Africa: Internally Generated Causes" (1995) 51 Int'l J. 27-53.

Huband, Mark. "The Power Vacuum" *African Report* (January-February 1991) 27-30.

–. *The Liberian Civil War* (London: Frank Cass Publishers, 1998).

Imobighe, T.A. "An African High Command: The Search for a Feasible Strategy of International Security" (1980) 79 African Affairs 315.

Jackson, Robert. *Quasi-States: Sovereignty, International Relations and the Third World* (Cambridge: Cambridge University Press, 1990).

–. "The Grotian Moment in World Jurisprudence" (1997) 13 Int'l Insights 35-56.

Jackson, Robert, and Carl Rosberg. *Personal Rule in Africa: Prince, Autocrat, Prophet, Tyrant* (Berkeley: University of California Press, 1982).

Jackson, Robert, and Doreen Jackson. *Contemporary Government and Politics: Democracy and Authoritarianism* (Scarborough, ON: Prentice Hall, 1993).

Jacob, Haruna, and Massoud Omar, eds. *France and Nigeria: Issues in Comparative Studies* (Ibadan: Credu Niger Press, 1992).

Jennings, R.Y. "The *Caroline* and the *McCleod Cases*" (1938) 32 A.J.I.L. 82.

Jessup, Phillip. *A Modern Law of Nations* (New York: Macmillan, 1948).

Jones, Christopher. *Soviet Influence in Eastern Europe: Political Autonomy and the Warsaw Pact* (Brooklyn: Praeger, 1981).

Johnston, Harry. *Liberia* (London: Hutchinson, 1906).

Knappman, Edward, ed. *Great American Trials* (Detroit: Gale Research Press, 1994).

Karlsrud, A. "The Seizure of the Danish Fleet, 1807" (1938) 32 A.J.I.L. 280.

Keesing's Contemporary Archives, annual volumes (London: Longman Publications, 1989-98).

Kelly, George, and Linda Miller. *Internal Wars and International Systems: Perspectives in Method* (New York: AMC Press, 1969).

Kelsen, Hans. "Recognition in International Law: Some Theoretical Observations" (1941) 35 A.J.I.L. 605.

–. "Collective Security and Collective Self Defence under the Charter" (1948) 42 A.J.I.L. 875.

–. "Is the North Atlantic Treaty in Conformity with the Charter of the United Nations?" (1951) 19 U. Kan. City L. Rev. 32.

–. *Collective Security at International Law* (Washington, DC: US Government Printing Office, 1957).

Kennedy, David. "A New Stream of Scholarship of International Law" (1988) 7 Wisc. Int'l L.J. 68.

Khare, Subhas. *Use of Force under the United Nations Charter* (New Delhi: Metropolitan Book Co., 1985).

Kirgis, F.L., ed. *International Organizations in Their Legal Setting* (St. Paul, MN: West Publishing, 1993).

Kissinger, Henry. *A World Restored* (Boston: Houghton Mifflin, 1957).

Kiwanuka, R. "The Meaning of 'People' in the African Charter of Human Rights" (1988) 82 A.J.I.L. 80.

Knop, K. "The Righting of Recognition of States in Eastern Europe and the Soviet Union" (1992) Can. Council Int'l L. Proc. 36.

Konneh, Augustine. *Religion, Commerce and the Integration of the Mandingo in Liberia* (New York: University Press of America, 1996).

Kufour, Kofi Oteng. "The Legality of the Intervention in the Liberian Civil War by the ECOWAS" (1993) 5 A.J.I.C.L. 528.

Kunz, Josef. "Individual and Collective Self Defence in Article 51 of the Charter of the United Nations" (1947) 41 A.J.I.L. 872.

–. "The Bogota Charter of the Organization of American States" (1948) 42 A.J.I.L. 508.

Kwakwa, Edward. *The International Law of Armed Conflicts: Personal and Material Field of Application* (Dordrecht, Netherlands: Martinus Nijhoff, 1992).

Larus, Joel. *From Collective Security to Preventive Diplomacy* (New York: John Wiley, 1965).

Lauterpacht, H. *The Function of Law in the International Community* (Oxford: Clarendon Press, 1933).

–. "The Grotian Tradition" (1946) 23 B.Y.I.L. 1.

–. *Recognition in International Law* (Cambridge: Cambridge University Press, 1947).

Liebenow, Gus. *Liberia: The Evolution of Privilege* (Ithaca, NY: Cornell University Press, 1969).

Little, Richard. *Intervention: External Involvement in Civil Wars* (London: M. Robertson, 1975).

Lloyd, Angela. "The Southern Sudan: A Compelling Case for Secession" (1994-95) 32 Colum. J. Transnat'l L. 419.

Lobel, Jules, and Michael Ratner. "Bypassing the Security Council: Ambiguous Authorizations to Use Force, Cease-Fires and the Iraqi Inspection Regime" (1999) 93 A.J.I.L. 1.

Lowenkopf, Martin. *Politics in Liberia: The Conservative Road to Development* (Stanford, CA: Hoover Institution Press, 1976).

Luard, Evan, ed. *The International Regulation of Civil Wars* (New York: New York University Press, 1972).

Luban, David. "Just War and Human Rights" (1980) 9 Philosophy and Public Affairs J. 160.

Lyons, Gene, and Michael Mastanduno, eds. *Beyond Westphalia? State Sovereignty and International Intervention* (Baltimore: Johns Hopkins University Press, 1995).

Lyons, Terrence. "Liberia's Path from Anarchy to Elections" (1998) 97 Current History 229.

MacDonald, Roderick. "Metaphors of Multiplicity: Civil Society, Regimes, and Legal Pluralism" (1998) 15 Ariz. J. Int'l L. 75.

Maksoud, Clovis. "The Arab World's Quandary" (1991) 8 World Policy J. 551.

Maoz, Zeer, and Nassim Abdolai. "Regime Types and International Conflicts 1816-1976" (1983) 33 J. Conflict Resolution 32.

Maugham, R.C.F. *The Republic of Liberia* (New York: Negro Universities Press, 1969).

Mazrui, Ali. *Toward a Pax Africana* (Chicago: University of Chicago Press, 1967).

McCoubrey, Hilaire, and Nigel White. *International Organizations and Civil Wars* (Aldershot, UK: Dartmouth Press, 1995).

McDougal, Myres, and Florentino Feliciano. *Law and Minimum World Public Order: The Legal Regulation of International Coercion* (New Haven, CT: Yale University Press, 1961).

–. *International Law of War* (New Haven, CT: Yale University Press, 1995).

McDougal, Myres, and Michael Reisman. "Rhodesia and the United Nations: The Lawfulness of International Concern" (1968) 62 A.J.I.L. 1.

Menon, Krishna. *India and World Politics: Krishna Menon's View of the World* (Toronto: Oxford University Press, 1968).

Miller, E. "Self Defense, International Law, and the Six Day War" 20 Isr. L.R. 49.

Minahan, James. *Nations without States: A Historical Dictionary of Contemporary National Movements* (London: Greenwood Press, 1996).
Moore, John Norton, ed. *Law and Civil War in the Modern World* (Baltimore: Johns Hopkins University Press, 1974).
Murdoch, James Oliver. "Collective Security Distinguished from Intervention" (1962) 56 A.J.I.L. 500.
Murphy, Sean. "The Security Council, Legitimacy and the Concept of Collective Security after the Cold War" (1994-95) 32 Colum. J. Transnat'l L. 201.
Mutua, Makau Wa. "Why Redraw the Map of Africa: A Moral and Legal Inquiry" (1995) 16 Mich. J. Int'l L. 1113.
–. "The Ideology of Human Rights" (1996) 36 Va. J. Int'l L. 589.
–. "Savages, Victims, and Saviours: The Metaphor of Human Rights" (2001) 42 Harv. Int'l L.J. 201.
Naidu, M.V. *Collective Security and the United Nations: A Definition of the UN Security System* (New York: St. Martin's Press, 1974).
Naldi, Gino, ed., *Documents of the OAU* (London: Mansel Publishing, 1992).
Neil, William. "Human Rights Monitoring versus Political Expediency: The Experience of the OAS/UN Mission in Haiti" (1998) 8 Harv. Hum. Rts. J. 101.
Nowrojee, Binaifer. "Joining Forces: United Nations and Regional Peacekeeping: Lessons from Liberia" (1995) 18 Harv. Hum. Rts. J. 50.
Nowrot, Karsten, and Emily Schabacker, "The Use of Force to Restore Democracy: International Implications of the ECOWAS Intervention in Sierra Leone" (1998) 14 Am. U. Intl. L. Rev. 321.
Nwachukwu, Ike, ed. *Nigeria and the ECOWAS since 1985: Towards a Dynamic Regional Integration* (Enugu, Nigeria: Fourth Dimension Publishers, 1995).
Ofodile, Anthony. "The Legality of ECOWAS Intervention in Liberia" (1994-95) 32 Colum. J. Transnat'l L. 381.
Ofuatey-Kodjoe, W. "Regional Organizations and the Resolution of Internal Conflicts: The ECOWAS Intervention in Liberia" (Autumn 1994) Int'l Peacekeeping 261-302.
Ojo, Olatunde. "Nigeria and the Formation of ECOWAS" (1988) 34 Int'l Org. 45.
Okafor, Obiora. "The Global Process of Legitimation and the Legitimacy of Global Governance" (1998) 10 A.J.I.C.L. 20.
–. *Redefining Legitimate Statehood: International Law and State Fragmentation in Africa* (The Hague: Martinus Nijhoff, 2000).
Okolo, Julius, ed. *West African Regional Cooperation and Development* (Oxford: Westview Press, 1990).
Okoye, F.C. *International Law and the New African States* (London: Sweet and Maxwell, 1972).
Olowu, C.A.B., and Victor Ayeni, eds. *A Nigerian Reader in the Policy Process* (Ife, Nigeria: University of Ife Press, 1991).
Onwuka, Ralph. *Development and Integration in West Africa: The Case of the Economic Community of West Africa (ECOWAS)* (Ife, Nigeria: University of Ife Press, 1982).
Otto, Pick, and Julian Critchley. *Collective Security* (London: Macmillan, 1974).
Perkins, John. "The Right of Counter-Intervention" (1986) 17 Ga. J. Int'l & Comp. L. 171.
Quashigah, E.K. "Protection of Human Rights in the Changing International Scene: Prospects in Sub-Saharan Africa" (1994) 6 A.J.I.C.L. 84.
–. "Legitimacy of Governments and Resolution of Intra-National Conflicts in Africa" (1995) 7 A.J.I.C.L. 284.
Reisman, Michael. "Rhodesia and the United Nations: The Lawfulness of International Concern" (1968) 62 A.J.I.L. 119.
–. "Coercion and Self Determination: Construing Article 2(4) of the UN Charter" (1984) 78 A.J.I.L. 642.
–. "Some Lessons from Iraq: International Law and Democratic Politics" (1991) 164 Yale J. Int'l L. 203-15.
–. "Humanitarian Intervention and Fledgling Democracies" (1995) 18 Fordham Int'l L.J. 794.
Reno, William. "Reinvention of an African State" (1995) 16 Third World Quarterly 16.

Rimmer, Douglas. *The Economies of West Africa* (New York: St. Martin's Press, 1985).

Rosenau, James, ed. *Governance without Government* (New York: Cambridge University Press, 1992).

–. *Along the Domestic-Foreign Frontier: Exploring Governance in a Turbulent World* (Cambridge: Cambridge University Press, 1999).

Rosenblum, Peter. "Irrational Exuberance: The Clinton Administration in Africa" (2002) 101 Current History 195.

Rothchild, Donald. "Ethnic Bargaining and State Breakdown in Africa" (1995) 1 Nationalism and Ethnic Politics 21.

Roxburgh, A. "The Sanction of International Law" (1920) 14 A.J.I.L. 26.

St. MacDonald, R. "The Developing Relations between Superior and Coordinate Bodies at International Law" (1964) 2 Can. Y.I.L. 21.

–. "The Nicaragua Case: New Answers to Old Questions" (1986) 34 Can. Y.I.L. 224.

Sandbrook, Richard. *The Politics of African Economic Recovery* (Cambridge: Cambridge University Press, 1993).

Savigny, Baron De. *Metternich and His Times* (London: Longman, Publications 1962).

Sawyer, Amos. *The Emergence of Autocracy in Liberia: Tragedy and Challenge* (San Francisco: ICS Press, 1992).

Schacter, Oscar. "The Right of States to Use Armed Force" (1984) 82 Mich. L. Rev. 1620.

–. "Self Defence and the Rule of Law" (1989) 83 A.J.I.L. 259.

Schermers, H.G. *International Institutional Law* (Alphen aan den Rijn, The Netherlands: Sijthoff and Noordoff, 1980).

Schick, F.B. "The North Atlantic Treaty and the Problem of Peace" (1950) 62 Juridical Rev. 26.

Schnably, Stephen. "The Santiago Commitment as a Call to Democracy: Evaluating the OAS Role in Haiti, Peru and Guatemala" (1994) 25 U. Miami Inter-Am. L. Rev. 393.

Schofield, Clive, ed. *World Boundaries,* vol. 1 (London: Routledge, 1994).

Schrijver, Nico. "Introducing Second Generation Peacekeeping: The Case of Namibia" (1997) 6 A.J.I.C.L. 1.

Schwarzenberger, G. *A Manual of International Law,* 6th ed. (South Hackensack, NJ: Professional Books, 1976).

Schwebel, Stephen. "The Effect of Resolutions of the UN General Assembly on Customary International Law" (1979) Proc. Am. Soc. Int'l L. 301.

Sesay, Ahmadu. "The Limits of Peace-Keeping by a Regional Organization: The OAU in Chad" (1991) 11 *Conflict Quarterly* 7-26.

–. "Collective Security or Collective Disaster? Regional Peace-Keeping in West Africa" (1995) 26 Security Dialogue 2.

Shaw, M. *International Law* (London: Grotius Publications, 1991).

Shawn, Walter. "Protecting the Avatar of International Peace and Security" (1996) 7 Duke J. Int'l & Comp. L. 93.

Shiner, Candy. "Peacekeepers Caught Up in Renewed War in Liberia" *Christian Science Monitor* (12 October 1991) 1.

Shiner, Roger. *Norm and Nature: The Movements of Legal Thought* (Oxford: Oxford University Press, 1992)

Simma, Bruno. "NATO, the UN and the Use of Force: Legal Aspects" (1998) 10 E.J.I.L. 1.

–, *et al.,* eds. *The Charter of the United Nations: A Commentary* (Oxford: Oxford University Press, 1994).

Snyder, Frederick, and Surakiart Sathirathai, eds. *Third World Attitudes toward International Law* (Dordrecht, Netherlands: Martinus Nijhoff, 1987).

Sohn, L.B. *Rights in South Africa: The UN and South Africa* (New York: Transnational Press, 1994).

Sorensen, Max. *A Manual of Public International Law* (London: Macmillan, 1968).

Soyinka, Wole. *The Open Sore of a Continent: A Personal Narrative of the Nigerian Crisis* (New York: Oxford University Press, 1996).

Starke, J.G. *An Introduction to International Law,* 9th ed. (London: Butterworths, 1984).

Stedman, Stephen. *Peacemaking in Civil War* (Boulder, CO: Lynne Rienner Publishers, 1991).

Steven, David. *Third World Coups d'état and International Security* (Baltimore: Johns Hopkins University Press, 1987).
Stowell, Ellery. *Intervention in International Law* (Washington, DC: John Byrne, 1921).
Szasz, Paul. "The Rise of Nationalism and the Breakup of States: The Fragmentation of Yugoslavia" (1994) 50 A.S.I.L. Proc. 33.
Tarr, Byron. "The ECOMOG Initiative in Liberia: A Liberian Perspective" (1995) 49 J. Opinion 3.
Taylor, Hannis. *A Treatise on Public International Law* (Chicago: Callaghan, 1901).
Thomas, Ann, and Aaron J. Thomas. *Non-Intervention: The Law and Its Import in the Americas* (Dallas: Southern Methodist University Press, 1956).
Toural, Souadia. *Somali Nationalism* (Cambridge, MA: Harvard University Press, 1963).
Tzeutschler, Gregory. "Growing Security: Land Rights and Agricultural Development in Northern Senegal" (1999) 43 J. Afr. L. 36.
Verzijl, J.W. *International Law in Historical Perspective* (Leyden, Netherlands: A.W. Sijhoff, 1968).
Vogts, Margaret, ed. *Liberian Crisis and ECOMOG: A Bold Attempt at Peacekeeping* (Lagos: Gabumo Publishing, 1992).
Waldock, C.M.H. "The Regulation of the Use of Force by Individual States" (1952) 18 Hague Recueil 455.
Wallerstein, Immanuel. *Africa: The Politics of Unity* (New York: Random House, 1965).
Wehberg, Hans. *The Outlawry of War* (Washington, DC: Carnegie Endowment for International Peace, 1931).
Weisburd, Mark. "The Emptiness of the Concept of *Ius Cogens* as Illustrated by the War in Bosnia-Herzegovina" (1995-96) 77 Mich. J. Int'l L. 1.
–. *Use of Force: The Practice of States since World War II* (University Park, PA: Pennsylvania State University Press, 1997).
Welch, R. "The OAU and International Recognition: Lessons from Uganda" in Yassin El-Ayouty, ed., *The OAU after Ten Years* (New York: Praeger, 1975) 103.
Weller, Mark. *Regional Peacekeeping and International Enforcement: The Liberian Crisis* (Cambridge: Grotius Publications, 1994).
Wheare, K.C. *Federal Government* (London: Oxford University Press, 1956).
Wheaton, H. *Elements of International Law* (Washington, DC: Carnegie Endowment for International Peace, 1936).
White, N.D. *Keeping the Peace: The United Nations and the Maintenance of International Peace and Security,* 2nd ed. (Manchester, UK: Manchester University Press, 1993).
Williams, Phil. *North Atlantic Treaty Organization* (London: Transaction Publishers, 1994).
Wilson, Charles. *Liberia* (New York: William Sloan Associates, 1947).
Wilson, Heather. *International Law and the Use of Force by National Liberation Movements* (Oxford: Clarendon Press, 1988).
Winfield, P.H. "The History of Intervention in International Law" (1922-23) 3 B.Y.I.L. 130.
Wippman, David. "Change and Continuity in Legal Justification for Military Interventions in Internal Conflicts" (1996) 27 Colum. H.R.L. Rev. 435.
–. "Military Intervention, Regional Organizations and Host-State Consent" (1996) 7 Duke J. Int'l & Comp. L. 156.
Wolfers, Michael. *Politics in the Organization of African Unity* (London: Methuen, 1967).
Wright, Quincy. "United States Intervention in Lebanon" (1959) 53 A.J.I.L. 120.
Wright, Stephen, ed. *African Foreign Policies* (Boulder, CO: Westview Press, 1999).
Yearbooks of the United Nations (New York: Martinus Nijhoff, 1991-97).
Zaya, Yeebo. *Ghana: The Struggle for Power – Rawlings: Saviour or Demagogue?* (London: New Beacon Books, 1991).

Index